Choosing a Hometown *in* North Jersey

A Milestones Guide

Choosing a HOMETOWN

NORTH JERSEY

A MILESTONES GUIDE

EDITED BY
Nan Goldberg

Record Books

Published by Record Books
150 River Street
Hackensack, NJ 07601

First published in 1997 by Record Books,
a division of The Bergen Record Corp.

ISBN: 0-9654733-0-9
CIP data available

First Edition
10 9 8 7 6 5 4 3 2 1

"Milestones" is a series of localized how-to guides, published annually by The Record, for the important events in North Jersey residents' lives.

Printed in the United States of America

Acknowledgments

Without the following people's hard work and commitment, this book would not have been possible:

John Zeaman, whose fine editing skills, excellent judgment, and dedication to the book gave it scope, consistency, and interest;

Marc Watrel, who supported the project in a hundred and one ways, editorial and otherwise;

Jennifer Cunningham, who designed the prototype and cover;

Maryellen Larry, whose design talent, resourcefulness, and unflagging energy were crucial;

Beverly Weintraub, Dorothy Fersch, and Brad Marks, copy editor, fact-checker, and artist extraordinaires;

Joanne Vero, who saw all of the possibilities and never stopped selling;

Chip McGregor and the entire prepress staff, without whose expertise I would have been lost;

Frank Hansen, George Geigengoltz, Ray Picano, Daniel Dembrosky, and Frank Swan of The Record manufacturing department, who turned film and galleys into a real book;

Chris Kapsalis and his staff of techies, especially Joy Sarnelli;

Writers Jan Barry, Kevin Byrne, Richard Cowen, Kelly David, Leslie Haggin, Hali Helfgott, Steven C. Johnson, Steve Marlowe, Tim May, Scott Moritz, Doug Most, DeQuendre Neeley, Jeff Pillets, Ed Reiter, Paul Rogers, Peter Sampson, David Schaublin, Jennifer Van Doren, Emily Wax, Barbara Williams, and Maria Zangaro;

Jill Schensul, whose advice and encouragement were essential;

Jon Markey, president of The Bergen Record Corp. and a real *mensch,* who listened, believed, and took a chance;

and Dean, Jordan, and Dagny Goldberg, for their love and patience.

Nan Goldberg
Editor

TABLE OF CONTENTS

INTRODUCTION

Most people search for the right house, rather than the right community. Realtors will show houses in three or four towns in their effort to make a sale, emphasizing physical features such as a deck, a sun room, or a third-floor office. Factors such as transportation, schools, and shopping may be taken into account — but in the end, buyers fall in love with a particular house and pay relatively little heed to the community where it is located.

And yet, community can make all the difference. More than the deck or the sun room, what matters are the quality of the neighborhood elementary school, the pleasures of the town pool, the breadth of the recreation program, the inspirational character of a church or a synagogue — or just that ineffable quality known as community spirit. New homeowners, especially young ones, often have no idea what kinds of things will matter to them as the years go by and their children mature.

One of North Jersey's unusual qualities is the many variations among its towns. The cliche about the sameness of the suburbs — identical ranch homes in treeless cul de sacs — is far from the picture here. Manhattan really has very little on North Jersey when it comes to variety.

True, North Jersey is an affluent region — Bergen is one of the nation's wealthiest counties — but the towns here span a wide socioeconomic range, from enclaves for the rich and successful, such as Alpine and Kinnelon's Smoke Rise, to working-class towns such as Passaic or Garfield, to the poorest neighborhoods of Paterson. Even within Bergen County, there is a continuum of affluence, with the wealthier towns located north of Route 4.

Geography offers even more contrast. People who want natural beauty, open spaces, and a rural lifestyle can find it to the west in towns such as West Milford or Ringwood, while those who prefer urban vitality will get everything they want in Hoboken, with its brownstone row houses, music clubs, and concentration of writers, artists, and musicians.

House-hunters in search of the quintessential old-fashioned suburb with great Victorian houses will be excited by Montclair or Ridgewood. Towns such as Teaneck and Hackensack offer an interesting ethnic mix. Some towns, such as Wyckoff, Westwood, or Englewood, have their own bustling shopping districts while others — Paramus and Wayne, for instance — boast instant access to malls such as Garden State Plaza, Paramus Park, Willowbrook, or Wayne Town Center.

Many of the state's best schools are located in North Jersey. Towns such as Demarest, Closter, and Old Tappan are part of regional school districts with high schools that, because of pooled resources and large student bodies, can offer a wealth of programs. Other towns insist on running their own high schools with as few as 500 students, providing more in the way of individual attention but sacrificing depth. Some, such as Tenafly, manage to have a top-flight high school without regionalizing.

The tiny town of Rockleigh, near the New York border, has enough historic charm to match anything in Vermont, while the high-rise communities of Fort Lee and Cliffside Park look and feel like a sixth borough of New York City.

There's hardly a town that doesn't claim to have community spirit, but some feel more strongly about it than others — as in Hillsdale, where volunteers built a new fieldhouse in barn-raising fashion, or Saddle Brook, where an annual picnic is attended by nearly 4,000 people.

For newcomers to the region, the variety of communities can be confusing. Bergen County poses a particular challenge because it's a checkerboard of 70 towns — many only a mile square — and lacks any central city. Passaic County has larger municipalities and some of these, such as Passaic, have Old-Worldish neighborhoods that maintain their own identities. Despite its greater distance from

New York City, Passaic County is more urban — Paterson is its queen city, though the luster is off its crown — but also more rural, as in the case of Pompton Lakes and West Milford.

The profiles in this book are intended to cut through this confusion, to convey the flavor and character of each town, while providing helpful facts and figures on such matters as SAT scores, recreation programs, and average household income.

But no town is an island, and all share in the character and resources of the region. Despite the density of development and the disappearance of much open space, North Jersey still has plenty of physical beauty, from the sheer cliffs of the Palisades to the gentle slopes of the Ramapo Mountains, from the often painted and poeticized Paterson Falls to the yellow expanses of the Meadowlands, where birds and other wildlife thrive within view of Manhattan skyscrapers.

North Jersey's history dates to the Colonial period and before, when the area was inhabited by peaceful Native Americans such as the Lenape, whose typical long-house dwellings have been reproduced in diorama form by countless elementary school students. No great Revolutionary War battles were fought here and, in fact, George Washington spent most of his time in North Jersey on one ignominious retreat or another, one of which was precipitated by a local farmer who saw British forces climbing the Palisades and ran to alert the Continental Army in Fort Lee. Not surprisingly, this local Paul Revere is claimed as a hero by several towns — Englewood Cliffs, Alpine, and Closter — each of which has its own version of the story.

Many of the eastern communities began as "bedroom towns" for New York City. One, Leonia, was partially developed as a community of scholars for Columbia University professors and other intellectuals. Today, however, North Jersey has a much more ambivalent relationship with New York. The George Washington Bridge, an engineering wonder of the 1930s, stands as an awesome architectural symbol of North Jersey's connection to Manhattan and is the most heavily traveled bridge in the nation. But a smaller percentage of people commute to the city than did 20 years ago, and instead travel from home to work without ever leaving the suburbs, creating unpredictable rush-hour traffic jams and a sprawling atmosphere reminiscent of Los Angeles.

If New York is no longer the place where everyone works, it is still the place where North Jersey residents — like tourists from all over the world — go for museum exhibits, theater, dance, or an elegant dinner. But as North Jersey has matured, it has begun to sprout its own cultural alternatives that make it possible to do those things right here. Serious French cuisine is served in places such as Ho-Ho-Kus or Bergenfield, and theaters such as Teaneck's American Stage Company and John Harms in Englewood offer drama and entertainment at less cost than Broadway, and with none of the hassle. And, whereas North Jersey sports fans once had to root for New York teams, we now have the Nets, the Devils, the Jets, and the Giants — and may, if George Steinbrenner has his way, some day get the Yankees.

The proximity to New York has endowed North Jersey with its share of celebrities. Former President Richard M. Nixon made his home in Saddle River and Park Ridge, where he wrote many of his books and regularly played host to statesmen and political pundits. Dizzy Gillespie lived in a modest house in Englewood for many years, and today the town is home to Eddie Murphy and Wilson Pickett. Alan Alda raised his children in Leonia even after he gained fame with "M*A*S*H," and still maintains his house there for when he's visiting New York or doing a Broadway show. Many North Jersey towns have been home to professional athletes, such as Lou Piniella, who lived in Allendale while he was with the Yankees; Fort Lee's Patrick Ewing; and Lawrence Taylor, of Upper Saddle River.

North Jersey boasts a number of fine hospitals that have the latest equipment and treatments. These include Holy Name in Teaneck, Hackensack University Hospital in Hackensack, Englewood Hospital, St. Joseph's in Paterson, and Wayne General, as well as smaller community hospitals such as The Valley Hospital of Ridgewood, Pascack Valley Hospital of Westwood, and Chilton Memorial Hospital in Pompton Plains.

North Jersey, like the rest of the metropolitan area, has experienced an enormous influx of immigrants during the last 15 years. Asians — Koreans in particular — have settled in great numbers in many towns here, particularly those in Bergen County. In some school systems, 20 percent of the students are Korean. Palisades Park has seen its business district largely transformed by Korean businesses, from restaurants to electronics stores to furniture stores. Other significant immigrant groups include Japanese, Indian, Pakistani, Colombian, Dominican, Irish, Russian, and Filipino. A movie theater in Ridgefield Park now shows exclusively Indian films. The domed roofs of mosques are not an exotic sight anymore. Hackensack has a Colombian festival every year, and Colombians regularly gather in the parks for organized soccer matches.

The influx of people speaking so many foreign languages has posed a challenge for local school systems, but most have risen to it, and the phrases "celebrating diversity" and "multiculturalism" have become Nineties cliches, just as "melting pot" was during an earlier period of immigration.

North Jersey awakened to overdevelopment in the late Eighties, when so many superfluous office buildings were put up on the assumption that business expansion would never level off. Neighborhoods suffered, too, as fine old homes were torn down so that their large lots could be subdivided for condominiums or multiple dwellings. The Nineties have seen increased concern for open space, historic preservation, and an issue infrequently raised in suburbia's halcyon days: pedestrian safety. Many North Jersey towns continue to grapple with the issue of affordable housing. Under the state's Mount Laurel ruling each town has a quota of such housing to fill, although some, like Wayne, have met the obligation by paying for units in inner cities, such as Paterson and Jersey City.

Crime, of course, is often what makes people flee from the city to the suburbs — and, for the most part, those who come to North Jersey find safer communities than those they left behind. Towns such as Ridgewood have an exceptionally low rate of violent crime, although burglary is a problem everywhere. Sometimes crime rates can be misleading. Paramus, for example, has a higher crime rate than surrounding towns, but only because of the pilferage and car thefts at the malls. Homeowners there experience no more crime than their counterparts elsewhere.

North Jersey has evolved into a complex region — still a suburb, but one with its own business base. There are more different kinds of people here than ever before, and more different kinds of communities. The quality of life is generally high — polls show that people like it here — despite some griping about taxes, or traffic, or crime. It's a nice place to live, and the variety ensures that just about everyone can find the right community — a place that matches their lifestyle and their aspirations, a place that feels like home.

It just takes a little research.

— John Zeaman

ALLENDALE

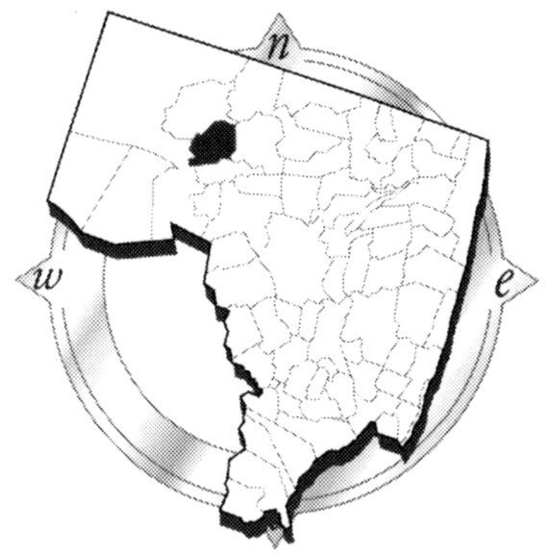

Allendale is one of the only North Jersey towns, it seems, where George Washington did not sleep. That does not, however, mean that it lacks historical significance.

In fact, an American patriot named John Fell — a member of the Continental Congress and a Bergen County judge — became a famous figure in Allendale during the American Revolution when he was imprisoned in a Provost jail in New York City by British Tories who raided his house. While in captivity, he kept a journal that documented the squalor of prison life and served to inspire other patriots.

That patriotic drive is very much alive today in Allendale, said borough historian Pat Wardell — especially when it comes to holiday observances.

"It's kept that small-town spirit," Wardell said. "It all started with a group of neighbors joining together to combine fireworks for the Fourth of July. Now it's everything, from Christmas to New Year's."

Like many other boroughs — Allendale, incorporated in 1894 — was first Indian territory. It later was named for Joseph Warner Allen, who surveyed the route of the Paterson and Ramapo Railroad, which ran through North Jersey during the late 1800s.

Two of the best-known areas of town, historically, are the Celery farm, now a nature preserve, and Crestwood Lake, which was once a public swimming area popular and large enough to draw crowds from all over the tri-state area. Later bought by the town, the lake is now strictly for residential use.

The neighborhoods mostly have a suburban, cozy feel, which makes it easier to build relationships.

"It's a small town, with kind of a rural setting," said Howard Ridkes, a nine-year resident and president of the local recreation commission."That's what we like about it. That's why we have a lot of community spirit here."

Noteworthy historical events

In the mid-1920s, a nefarious Irish hoodlum, believed to have been involved in bootlegging liquor, was blown up in his car as it sat parked at Allendale Manor on Franklin Turnpike.

Schools

Educational standards in Allendale are high, with high school test scores serving as the jewel in the crown.

Two schools serve 950 students in grades kindergarten through 8; the regional high school population is about 750. Northern Highlands Regional High has solidified the city's reputation, with New Jersey Monthly magazine ranking it No. 4 in the state in its 1996 report and fifth in the 1994 report. The school system had the highest scores in the state on the eighth-grade Early Warning Test. The average combined SAT score was 1075.

Ninety percent of the students enrolled in the district go on to attend college, with 5 percent going to Ivy League schools.

"The value of education is held very highly in the community," said Dr. J. Thomas Morton, superintendent of schools. "You often find that at any given event for youngsters, parents are there, whether it's a high school game or a kindergarten recreation program. We take a great deal of pride in our activities here."

Houses of worship

Archer United Methodist; Calvary Lutheran Church of Allendale; (Episcopal) Church of the Epiphany; Guardian Angel Roman Catholic (R.C.) Church; and Highland Presbyterian Church.

Houses

Houses are medium-size to large and range in style from split-level homes to ranch-style houses to some old Victorian-style spreads.

TRANSPORTATION

New Jersey Transit trains run from the town to Hoboken, where you can pick up the PATH train to Manhattan and other destinations, but there is no bus service. In town, it's easy to get anywhere on foot, by bike, or by car.

RECREATION

After receiving funding from the Green Acres project in the late Sixties, one of the borough's most famous landmarks, the Celery farm, was turned into a nature preserve. The farm was founded in the 1800s by Henry J. Appert, who cultivated onions and celery on land off an area known as Wolf Lake, formerly Indian stomping grounds. The farm now serves as a wildlife refuge where residents can hike trails and observe animals in their natural habitat. Crestwood Lake also features baseball fields and an ice hockey rink for use in late fall and winter.

ARTS AND CULTURE

No programs specific to Allendale.

CHILD CARE SERVICES

Allendale provides no child care services; however, the YWCA runs before- and after-school programs at Hillside Elementary School. There also are two private child care facilities in town.

SENIOR SERVICES

None provided in the township.

RECENT DEVELOPMENTS

Superintendent of Schools Morton said the school board is working on a proposal to upgrade computer technology in the district, giving students access to the Internet. Also, in August 1996 state Education Commissioner Leo Klagholz granted the borough of Ho-Ho-Kus permission to send its students to Northern Highlands Regional High School instead of Midland Park High, which Ho-Ho-Kus students have attended for 23 years.

Drawbacks

A longstanding controversy rages over the resounding blasts of gunfire from a Waldwick-based police pistol range. Residents complain that the noise disturbs their peace, and 29 Allendale residents have filed a lawsuit against Waldwick, its police chief, and the Waldwick Pistol and Rifle Club.

The Allendale residents charge that "unreasonable use" of the pistol range has increased over the years, "without due regard to the effects it has on surrounding property owners." As of the end of 1996, they were seeking to have the facility closed.

Prominent residents

Former New York Yankee player and manager Lou Piniella.

Phone numbers

Township clerk (201) 818-4404
School district (201) 327-2020
Public library (201) 327-4338

— *Kevin Byrne*

Demographics

County: Bergen
Size: 3.1 square miles
Population: 5,900
Density: 1,884/square mile
Median age: 40.6 years
White: 95.4 percent
Asian: 3.7 percent
Black: 0.4 percent
Median house value: $317,800
Upper 25 percent: $447,500
Lower 25 percent: $244,700
Median year built: 1957
Median rent: $902
Single-family homes: 584
Condominiums: Approximately 170 units
Median property taxes per household (1994): $6,668
Median household income: $78,361
Industrial property: 11 parcels
Sewers: Mostly public, some private
Library: 43,633 volumes, 127 periodicals, 1,462 audio materials, and 681 videos
Media: The Record covers the town, as well as the Town Journal, a weekly. TCI provides cable service.
Fire and ambulance: Volunteer
Police: Paid
Crime rate per 1,000 (1994): 14.6
Violent crime rate per 1,000 (1994): 0.7

ALPINE

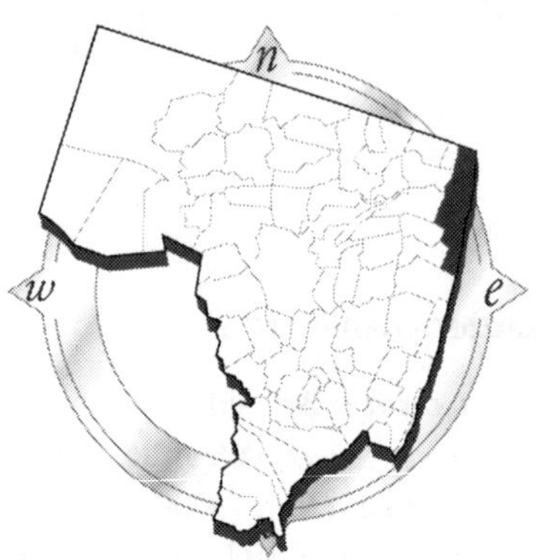

Perched atop the cliffs of the Palisades and marked by opulent houses set on large tracts, Alpine typically attracts educated and successful professionals. Despite its proximity to New York City, its idyllic setting gives Alpine the atmosphere of a mountaintop hamlet, rather than a suburb in a bustling metropolitan county.

Alpine's municipal government does not provide a lot of services for its wealthy citizens. It doesn't have its own library or high school, and it relies on neighboring Cresskill for many recreation programs. Instead, the Borough Council strives to keep the tax rate low, and succeeds: Although the median house in Alpine is valued at more than $500,000, the average household pays only $4,501 in property taxes. Still, the borough lavishes money on its one elementary school, spending $11,915 per student. (After grade 8, students attend Tenafly High School). Nor does it scrimp on security, maintaining a police force of 13 for Alpine's tiny population of less than 2,000.

Alpine also maintains tight control over development. Industry has long been restricted. More than half the borough's 4,100 acres are in conservation areas or parks — much of it part of the Palisades Interstate Park system and the Alpine Boy Scout Camp — and will stay forever wild. The rest of Alpine's 6.4 square miles is dotted with homes on one- and two-acre lots.

Privacy is apparently a big issue for Alpine residents, who would rather pick up their mail at the post office than have it delivered to their property. This tradition has, in turn, created a de facto town center through which nearly everyone passes on a daily basis, and which serves as a local forum for residents to greet one another and discuss politics and community issues. The post office stays open till 7 p.m. weekdays and till 4 p.m. on Saturdays.

Alpine is not exclusively a town for the wealthy. People of middle-class means live in the Old Alpine neighborhood of smaller wood-frame houses, and, as Mayor Lawrence Manus observed, "the very affluent rub shoulders with people living in more modest homes."

Despite its opulence and elitism, Alpine is not a community of wealthy recluses. "There is an extraordinary sense of community pride," noted area real estate saleswoman Marlyn Friedberg.

Noteworthy historical events

In a surprise attack, British Gen. Cornwallis crossed the Hudson River from Yonkers on Nov. 19, 1776, landing on the shores of Alpine with an army of several thousand troops. Local lore holds that a country farmer, while plowing his fields, spied the oncoming troops and raced to Fort Lee to warn the patriot forces. This attack, had it been successful, might have proved a perilous turning point for the Colonial rebels.

Schools

"Because Alpine's school is small, a lot of attention is paid to each child," said School Superintendent Mathew Glowski. One elementary school serves all Alpine students from grades kindergarten through 8.

With a student-to-teacher ratio of 17 to 1, the district can afford its 180 or so students some singular educational opportunities. French and Spanish are taught three times a week beginning in kindergarten and continuing through grade 5. Computers also are introduced in kindergarten. Advanced courses enable many teens to enter high school above grade level, and weekly progress reports in each of the major subjects keep parents apprised of their children's progress.

A cooperative program with students from Englewood Cliffs and Tenafly grammar schools brings together children from different socioeconomic backgrounds to work in nearby food banks and for problem-solving sessions related to community issues.

After eighth grade, Alpine students attend Tenafly High School, which in 1996 was ranked the sixth-best high school in the state by New Jersey Monthly magazine. (For more details on Tenafly High School, see the Tenafly profile.)

Houses of Worship

Alpine Community Church (non-sectarian), which celebrated its 125th anniversary in 1996.

Houses

Many of Alpine's older Cape Cods have been razed to make way for large colonial or modern-style houses, said real estate saleswoman Marlyn Friedberg. The most exclusive residential neighborhoods are the borough's three subdivisions off Route 9W — Rio Vista, Glen Goin, and Timberline — where custom-built homes on large lots sell for in excess of $1 million.

Transportation

Bus transportation to Manhattan is provided along Route 9W, which runs through Alpine.

Recreation

Alpine has large areas of natural woodland for hikers and outdoor enthusiasts. The borough also offers a municipal swimming pool, tennis courts, and several bicycle trails. The borough coordinates its recreational programs with Cresskill, where youngsters can choose basketball, soccer, and baseball in addition to the sports provided through the public school system. The Memorial Day Parade followed by the annual barbecue hosted by the Alpine Fire Department is a community tradition.

The privately run Alpine Country Club is located in the borough.

Arts and Culture

The Community House, run by the Alpine Community Church, hosts cultural events, including an annual theatrical production and rehearsal and performance space for a local choir. Alpine's Historical Society, staffed by volunteers, chronicles the culture and times of the borough.

Child care services

A prekindergarten program and summer camp are available to residents, for a fee. Students in grades 3 and up may participate in an after-school study hall.

Senior services

Although not aimed specifically at the borough's senior citizens, the Community House's cultural activities attract many of Alpine's older residents.

Recent developments

Bergen County officials recently voted to preserve 134 acres in Alpine and Rockleigh as parkland. By the 1997-98 school year, the elementary school will have completed construction of a new auditorium stage and a new computer room.

Drawbacks

The number of fatalities along Route 9W has been of great concern to Alpine Borough officials. Recently, under a half-million-dollar grant from the state Department of Transportation, long-range safety changes have been implemented, including a reduced speed limit. Repavement of the highway is ongoing.

Prominent residents

Stevie Wonder, musician; Mike Schneider, Fox network newscaster.

Phone numbers

Township clerk (201) 845-2900
School district (201) 845-9114

— *Maria C. Zingaro*

DEMOGRAPHICS

County: Bergen
Size: 6.4 square miles
Population: 1,716
Density: 270/square mile
Median age: 39.7 years
White: 87.3 percent
Asian: 11.4 percent
Black: 1.1 percent
Median house value: $500,001
Upper 25 percent: Not available
Lower 25 percent: Not available
Median year built: 1968
Median rent: $979
Single-family homes: 561
Condominiums: None
Median property taxes per household (1994): $4,501
Median household income: $106,330
Industrial property: None
Sewers: 77 public, 511 septic
Library: None. Alpine residents may buy membership at libraries in neighboring towns.
Media: The Record covers the borough in addition to the Suburbanite and the Englewood Press-Journal, both weeklies. TCI provides cable service.
Fire and ambulance: Volunteer
Police: Paid
Crime rate per 1,000 (1994): 22.7
Violent crime rate per 1,000 (1994): 1.2

BERGENFIELD

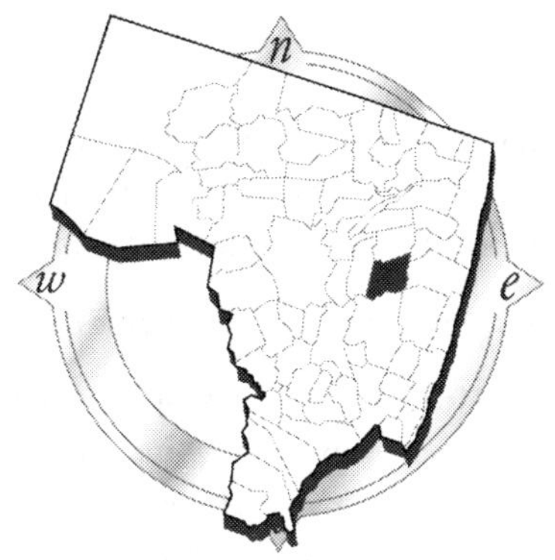

With unparalleled citizen activism, networks of closely knit neighborhoods, and a growing immigrant population, the borough of Bergenfield is one of Bergen County's most spirited and diverse communities.

The 2.9-square-mile borough is bounded by Dumont to the north, Tenafly and Englewood to the east, Teaneck to the south, and New Milford to the west.

Many of the borough's newest residents are of Indian, Central American, South American, and East Asian origin. A broad program of borough services and businesses have sprung up to meet the needs of those groups — giving Bergenfield a wide appeal to newcomers.

Bergenfield residents take a strong interest in the borough's political and social affairs. Rarely are council meetings sparsely attended here, and the borough's administrations generally have fostered an atmosphere of open dialogue with the community.

Ordinary residents have taken initiatives that have led to improved borough services such as leaf recycling and the rehabilitation of the swim club.

Bergenfield makes an effort to provide services to young and old alike. New families are bountiful in these parts, but the town also has a large elderly population. It has abundant recreation programs for children and programs to help senior citizens maintain independent living in their homes, while providing others with assisted-living centers.

Entrepreneurs also have good reason to look to Bergenfield. The borough has a strong, healthy business district. Its main thoroughfare, Washington Avenue, has national franchises as well as thriving, family-owned businesses. Almost 160 local businesses belong to the Chamber of Commerce.

Noteworthy Historical Events

Much of the borough was part of Camp Merritt in the World War I era. More than one million American troops passed through Camp Merritt, which served as an embarkation camp for overseas service and other training camps.

Schools

The Bergenfield school system is one of the major reasons young families move into the borough. Serving 3,261 students, with five elementary schools, one middle school, and one high school, the district offers a vast array of programs and classes. Its high school marching band has won national acclaim, and the high school graduation rate is more than 95 percent, with nearly three-quarters of those students going on to either two- or four-year colleges. Average SAT scores in 1995 were 405 verbal, 464 math. The high school offers about 30 advanced placement and honors courses. The district meets the needs of gifted and talented and disabled students. The average class size is 25, but one elementary school offers smaller classes for students who are recent immigrants.

The Board of Education also operates an adult community school at the high school, including practical courses in computer science, languages, and English as a Second Language. Recently, school trustees allocated $250,000 to upgrade computers and integrate the equipment into the curriculum at all the district's schools. The money will put computers into fifth-grade classrooms and school libraries, and add another computer lab at the high school.

Parochial and private schools include St. John the Evangelist Roman Catholic School and Montessori Learning Center.

Houses of Worship

All Saints Episcopal Church; Bergenfield Community Assembly of God; Calvary Lutheran Church; Church of the Good Shepherd United Methodist; Church of God of Englewood Inc.; Clinton

Avenue Reformed Church; Congregation Beth Abraham of Bergenfield; Congregation Beth Israel of Northern Valley; First Baptist Church of Bergenfield; St. Anthony's Orthodox Church; St. John the Evangelist R.C. Church; St. Stephen's Church; Malankara Orthodox; Sang Myung Korean Presbyterian Church; and South Presbyterian Church of Bergenfield.

HOUSES

Even the highest-priced houses in Bergenfield are moderate compared with other Bergen County towns.

TRANSPORTATION

New Jersey Transit services the borough, with all-day bus service to Port Authority in Manhattan (a 45-minute trip) and the terminal at the George Washington Bridge in Manhattan (about 25 minutes). There is also bus service to Hackensack, the county seat.

RECREATION

The borough's park system is one of its most treasured features. The town has more than 10 neighborhood parks and playgrounds, and the recreation department offers year-round activities for the whole family. Groups that wish to create leagues or programs can receive space, supplies, and funding from the borough.

Picturesque Cooper's Pond is a popular wedding-photo location, and many residents have fond memories of fishing, picnicking, and ice-skating there.

There are several athletic clinics for students, including basketball, weightlifting, softball, and baseball. The town runs a summer day camp for children, and swimming is available to all residents.

ARTS AND CULTURE

During the summer, the recreation department sponsors an outdoor Summer Concert Series, often including barbershop quartets, bluegrass, and a cappella performances. The Bergenfield Council for the Arts offers arts and crafts shows, dances and theatrical and musical performances, with an annual gala in June. The Bergenfield Museum Society mounts two to three exhibits every year.

CHILD CARE SERVICES

Bergenfield has seven private child care facilities.

SENIOR SERVICES

Bergenfield has several senior citizen housing complexes, the largest being the quiet Brookside Gardens on Murray Hill Terrace. A transportation program provides rides to doctors, hospitals, and clinics. A borough-sponsored bus service, called BEST, takes seniors to the downtown business district and municipal offices every Wednesday. The local chapter of the American Association of Retired Persons and the Sunshine Club offer information and activities.

RECENT DEVELOPMENTS

The town is securing grants to build a new community center that will house several recreational and cultural facilities, including the Bergenfield Museum Society.

DRAWBACKS

In 1994, the borough administration switched from a calendar year budget to a fiscal year budget, allowing the town to bond $7.7 million, some of which was to pay for early retirement for several borough employees. The borough intends to repay the retirement funds over 10 years at an interest rate of close to 9 percent. While the 1996-97 fiscal year saw only a minute municipal tax increase, analysts say the payments will increase and affect tax bills.

PROMINENT RESIDENTS

Milwaukee Brewers pitcher Ron Villone lives in the borough during the off season.

PHONE NUMBERS

Borough clerk (201) 387-4055
School district (201) 385-8202
Public library (201) 387-4040

— *DeQuendre Neeley*

Demographics

County: Bergen
Size: 2.9 square miles
Population: 24,458
Density: 8,456/square mile
Median age: 36.5
White: 83.9 percent
Asian: 9 percent
Black: 4.2 percent
Median house value: $184,000
Upper 25 percent: $211,700
Lower 25 percent: $162,000
Median year built: 1949
Median rent: $647
Single-family homes: 5,950
Condominiums: Not available
Median property taxes per household (1994): $5,127
Median household income: $45,713
Industrial property: 55 parcels
Sewers: Public
Library: 112,000 volumes (est.)
Media: The Record covers the town, as do the Twin-Boro News and the Town News. Cable service is provided by Cablevision.
Fire and ambulance: Volunteer
Police: Paid
Crime rate per 1,000 (1994): 18.3
Violent crime rate per 1,000 (1994): 2

Cliffside Park

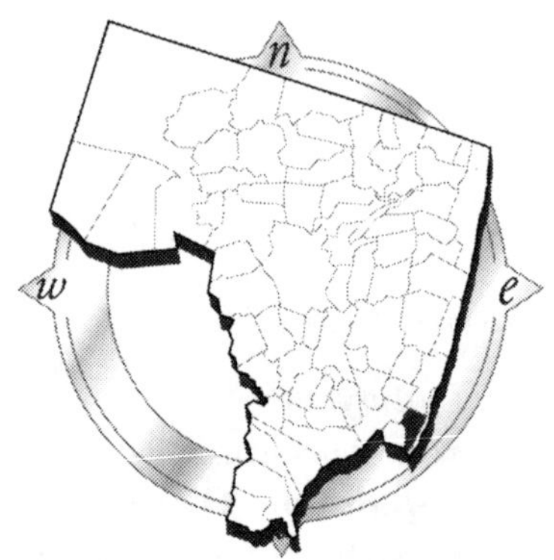

Cliffside Park lies at the crest of the Palisades in southeastern Bergen County, conveniently situated between the George Washington Bridge and the Lincoln Tunnel, and just a stone's throw from the ferry to midtown Manhattan.

With some 20,800 residents within its square-mile borders, it is the most densely populated community in the county.

Once a heavily blue-collar town that drew Italian, Polish, and Irish immigrants, Cliffside Park in recent decades has evolved — at least in certain sections — into a bedroom community for an upscale, white-collar population attracted by its Hudson River high-rises and the short commute to New York City.

The town today is known for its scenic views, clean and safe streets, quality municipal services, variety of restaurants, and its combination of small-town and cosmopolitan atmosphere.

Cliffside Park's main street is Anderson Avenue, a commercial strip with a strong ethnic flavor. Off Anderson stretch neat blocks of one- and two-family homes. Heading east toward the cliffs are the larger homes and high-rises with a view of the Manhattan skyline.

The town's trademark luxury skyscrapers, the twin 31-story Winston Towers, were built in the 1970s on the site of the former Palisades Amusement Park, sparking a high-rise boom. In recent years, the distinctive Carlyle Towers joined the skyline, occupying the last undeveloped site in town.

Some high-rise dwellers have become involved in politics in recent years, trying unsuccessfully to topple the town's mayor of 33 years, Democrat Gerald Calabrese. Republicans haven't fared any better in their attempts to topple the mayor; the last time a

Republican even won a council seat was in the 1970s.

Noteworthy historical events

In 1781, Brigadier Gen. Anthony Wayne and 1,000 Continental Army troops passed through Cliffside Park on their way to the Bull's Ferry blockhouse (in Guttenberg). They surrounded the log fortification on July 21 but were forced to withdraw by nightfall, soundly defeated by fewer than 90 British sympathizers.

On Oct. 4, 1951, North Jersey bootlegger and gambling chief Willie Moretti, an associate of such kingpins as Abner "Longy" Zwillman, Meyer Lansky, Lucky Luciano, and Frank Costello, was gunned down at Joe's Elbow Room, a local restaurant, shortly after testifying before the Kefauver Crime Commission. Vito Genovese, late don of one of New York's largest crime families, was widely credited with orchestrating the murder during his climb to power.

In 1971, Palisades Amusement Park, world famous for its giant Ferris wheel, roller coasters, huge salt-water pool, beauty pageants, contests, and other attractions, closed its doors after 73 years.

Schools

The Cliffside Park school district had 2,366 students enrolled for the 1996-97 school year, including 1,329 in grades kindergarten through 8. The district has four elementary schools, one of which also doubles as a middle school for the seventh and eighth grades. The high school also serves about 370 tuition-paying students from Fairview. Enrollment has been climbing in recent years.

The high school offers 123 courses, 14 honors programs, and five advanced placement programs. It is a charter member of the Bergen County Interactive Television Network consortium, which broadcasts high school and college courses that are offered elsewhere. The school also broadcasts its Latin class on the network and in the past has beamed in a Russian language class. The school also offers programs for students with special needs, vocational classes such as drafting, woodworking, and auto mechanics, and a shared-time program with the county vocational school. In 1995, the district sent 71 percent of its graduates to two- or four-year colleges. Average SAT scores in 1996 were 375 verbal and 463 math.

School No. 4 was recognized in 1995 under the state's Star School program for developing its writing workshop for seventh- and eighth-graders.

Epiphany Roman Catholic School is located in Cliffside Park.

Houses of worship

Christian Science Reading Room; Epiphany Roman Catholic Church; First Baptist Church-Grantwood; Grantwood Congregational Church; New Jersey Bible Church; Sacred Heart Parish of North Bergen; Sarang Presbyterian Church; St. Demetrius Melkite; Temple Israel Community Center; Trinity Episcopal Church; and Trinity Evangelical Lutheran Church.

Houses

The housing stock is typical of the area, with many brick and stone homes, wood-frame houses, two-family homes, mid-rise apartment buildings, and high-rise condominiums and cooperatives. The styles vary from Cape Cod to Victorian.

Transportation

New Jersey Transit provides three bus routes on Palisade and Anderson avenues that link commuters with Port Authority in midtown Manhattan and the George Washington Bridge. Another route terminates at the Bergen Mall in Paramus.

Recreation

Cliffside Park offers a variety of programs, including basketball, baseball, roller hockey, football, cheerleading, soccer, wrestling, and track and field.

The summer program includes arts and crafts, field trips, and nature hikes, plus football, basketball, and tennis clinics.

The recreation department operates a state-licensed preschool on weekdays at the recreation building at West Grantwood Park, the borough's largest park and playground area.

Other parks include Columbus Park, Zalewski Park, Memorial Park, Honor Park, the Gus Lesnevich Memorial Park, and the Little League field.

Arts and culture

There are no museums or professional performing groups.

Child care services

The town recreation department runs a small preschool program. The town has four licensed child care facilities, and the planning board has given approval for another.

Senior services

The borough has two senior residences with 354 units combined and a Nutrition Center sandwiched between them. The center is open daily and provides a hot lunch. A homebound lunch program also is available for those who qualify. There are dances, parties, crocheting, and other activities. A county van assists in transporting participants to and from the center and on weekly shopping trips.

Recent developments

In an effort to control traffic, Cliffside Park closed Oxenhill Road at its border with neighboring Edgewater in late 1996. Edgewater residents were outraged, as the road is one of four thoroughfares into town.

Drawbacks

Traffic congestion and a shortage of parking in the shopping district are growing problems.

Prominent residents

Gloria Gaynor, pop singer and queen of the Seventies' disco craze. Frank Lautenberg, U.S. senator.

Phone numbers

Township clerk (201) 945-3456
School district (201) 313-2310
Public library (201) 945-2867

— *Peter Sampson*

Demographics

County: Bergen
Size: 1 square mile
Population: 20,393
Density: 21,153/square mile
Median age: 38.8
White: 88.1 percent
Asian: 7.4 percent
Black: 1.8 percent
Median house value: $221,200
Upper 25 percent: $278,600
Lower 25 percent: $181,100
Median year built: 1958
Median rent: $633
Single-family homes: 1,674
Condominiums: Not available
Median property taxes per household (1994): $4,227
Median household income: $40,600
Industrial property: 15 parcels
Sewers: Public
Library: 58,821 volumes, 167 periodicals, 822 videos, 2,021 audiotapes and CDs
Media: The Record and the Jersey Journal cover the town, as do the weeklies the Palisadian, Sun Bulletin, and Bergen News. Time Warner Cable provides cable service.
Fire and ambulance: Paid
Police: Paid
Crime rate per 1,000 (1994): 21.4
Violent crime rate per 1,000 (1994): 1.2

Clifton

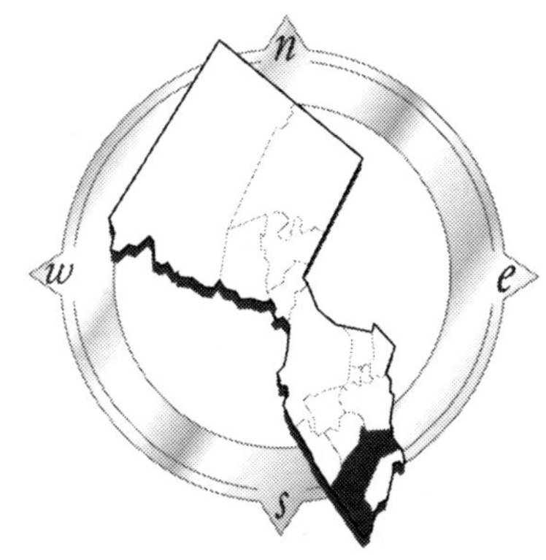

One of the largest municipalities in New Jersey, the City of Clifton offers many of the benefits of an urban community with few of the drawbacks. Largely residential, it flows seamlessly into the small suburban townships around it.

The city has four distinct sections: Allwood, Delawanna, Athenia, and Richfield. These were once separated from each other by farmlands, but as the farmlands were developed, the neighborhoods gradually blended together.

Fully developed today, Clifton offers a diversity of services to its increasingly diverse residents. Young families, drawn to Clifton because of its affordable housing, co-exist happily with the city's large senior citizen population. Similarly, Clifton residents of Western European descent have made room for people from Eastern Europe, India, the Middle East, and South and Central America; the city's Cultural Awareness Committee works to promote this variety as one its best assets.

Economically, local merchants have joined together to improve the downtown shopping district. The mayor and City Council have actively recruited outside industries and retailers for unused city properties. The influx of business has helped keep residential property taxes moderate.

Though technically designated a city, Clifton — thriving, vital, and geared toward its residents — contentedly carries on, well disguised as a seemingly typical suburb.

Noteworthy historical events

During the American Revolution, Clifton was an essential part of the Continental Army's retreat route toward the Delaware River. In pursuit of the fleeing rebel troops, British Gen. Cornwallis spent the night of Nov. 25, 1776, in a Clifton (then Acquackanonk) home.

In its more recent history, Clifton was the site of the nation's first strip mall, Styertown, built in 1952 and still flourishing.

Schools

The Clifton school district serves about 8,200 students in its 13 elementary schools, two middle schools, and one high school. "We provide for all needs here," said Schools Superintendent William Liess. "Given the size of the district, we can do that." In recent years, every school has been renovated and in some cases expanded to meet the needs of an increasing student population.

In the elementary schools, curricula have been updated and include new reading and mathematics programs. A new, more hands-on science program was scheduled to be implemented in 1997. A referendum also was being prepared that proposed technological improvements for all Clifton's schools.

Also at the elementary level, the district offers a highly individualized gifted and talented program. Families with special-needs students often move to Clifton because of its in-district special-needs programs.

The middle schools use a team-teaching approach to provide students with more personalized and concentrated instruction. Foreign language instruction is available to seventh-grade students, and both middle schools run an after-school enrichment program.

Liess described Clifton High School as "the most comprehensive in northern New Jersey ... with the most extensive advanced placement program." By taking specially designed courses, students can earn up to 20 college credits while in high school. Construction of a wing containing a fully computerized science and media center is under way. About 80 percent of Clifton's graduating seniors go on to attend two- or four-year colleges. Average SAT scores in 1995 were 409 verbal, 474 math.

Parochial schools include Pope John Paul II Roman Catholic (R.C.) School; Sacred Heart R.C. School; St. Andrew the Apostle R.C. School; St. Brendan R.C. School; St. Clare R.C. School; St. Cyril and

Methodius R.C. School; St. John Kanty R.C. School; St. Paul R.C. School; and St. Philip the Apostle R.C. School.

Houses of worship

Allwood Community Church (Reformed); Athenia Reformed Church; Beth Shalom Reformed Temple; Cavalry Baptist Church; Clifton Jewish Center; Crossroads Free Methodist Church; Evangelical Fellowship Chapel of the Fellowship Deaconry; Faith Gospel Church; Fellowship Chapel of the Fellowship Deaconry; First Lutheran Church; First Presbyterian Church of Clifton; Free Reformed Church; Grace Bible Church; Holy Face Monastery; Hope Reformed Church; Israel Memorial AME Church; Lakeview Heights Reformed Church; Netherland Reformed Church; New Jersey Reformed Presbyterian Church; Northside Christian Reformed Church; Richfield Christian Reformed Church; Russian Orthodox Church of the Assumption; Sacred Heart Roman Catholic (R.C.) Church; St. Andrew the Apostle R.C. Church; St. Brendan's R.C. Church; St. Clare's R.C. Church; St. Cyril and Methodius R.C. Church; St. George's Greek Orthodox Church; St. John Kanty R.C. Church; St. John's Evangelical Lutheran Church; St. Mary Protectress Ukrainian Orthodox Church; St. Paul's R.C. Church; St. Peter's Episcopal Church; St. Philip the Apostle R.C. Church; Trinity Church of the Nazarene; Trinity United Methodist Church; Ukrainian Orthodox Holy Ascension Church; Unification Church; United Reformed Church; and Valley Chapel Assembly of God.

Houses

Home styles generally include Cape Cods, colonials, Tudors, and split-levels. Housing prices are affordable, and resale values are strong.

Transportation

New Jersey Transit provides bus service from Clifton to Port Authority in Manhattan, as well as train service to Hoboken, where connections can be made to southern New Jersey, the PATH system, and ferries to lower Manhattan. There is also bus transportation within Clifton and to nearby communities including Passaic,

Paterson, and Newark. Local van transportation is also available, and there is shuttle bus service for Clifton's seniors.

Recreation

Clifton has 36 parks and playgrounds, and the city's recreational programs are among its most valuable assets. Sports programs for adults include two softball leagues, aerobics, archery, and men's basketball. For children, baseball, bowling, basketball, and gymnastics are available during the school year. In the summer, the city sponsors a six-week combination sports and arts day camp, and a preschool camp. Additional sporting and recreational activities are offered by the Clifton YM-YWHA.

The Department of Recreation sponsors special-interest clubs including a coin club, a stamp club, and a garden club, as well as programs for preschoolers, mothers and children, and disabled adults. Annual Clifton events include an Easter egg hunt, a Halloween parade, and a Christmas tree-lighting ceremony.

Clifton also sponsors an annual Youth Week, which includes athletic and artistic competitions. As part of Youth Week, Clifton students can be paired up with city officials to participate in municipal governance.

Arts and culture

The Clifton Choral Society, the Clifton Association of Artists, and the Summer Actors' Workshop operate through Clifton's Department of Recreation.

The Hamilton House Museum is the museum of the City of Clifton. Staffed by volunteers and situated in a house built in 1817 by the Vreeland family, the museum is open to the public Sundays from 2 to 5 p.m.

Child care services

The Boys' and Girls' Club of Clifton coordinates after-school child care in many of the city's elementary schools. The programs, which run from the end of the school day until 6 p.m., are available for a nominal fee.

Several private day-care centers are also available in Clifton.

Senior services

Clifton offers a multitude of services to its senior population of approximately 20,000. The city's Senior Center provides information and referrals for a variety of issues and problems, and assists with grant applications for special funds to low-income seniors. The city also offers seniors shuttle bus transportation to doctors and supermarkets and operates a Meals-on-Wheels program and two sites that provide lunchtime meals.

The city has more than 25 independently run social clubs for seniors; they sponsor luncheons, recreation, and trips. The city is investigating development of a large assisted housing complex with an on-site nursing home facility and small shopping center.

Daughters of Miriam Center for the Aged is located in Clifton.

Recent developments

Clifton Commons — a massive, $200 million shopping and recreational complex — will be built over the next three to four years on property formerly occupied by large corporations. The development will include a supermarket and other retail space, several restaurants, a multiplex movie theater, a hotel, office space, and more than 235 housing units.

Drawbacks

In recent years, Clifton, like many Northeastern communities, has lost much of its manufacturing and industrial base, with a resulting loss of jobs. According to Mayor James Anzaldi, the challenge is to maintain the property tax base by continuing to attract business to the community. In planning Clifton Commons, the city has taken steps to develop retail space on now-empty property.

Phone numbers

Township clerk (201) 470-5800
School district (201) 470-2260
Public library (201) 772-5500

— *Maria C. Zingaro*

Demographics

County: Passaic
Size: 11.3 square miles
Population: 71,742
Density: 6,347/square mile
Median age: 39 years
White: 92.8 percent
Asian: 3.5 percent
Black: 1.4 percent
Median house value: $185,000
Upper 25 percent: $223,700
Lower 25 percent: $159,600
Median year built: 1947
Median rent: $537
Single-family homes: 13,937
Condominiums: Approximately 750 units
Median property taxes per household (1994): $3,954
Median household income: $39,905
Industrial property: 456 parcels
Sewers: 29,869 public, 79 septic
Library: 165,225 volumes
Media: The Record and the New Jersey Herald & News cover the town.The Daily Journal is Clifton's twice-weekly local newspaper. Cable service is provided by TCI.
Fire and ambulance: Paid
Police: Paid
Crime rate per 1,000 (1994): 11.3
Violent crime rate per 1,000 (1994): 0.2

Closter

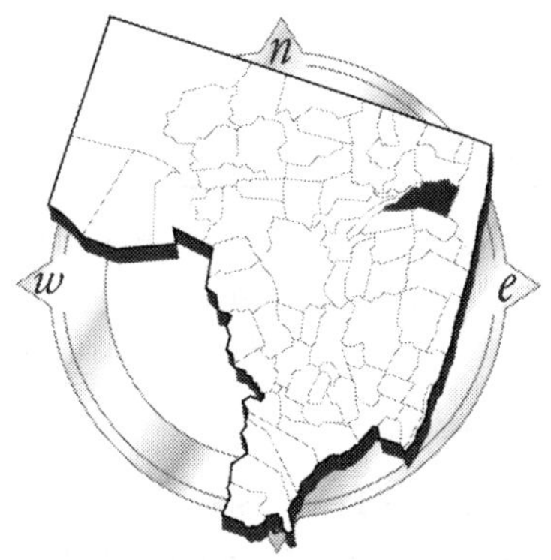

Just 10 minutes from the George Washington Bridge, with charming 18th and 19th century houses scattered around town, Closter is the ideal spot for the commuter with a big-city job who's looking for a small-town lifestyle.

"I love the old roadways like Piermont, the old buildings, the stone houses," said Pat Garbe Morillo, president of the Closter Historical Society and the borough's official historian. "The historic downtown area has so much charm. A lot of the buildings are from the 1800s, and the old houses haven't been altered too much."

But even Morillo admitted that charm alone is rarely enough to persuade out-of-towners to move in.

"I'm sure the location — 10 minutes to the George Washington Bridge — is why a lot of people like to live here," she said. "Historically, it's been a commuter town. Its nickname is the Hub of the Northern Valley."

Sprawled over 3.2 square miles, with the heavily traveled Closter-Dock Road slicing through its middle, the borough is a mixture of quaint shops, mini-malls, and quiet neighborhoods. Borough Hall, in the center of town on Closter-Dock Road, is impossible to miss.

Noteworthy historical events

The borough seal is the Lone Horseman with a three-cornered hat. "Closter has the Paul Revere of Bergen County," Morillo said. This anonymous hero was a Closter farmer who alerted the area to the approach of several thousand Redcoats who had crossed the Hudson River in flatboats and scaled the Palisades early in the morning of Nov. 20, 1776. The warning gave George Washington time to ride to Fort Lee from his Hackensack headquarters and retreat across the Hackensack River. The farmer had been plowing his field when he saw the first British scouts advancing down Closter-Dock Road. He rode to Fort Lee to report his sighting.

Schools

The Closter school system has some 900 students, spread among grades kindergarten through 8 at the Hillside and Tenakill elementary schools and at the Village Middle School. Closter has a low ratio of teachers to students — about 1:15 — and its $8,321 per-pupil cost is a little above the state average. The median teacher salary in Closter is approximately $65,000.

Closter high school students attend Northern Valley Regional High School in Demarest, which was ranked 19th among New Jersey high schools by New Jersey Monthly magazine in 1996. The magazine reported that 85 percent of the school's graduates go on to four-year colleges and 9 percent go on to two-year colleges.

The high school's 1995 SAT scores averaged 459 verbal, 555 math. The school, which offers some 200 courses, including 11 advanced placement, had three National Merit Scholars in the 1996-97 school year.

With 300 computers, another 100 on the way, and Internet access, the high school is one of the most technologically advanced in the country, Principal Bert Ammerman said. It was one of 29 high schools nationally to receive Blue Ribbon honors in technology.

Houses of worship

Centennial AME Zion Methodist; Emmaus Mission Church; First Congregational Church; Jehovah's Witness Congregation of Closter; Korean Gillbott Church; Reformed Church of Closter; St. Mary's Roman Catholic Church; St. Paul's Evangelical Lutheran Church; and Temple Beth-El of Northern Valley.

Houses

A diverse selection, from century-old cottages to modern colonials to apartments in the downtown area.

Transportation

Rockland Coaches Inc. provides daily bus transportation to and from New York City, with reduced fares for riders over age 62.

Recreation

The spring baseball and softball leagues are among the town's most popular youth programs. There are leagues for all ages, and all-star teams are selected at the end of each season.

In the winter, the town joins with Demarest and Haworth to run basketball leagues for girls and boys grades 4 through 6. A seventh- and eighth-grade boys basketball team plays in the North Jersey League. Soccer and wrestling are also popular.

Arts and culture

Closter often displays the works of local artists at the Closter Public Library. A separate wing of the library houses works by Abram Belskie, a noted sculptor who lived in town until his death in 1988. Closter residents can drive a few minutes to catch shows for all age groups at the Oradell Playhouse.

The Closter Nature Center sponsors monthly programs for youth and community groups.

Child care services

There are five private child care facilities in Closter, not including summer recreation programs.

Senior services

In addition to a number of seniors' residential units, Closter has Spectrum for Living, a long-term residential care facility for developmentally disabled adults.

The Closter Senior Citizens' Club, formed in 1957, meets bimonthly for residents 60 and over. The group plays bingo and cards, does crafts and line dancing, and takes trips.

Recent developments

After a lengthy controversy that included death threats against the mayor and a local attorney, Temple Emanu-El appears on the verge of completing a move from its home in Englewood to Closter. The battle involved the location of the temple in Closter, but a compromise seems to have been reached to build it on Piermont Road.

Drawbacks

At the top of the short list of drawbacks for living in Closter is the rising price of homes. Developers are tearing down many of the older homes in town and building larger houses, unaffordable for many, for as much as $600,000. The average home price in town has climbed to close to $300,000, above the average of surrounding towns, according to several real estate agencies.

Prominent residents

Marcel Jovine, artist.

Phone numbers

Township clerk (201) 784-0756
School district (201)768-3001
Public library (201) 768-4220

— *Doug Most*

Demographics

County: Bergen
Size: 3.2 square miles
Population: 8,094
Density: 2,544/square mile
Median age: 38.3 years
White: 81 percent
Asian: 17.4 percent
Black: 1.1 percent
Median house value: $275,200
Upper 25 percent: $376,900
Lower 25 percent: $216,900
Median year built: 1954
Median rent: $892
Single-family homes: 2,492
Condominiums: None
Median property taxes per household (1994): $5,767
Median household income: $62,555
Industrial property: 7 parcels
Sewers: Public and private
Library: 42,000 volumes
Media: The Record and two weeklies, the Suburbanite and the Englewood Press-Journal, cover the town. Cable service is provided by Cablevision.
Fire and ambulance: Paid
Police: Paid
Crime rate per 1,000 (1994): 17.5
Violent crime rate per 1,000 (1994): 1

CRESSKILL

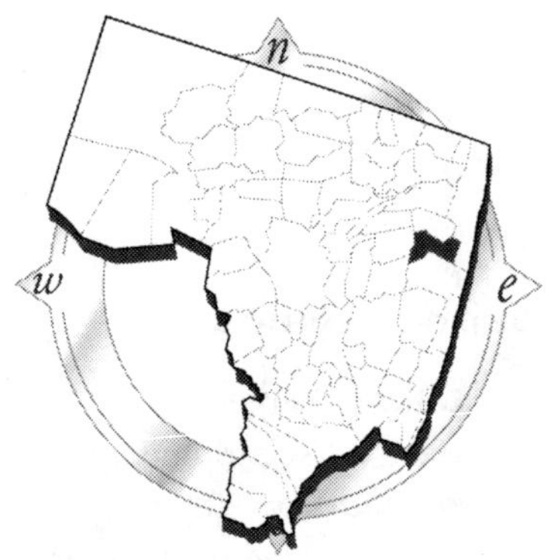

Once a blue-collar town, the borough of Cresskill is now a white-collar bedroom community with a large majority of wage-earners who commute to New York City. Named for the watercress that grows along its Tenakill Brook, the town is known today for its attractive, tree-lined streets, a low crime rate, quality municipal services, and high-priced homes on large lots.

It also has plenty of small-town charm, with a well-stocked library, a prekindergarten program run out of the Bryan School as a cooperative venture with parents, a municipal swimming pool, and a strong sense of neighborhood pride.

"It's just a safe, friendly, close-knit community," said Mayor John Bergamini. "When people move here, they stay."

Cresskill was a quiet farming community in the township of Palisades until 1859, when the Northern Railroad of New Jersey linked it to Jersey City and the ferry to New York City. In the late 1800s, it was home to the largest chicken hatchery in the world, which produced 10,000 chickens a week.

Cresskill's development boom came right after World War II to accommodate returning veterans. The population doubled, to 7,290, between 1950 and 1960.

Building was easy in Cresskill because much of the land had been cleared during World War I for the construction of Camp Merrit, an embarkation center for troops. Today almost all the available land has been developed.

Cresskill's small downtown, along Union Avenue and Piermont Road, has a supermarket, several banks, a half-dozen restaurants, and a number of clothing stores.

Noteworthy historical events

One of the town's oldest buildings is the Dutch-style Huyler Homestead at 50 County Road. The house, now a private residence, is on the National Register of Historic Places.

Schools

Cresskill prides itself on its schools. About 95 percent of the high school graduates go on to two- or four-year colleges each year, and the high school was ranked 65th in the state in 1996 by New Jersey Monthly magazine. The 1995 average SAT verbal score was 444; in math, 512.

The system is very small, with 1,152 students divided between the combined 501-student Cresskill Junior/Senior High School and two elementary schools, the Merritt School and Edward H. Bryan School. There is one parochial school in the borough: St. Therese Roman Catholic School, for kindergarten through grade 8.

The small student population, and an average class size that hovers around 15 students, allows the district to give special attention to students with outstanding ability and those with special needs. The high school offers advanced placement courses in English literature, history, mathematics, and foreign languages, and fields 15 varsity athletic teams, including baseball, football, tennis, volleyball, and basketball.

Houses of worship

Cresskill Congregational Church; Northern Valley Evangelical Free Church; Reformed Church on the Hill; Social Concerns; and St. Therese Roman Catholic Church.

Houses

Typical Cresskill houses are the split-level and ranches that defined the post-war building boom. Houses in the borough start around $200,000 for some small two- to three-bedroom Cape Cods or colonials on 50-by-100-foot lots on the west side of town. The priciest neighborhoods are the Rio Vista and Tammy Brook Estates developments on the eastern side of town. There, custom homes, some with private tennis courts and pools, are built on nine-tenths of an acre, known as a builder's acre. These homes sell for $1 million to $2 million.

Transportation

The Red and Tan Lines offers 45-minute rush-hour transportation to Port Authority in Manhattan. Train connections to the PATH system in Hoboken can be made in neighboring Tenafly.

Recreation

When Cresskill began its baton-twirling competition a few years back, it was a strictly local affair. But the annual competition has blossomed so thoroughly that the town now hires a hall at Bergen Community College for the event. Last year, it attracted 1,000 participants and fans. The municipal recreation program offers swimming, karate, softball, and baseball, as well as a local Little League. Programs are offered for everyone from kindergarteners to adults.

The main recreational complex covers a three-block area running from Madison Avenue southward to the Tenafly line, between Third and Fourth streets, and includes the two-block William Cook Park, with three tennis courts, a soccer field, baseball diamond, and play area. The southern part of the area is the municipal pool.

Arts and culture

There are no museums or professional performing groups in Cresskill.

Child care services

Cresskill Cooperative Preschool, operated by parents, is offered at the Bryan School. There are two private child care facilities in town.

Senior services

The Cresskill Senior Citizen Club meets twice a month at the American League. It takes bus trips to various destinations including Atlantic City and regional dinner theaters, with transportation costs funded by the municipality. Cresskill's health department offers flu shots and blood pressure tests free of charge to seniors, in addition to hearing and eye testing. Members of the Senior Citizen Club meet for line dancing.

RECENT DEVELOPMENTS

Residents and town officials are concerned over what may happen to a 4.6-acre property that was once the site of the Quirk Funeral Home. The century-old Gothic revival mansion — thought to be the home of Gen. John J. Pershing before World War I, when the area was the site of an Army training base — was considered an important historic landmark in town, but was torn down two years ago by a developer. The developer wants to build a 100-unit apartment complex that would contain some low-income units, required under the state's Mount Laurel mandates. The inclusion of the low-income units is seen in town as a ploy to circumvent local zoning regulations.

DRAWBACKS

Housing is expensive in Cresskill. Also, both the lack of industry and the necessity of supporting its own non-regionalized school system keep taxes high.

PHONE NUMBERS

Township clerk (201) 569-5400
School district (201) 567-5921
Public library (201) 567-3521

— John Zeaman

DEMOGRAPHICS

County: Bergen
Size: 2.1 square miles
Population: 7,558
Density: 3,577/square mile
Median age: 39.8
White: 85.5 percent
Asian: 13.6 percent
Black: 0.7 percent
Median house value: $245,800
Upper 25 percent: $319,800
Lower 25 percent: $202,200
Median year built: 1954
Median rent: $1,001
Single-family homes: 2,342
Condominiums: 63 units
Median property taxes per household (1994): $5,242
Median household income: $42,464
Industrial property: None
Sewers: Public and private
Library: 47,862 volumes
Media: The Record covers the town, as does the weekly Suburbanite. Cablevision provides cable service.
Fire and ambulance: Volunteer
Police: Paid
Crime rate per 1,000 (1994): 12.6
Violent crime rate per 1,000 (1994): 0.9

DEMAREST

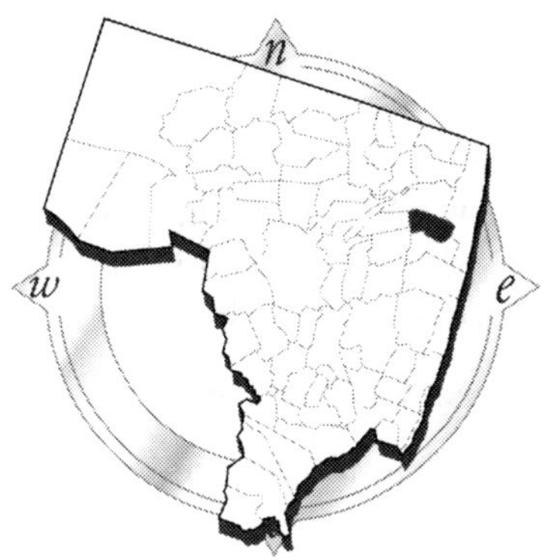

Though not yet into its second century, Demarest projects an old-fashioned warmth, charm, and cohesiveness of spirit uncommon in even the most established communities. "Community spirit and community togetherness make for lasting relationships and lasting friendships," said Councilwoman Carole Cardinale.

Many residents participate in one or more of the borough's recreational and cultural activities. Others volunteer with the garden society, fire department, or ambulance corps. Even Demarest's library is privately supported. And this sense of community spirit is not unique to the borough's older citizens, but can also be seen among Demarest's youth.

Demarest's center, at least figuratively, is the picturesque pool known locally as the Duck Pond. It was created in the late 1800s, when residents dammed up a stream for ice skating in the winter and rowing in the summer. Today, Demarest's tiny commercial district, Borough Hall, and fire department are clustered around the Duck Pond.

Residents actively work to maintain the character of their community. The borough is "a little bit of Americana that we are trying to keep natural-looking," Cardinale said. "It has remained much the same over the past 30 years." The borough is surrounded by woodlands, for example, and that rural beauty has not been sacrificed to further town development. No industry has been permitted, and although there are a handful of small shops in town, residents must travel to neighboring Cresskill or Closter for most necessities.

Parents still let their children ride all over town on bicycles.

Neighbors still offer one another wild raspberries picked from their backyards. People might be drawn to the town because of its quick access to New York City, but they'll likely be sold on it for the kind of security that only a true, old-style community can offer.

Noteworthy historical events

In the 1850s, State Sen. Ralph Demarest was instrumental in the building of a railroad that ran from Jersey City to Piermont, N.Y., and was a major factor in the region's development. The local railroad stop was named Demarest Station, and later, when the borough was incorporated, it adopted the name. In 1909, Demarest Station was outfitted with an elegant stationhouse built from locally quarried sandstone. The building, which still stands, was designed by Cleveland Cady, a famed architect (and the father of Elizabeth Cady Stanton, the suffragette).

Schools

The Demarest school system is a compelling reason for families with children to make their home in the borough. The district operates three elementary schools, each with an uncommonly low student-teacher ratio.

Demarest teenagers attend Northern Valley Regional High School, which was ranked 19th in the state in 1996 by New Jersey Monthly magazine. Situated within the Demarest borough limits, the high school serves some 1,000 students from Demarest and neighboring towns.

Northern Valley offers advanced placement classes in U.S. and European history, biology, chemistry, physics, calculus, Spanish, French, English literature and composition, and economics. The 1995 average SAT scores — 468 verbal and 532 math — are at least 50 points above the state averages. Ninety-two percent of the high school students go on to attend two- or four-year colleges.

St. Joseph-Sacred Heart School and Academy of the Holy Angels High School are also located in Demarest.

Houses of worship

Demarest Baptist Church ABC; Demarest United Methodist

Church; Han In Korean Church of New Jersey; St. Joseph's Korean Catholic Mission; and St. Joseph's Roman Catholic Church.

Houses

No one style of construction typifies the houses found in Demarest. Cape Cods, colonials, split-levels, and large contemporaries are well interspersed. Prices vary widely, ranging from $220,000 for an older, smaller home to more than $1 million for a large modern house.

Transportation

The Red and Tan Bus Lines provides transportation into Port Authority in Manhattan.

Recreation

The Nature Center, a large property maintained by the borough on its northern side, provides residents with pristine fields and woodlands for hiking and wandering. The center also sponsors the borough's annual Octoberfest, an outdoor, family-oriented festival with canoe and pony rides for children and games of chance and display booths for adults. The Demarest Garden Society maintains Davies Arboretum. A children's park and baseball diamond can be found in Wakelee Field.

Recreational activities offered to Demarest residents include baseball, softball, soccer, and tennis for children; basketball, tennis, and volleyball for adults. Residents may also join the privately run Demarest Swim Club. Each summer, the borough sponsors free concerts. The borough holds a Memorial Day parade, a Ragamuffin parade, and a tree-lighting ceremony each year.

Arts and Culture

The Old Church Cultural Center in Demarest, an art school located on the site of a burned-out church, runs more than 60 arts and crafts courses throughout the year. Classes include drawing, painting, ceramics, photography, jewelry-making, children's book illustration, print-making, stained glass, basket-weaving, portfolio development, dance, and tai chi.

In addition to displaying the work of its students, the center rents its gallery space to artists who wish to show their work locally. For the past eight years, the center also has hosted the New Jersey Annual Small Works festival, which features work from artists from all parts of the state.

Other programming includes classical and jazz concerts, a pottery show and sale (held annually), and a show for polymer clay artists that includes workshops and lectures.

A community effort is under way to preserve and restore the Tenakill Bridge and to list it on the state and national registers of historic places.

Child care services

The Demarest Parent Teacher Association runs a tuition-based after-school program from 3 to 6 p.m. for children grades kindergarten through 5. Northern Valley Regional High organizes a Teens and Tots program, where high school students care for youngsters under faculty supervision. Privately run child care is also available.

Senior services

The Demarest Recreational Center, used primarily by the borough's seniors, is located in the former Demarest stationhouse. Activities include folk dancing, games, chorus, exercise classes, yoga, line dancing, arts and crafts, and stained-glass making. The center organizes trips to Atlantic City and other nearby points of interest. Additionally, the Demarest Senior Citizens Club sponsors luncheons and trips.

Recent developments

Restoration is being planned for the Hardenburgh Bridge, built in 1909. The brick arch bridge, held together without mortar, is the last of its kind in the county. Refurbishment plans include strengthening the construction and widening the road without tampering with the structure's essential design and appearance. The Wakelee Field ball park is also slated for improvements. Renovation has just been completed on the children's playground.

Drawbacks

The borough's high tax rate, while not uncommon in Bergen County, is the principal drawback to living in the borough.

Prominent residents

Television announcer Don Pardo; State Sen. Gerald Cardinale.

Phone numbers

Township clerk (201) 768-0167
School district (201) 768-6060
Public library (201) 768-8714

— *Maria C. Zingaro*

Demographics

County: Bergen
Size: 2.07 square miles
Population: 4,800
Density: 2,320/square mile
Median age: 39.9 years
White: 81.4 percent
Asian: 17.6 percent
Black: 1 percent
Median house value: $322,800
Upper 25 percent: $450,000
Lower 25 percent: $246,100
Median year built: 1956
Median rent: $1,001
Single-family homes: 1,557
Condominiums: None
Median property taxes per household (1994): $6,896
Median household income: $68,043
Industrial property: None
Sewers: 1,589 public, 9 septic
Library: 23,460 volumes
Media: The Record covers the town, as do the Suburbanite and the Englewood Press-Journal, both weeklies. Cablevision provides cable service.
Fire and ambulance: Volunteer
Police: Paid
Crime rate per 1,000 (1994): 11.3
Violent crime rate per 1,000 (1994): 0.2

DUMONT

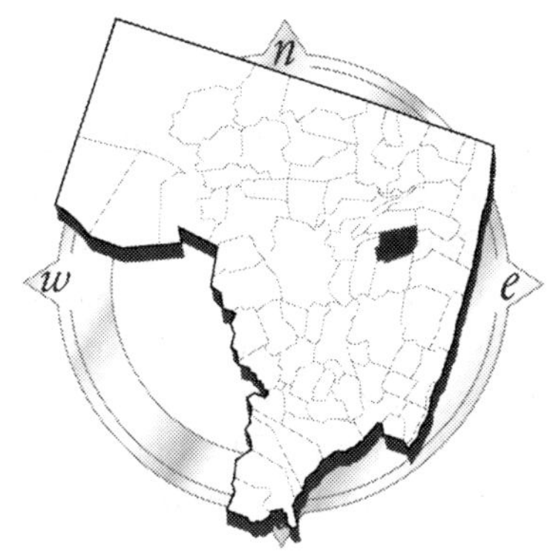

"In Schraalenburgh the [18]80s and '90s were years of innocent pleasures and quiet contentment. Life ... moved at a leisurely pace."

— **H. Jeanne Altshuler,**
"Dumont Heritage: Old Schraalenburgh"

Though smaller than Bergenfield, its twin borough to the south, Dumont has carved out a unique spot in Bergen County, rich in history and culture while preserving a touch of the rural simplicity evoked in the above passage.

H. Jeanne Altshuler, in her book on Dumont history, described women crocheting around the fire while men tended to borough affairs. Although times have changed radically, residents today praise the borough for its small-town charms and pleasant lifestyle.

Named for its first mayor, Dumont Clarke — a wealthy, civic-minded New York banker — the 1.79-square-mile borough is bounded by Cresskill to the east, Haworth to the north, Bergenfield to the south, and New Milford to the west.

Once known as the Dutch settlement of Schraalenburgh, or "scraggly hill," Dumont in its early days comprised three sections — Fleetwood, Fairfield Manor, and Sanhurst. With time, however, the distinctions among them have eroded.

Dumont may be best known as the home of the Old North Reformed Church, one of the finest examples of early American church architecture in the country.

"Don't forget the library," said its director, Elizabeth Stewart. "A town's most prized possession is its library." The borough library has almost 50,000 volumes and offers lectures, late-night hours for research, and services for shut-in readers.

Dumont, nine miles west of New York City, was cited in a survey of American suburbs, "Safest Places for the '80s" by David and Holly Franke, as one of the nation's safest places to live. The authors attributed the borough's low crime rate to its distance from any major highways. The book noted that Dumont scored lower than rural areas in all types of crime except larceny and auto theft.

Noteworthy historical events

A World War I army camp was hastily erected in the borough in 1917. Camp Merritt served as an embarkation point for more than a million soldiers going and returning from overseas.

Schools

The public school system in Dumont began in 1800 when a one-room schoolhouse was built on a lane near Old North Reformed Church. Today, the school district has five schools and serves more than 2,000 students.. The median teacher salary was $58,300 in 1995.

In addition to standard courses, Dumont schools offer advanced placement, honors, and gifted and talented courses as well as a slew of extracurricular activities.

Dumont has begun integrating computers and the latest technology into the curriculum; last year the Honiss and Selzer Schools each received a state-of-the-art computer lab. Every school has computers, and Dumont has updated its technology without significant bond-raising.

More than 95 percent of the high school students graduate, with more than two-thirds continuing on to a four-year college. Average SAT scores were 422 verbal, 474 math in 1995.

St. Mary's Roman Catholic School is located in Dumont.

Houses of worship

Calvary United Methodist Church; End of the Earth Church; Iglesia Bautista Resurreccion; Living Word Community Church; Our Redeemer Lutheran Church; Old North Reformed Church; and St.

Mary's Roman Catholic Church.

Houses

Dumont's housing is mostly single-family. Although Cape Cods and colonials abound, the borough does have a few garden apartment complexes as well as two senior living facilities.

Transportation

New Jersey Transit has three bus routes to Manhattan and two local buses, one that goes to Hackensack (the county seat) and one that goes to Carlstadt.

Recreation

With 11 parks and lots of activities for children and adults, the borough has maintained a commitment to athletics, open spaces, and safety.

Several of the parks have one or more baseball/softball diamonds, basketball, and tennis courts. One park has a hockey arena that's also available for in-line skating.

The recreation commission sponsors baseball, basketball, softball, football, wrestling, cheerleading, and volleyball. During the summer, there are several trips, crafts classes, and more sports. For adults, the borough offers aerobics, soccer, and open gym nights. A private swim club is available to all residents for a fee.

Arts and culture

The New Jersey Symphony Orchestra performs three to four concerts in Dumont each year. The high school has an award-winning marching band, part of an extremely popular music department that performs frequently for the public.

The library, senior center, and several community organizations showcase the work of local artists. Dumont is also home to Evelyn Swartz, a quiltmaker whose patterns were inspired by primitive cave drawings.

Child care services

The borough has no municipally run day care centers, but there are several privately run facilities. One, Northern Valley Preschool, runs an after-school program at the elementary schools.

Senior services

The popular new senior citizen center is hooked up to ITV, or Interactive Television. The cable hook-up allows seniors to take courses for credit at area community colleges. Mayor Don Winant, who spearheaded the project, hailed the connection as an excellent example of intergenerational learning.

The senior center provides transportation to doctors' offices, downtown, and municipal buildings. It has a boccie ball court, bingo room, lounge, and library. The center offers several trips annually.

Dumont is home to two senior living facilities. The Dumont Senior Citizen Housing has 40 one-bedroom apartments in a beautiful complex convenient to downtown and Borough Hall. The other, the David Roche apartments, offers dozens of units for Dumont seniors.

Northern Valley Adult Day Health Center is located in Dumont.

Recent developments

The borough is seeking funding for a roller-blading arena to accommodate the overflow from the hockey/roller-blading rink.

Drawbacks

With the amount of undeveloped land dwindling, density may become a problem for the tiny borough.

Prominent residents

Ultramarathoner Stu Mittleman.

Phone numbers

Township clerk (201) 387-5022
School district (201) 387-3082
Public library (201) 384-2030

— Dequendre Neeley and Marc Warren Watrel

Demographics

County: Bergen
Size: 2 square miles
Population: 17,187
Density: 8,660/square mile
Median age: 36.6
White: 91.2 percent
Asian: 6.8 percent
Black: 1.1 percent
Median house value: $188,400
Upper 25 percent: $220,100
Lower 25 percent: $165,700
Median year built: 1947
Median rent: $630
Single-family homes: 4,505
Condominiums: 47 units
Median property taxes per household (1994): $4,850
Median household income: $48,776
Industrial property: 11 parcels
Sewers: Public
Library: 49,398 volumes
Media: The Record covers the town, as does the weekly Town News. Cable service is provided by Cablevision.
Fire and ambulance: Paid
Police: Paid
Crime rate per 1,000 (1994): 16.8
Violent crime rate per 1,000 (1994): 0.9

Elmwood Park

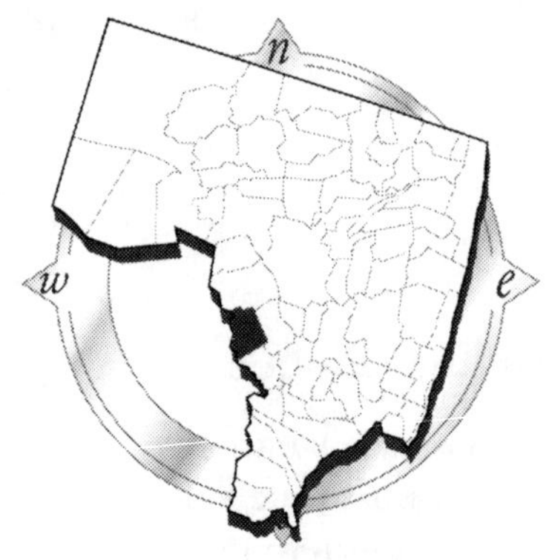

In 1962, newlywed Richard Mola found a small Cape Cod house in East Paterson and decided to settle down. Ten years later, Mola ran for mayor of the small, 2.7-square-mile community and won. One year into his term, voters decided they wanted to change the name of the town to Elmwood Park.

"I was the last mayor of East Paterson and the first mayor of Elmwood Park," Mola said. "The community felt that we were in Bergen County and that we should disassociate ourselves from the large City of Paterson."

Today, first-time buyers often choose Elmwood Park. "Buying a home here allows for a quick commute and an inexpensive Bergen County community," explained Bill Luzzi, of Re/Max real estate. Elmwood Park is about eight miles from Manhattan and is bordered on the west by Paterson, on the north by Fair Lawn, on the south by Garfield, and on the east by Saddle Brook. An old-fashioned business district on Market Street includes a florist, a funeral parlor, a tiny diner, a card store, and a deli.

Noteworthy Historical Events

There was a thriving race track — the only mile-long track in the state — in East Paterson around 1890. Visitors would come from as far as New York and Pennsylvania to enjoy harness racing from a grandstand a block long. But blue laws outlawing racing and drinking closed the track a decade after it opened.

Schools

The district serves 1,800 students, with three primary schools, one middle school, and Elmwood Park high school. There are also several special-needs programs, including a gifted and talented program that begins at the elementary level.

The high school offers more than 100 courses, 12 honors programs, and six advanced placement programs. Eighty-three percent of Elmwood Park High School graduates go on to two- or four-year schools. In 1995, the average verbal score on the Scholastic Assessment Test was 483; math scores averaged 513. Students can study Italian, Spanish, and French.

St. Leo's Roman Catholic School is located in Elmwood Park.

Houses of worship

Christian Victory Fellowship; Elmwood Park Jewish Center; First Presbyterian Church of Elmwood Park; and St. Leo's Roman Catholic Church.

Housing

Starter homes can cost as little as $100,000. There are also 1,000 apartments.

Transportation

New Jersey Transit provides a 20- to 30-minute commute into New York by bus. A train to Hoboken runs from the nearby Fair Lawn station. From Hoboken, PATH connections are available to Jersey City, Newark, and New York.

Recreation

The town provides a full range of team sports for children as well as programs for adults. The Rosemont Park has swings for kids, and Elmwood Park has swings and a basketball court. Cherry Hill Park has a walking path, and the high school has tennis courts that residents can use after hours.

During the summer, some roads are closed off for biking on Sunday afternoons.

Arts and culture

The library offers lectures and programs on art and books.

Child care services

The town's recreation department runs an after-school care program where kids can do homework. Elmwood Park also has four private child care facilities.

Senior services

There is a meeting room for seniors in the recreation center. Health programs and services are offered throughout the year, including seminars on diet and aging, flu shots, and blood pressure tests. Senior clubs offer day trips throughout the year.

Drawbacks

There is an overflow of traffic from Route 4.

Recent developments

Two large office buildings are scheduled to be constructed along River Road.

Prominent residents

Dick Vitale, TV sports commentator.

Phone numbers

Township clerk (201) 796-1457
School district (201) 794-2933
Public library (201) 796-8888

— *Emily Wax*

Demographics

County: Bergen
Size: 2.7 square miles
Population: 17,623
Density: 6,639/square mile
Median age: 38.4
White: 93.7 percent
Asian: 3.4 percent
Black: 0.8 percent
Median house value: $185,600
Upper 25 percent: $210,100
Lower 25 percent: $164,900
Median year built: 1950
Median rent: $542
Single-family homes: 3,258
Condominiums: 57 units
Median property taxes per household (1994): $3,695
Median household income: $38,248
Industrial property: 59 parcels
Sewers: Public
Library: 70,143 volumes
Media: The Record covers the town, as does the Shopper News, a weekly. TCI provides cable service.
Fire and ambulance: Volunteer
Police: Paid
Crime rate per 1,000 (1994): 42.2
Violent crime rate per 1,000 (1994): 1.9

EMERSON

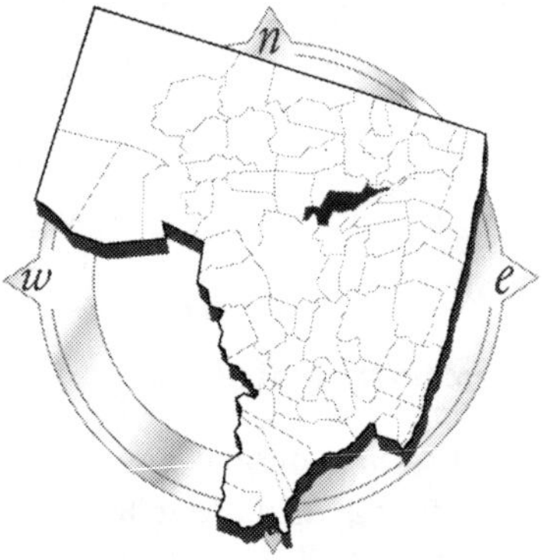

A small sign on the road into Emerson reads, "Emerson the Family Town." Residents of this 2.2-square-mile municipality still feel their children can safely ride their bikes around town, and describe their community as "delightfully quiet."

For families, the town has several benefits: a good school system in a small yet ethnically diverse community, and an easy commute into New York City.

On a clear night in Emerson you can see the glow of the George Washington Bridge from the Bird Hill Emerson Golf Club.

"We have very little commerce and industry. We are very close to the city, and at the same time we are a very small town," Mayor Owen Cassidy said.

Residents recently joined together to raise funds to rebuild a park. It was renamed in honor of Leo Rosengart, an Emerson resident who died in a plane crash.

The community has a mixed population of middle-class Catholics and Jews and a thriving Armenian population.

"It's the United Nations here," Cassidy said. "Everyone helps each other. After the local Roman Catholic parish permitted members of the Jewish temple in town to worship at the Catholic school while their building was in construction, the Jewish members of the community said they would watch the Catholic children during midnight Mass."

"At the time we moved in, it was starting to really grow. I thought it was nice to be part of a town becoming bigger and better," said Muriel Wassmann, the borough historian, who has lived in Emerson for more than 35 years. "The township split from Washington Township in 1903, and I'm sure no one regrets it. It's nice to have home rule in a small town."

Noteworthy historical events

There was a famous duel between Gen. Enoch Poor and Major James Porter during the American Revolution. Legend has it that Poor died from his wounds shortly after the fight, but the episode was covered up. "It was like a hidden secret for a long time; no one wanted anyone to know that a major might have killed a general," Wassman said. Emerson residents also were reluctant to publicize the duel, thinking it would detract from the town's reputation.

Schools

Emerson's tiny school district is the pride of residents here. The district, which serves 1,000 students, has two elementary schools. Emerson Junior High School (grades 7 and 8) is housed in the high school. In 1996, there were only 412 students in grades 7 through 12. Nevertheless, the high school offers more than 100 courses, five honors programs, and advanced placement courses in calculus and foreign languages. There are also several special-needs programs, including a gifted and talented program that begins at the elementary level. The high school also has an independent study program for seniors with special interests. About 92 percent of Emerson High School graduates go on to attend two- or four-year colleges. The average SAT score is 519 verbal, 542 math.

Assumption of the Blessed Virgin Mary Church has a private school program for preschool through eighth grade.

Houses of worship

Assumption of the Blessed Virgin Mary Roman Catholic Church; Church of Jesus Christ of Latter Day Saints; Emerson Assembly of God; Emerson Bible Church; Emerson Jewish Center; Congregation B'nai Israel; and First Korean Presbyterian Church of New Jersey.

Houses

"There is a pretty broad range in Emerson," said Bill Teubner, president of Prudential Higgins Realty.

TRANSPORTATION

Residents commute on the Main Bergen line into Hoboken, where they can pick up PATH connections to Newark, Jersey City, and New York. New Jersey Transit also provides bus service to Port Authority in Manhattan.

RECREATION

There is an active sports program and children's football and Little League baseball teams. There are also two private golf clubs: The Bird Hills Emerson Golf Club and the Hackensack Golf Club. Hillman Park is the biggest in the borough, with ball fields and swings. There are also smaller pocket parks and Leo Rosengart Memorial Park, formerly called Sunset Park.

ARTS AND CULTURE

The library has lectures and art exhibits.

CHILD CARE SERVICES

There are several privately run child care centers in Emerson.

SENIOR SERVICES

There is an active senior citizens club at the Emerson Senior Citizens Center.

RECENT DEVELOPMENTS

Recently, 59 $400,000 homes were built in the borough.

DRAWBACKS

Some residents say traffic lights are needed at some intersections in town.

PHONE NUMBERS

Township clerk (201) 262-6086
School district (201) 262-2828
Public library (201) 261-5604

— *Emily Wax*

Demographics

County: Bergen
Size: 2.22 square miles
Population: 6,859
Density: 3,115/square mile
Median age: 39.6
White: 93.2 percent
Asian: 6 percent
Black: .01 percent
Median house value: $227,800
Upper 25 percent: $275,400
Lower 25 percent: $190,400
Median year built: 1956
Median rent: $861
Single-family homes: 2,076
Condominiums: 25 units
Median property taxes per household (1995): $5,324
Median household income: $65,184
Industrial property: None
Sewers: Public
Library: 30,732 volumes
Media: The Record covers the town, as does Community Life, a weekly. Cablevision provides cable service.
Fire and ambulance: Volunteer
Police: Paid
Crime rate per 1,000 (1994): 16.9
Violent crime rate per 1,000 (1994): 0.7

ENGLEWOOD

Englewood is a city of contrasts, from the stately mansions that line the East Hill section to the low-rise public-housing complexes that lie west of the railroad tracks on South Van Brunt Street; from the busy concrete sprawl downtown to the wildflower fields that line the peaks of the Palisades.

Class differences aside, Englewood is a cultural melting pot. Residents of the city of 25,000 represent every faith and nationality, with large contingents of Jews, African-Americans, Latinos, and West Indians.

Englewood has all the advantages of a city, with trains and buses that will take you across the George Washington Bridge in about 20 minutes. It also has the feel of a small town: Thousands of people gather each July for the city's jazz concert, which honors the memory of its favorite musical son, Dizzy Gillespie.

Thus, it is both cultural and cutting-edge: Englewood boasts a modern medical facility, Englewood Hospital; and the John Harms Center for the Performing Arts, which hosts an array of stars, from the Russian ballet to Jay Black and the Americans.

Although it is designated a city, Englewood also has the Flat Rock Nature Center, 150 acres of woods and greenery off Van Nostrand Avenue. Flat Rock is open to the public year-round and is filled with hiking trails and animal sanctuaries.

Englewood is primarily a residential community, although a large industrial area occupies the southern end of town near Route 4. A large retail district, located on Palisade Avenue, runs through the center of town past City Hall at North Van Brunt Street.

The eastern side of Palisade Avenue is an upscale mix of specialty shops, including furriers, chocolatiers, and apparel stores. The western side of the avenue is downscale, a mix of beauty supply outlets, fast food restaurants, and casual clothing stores.

Noteworthy historical events

The Revolution nearly ended in Englewood in November 1776. George Washington beat a hasty retreat through town with the British, under Cornwallis, hot on his heels. Eventually, the British caught sight of Washington at the corner of Palisade Avenue and Tenafly Road. But Washington's rear guard was able to hold off the British advance long enough for the Continental Army to escape. Aviator Charles Lindbergh lived at the mansion of Sen. Dwight Morrow, which is now the campus of Elizabeth Morrow School. Writer Upton Sinclair opened a Utopian Socialist commune, Helicon Hall, on Walnut Street near the intersection of Woodland Court in 1906. It burned down a year later.

Schools

Although Englewood's population is roughly 50 percent white, the public school population is more than 95 percent minority. The problem of white flight was exacerbated when the neighboring town of Englewood Cliffs, which sends its students to Englewood's Dwight Morrow High, tried to pull out of the arrangement in 1986 and send its students to Tenafly High School. The case dragged on in court for years, while most Englewood Cliffs students were enrolled in private schools. In 1996, however, the state ordered Englewood and surrounding towns to come up with a plan to desegregate Dwight Morrow. A magnet plan has been proposed that would draw students from all over Bergen County, but it has not been finalized.

Some 81 percent of Englewood students took the Scholastic Assessment Test in 1995. Average scores were 353 in verbal, 400 in math. Englewood sends 59 percent of its students to four-year colleges and 16 percent to two-year colleges.

Englewood has several private and parochial schools that offer primary and secondary education, including Elisabeth Morrow and Webster Cooperative; Dwight-Englewood High School; Solomon Schechter Day School; Moriah Hebrew Day School; and St. Cecelia's.

HOUSES OF WORSHIP

Assembly of God New Jersey Central Church; Back to the Bible Church; Bethany Presbyterian Church; Christian Science Reading Room; Church of God of Prophecy; Community Baptist Church; Community Seventh Day Adventist Church; Congregation Ahavath Torah; Congregation Shomrei Emunah; Ebenezer Baptist Church; Englewood Assembly of God; Englewood Baptist Church; Englewood Church of God in Christ; Englewood Church of God Mission; Eruv Commitee of Englewood; First Baptist Church of Englewood; First Presbyterian Church of Englewood; First United Methodist Church; Galilee United Methodist Church; Genesis Community Baptist Church; Hackensack Pentacostal Assembly; Impact Ministry; Jehovah's Witness Congregation of Englewood; Jesus Christ is God's Church; Korean Community Church of N.J.; Mehfile-Shahe-Khorasan Charitable Trust; Mikva Association of Englewood; Mt. Calvary Baptist Church; Mt. Olive Baptist Church; New Jerusalem Baptist Church; Refuge Temple Church of God in Christ; St. Cecilia's Roman Catholic Church; St. John's Lutheran Church; St. Paul's Episcopal Church; Shiloh A.M.E. Zion Church; Temple Emanu-El; True Vine Christian Center; Unitarian Universalist Society of the Palisades; West Side Presbyterian Church, and The Young Nak Presbyterian Church.

HOUSES

Homes run the gamut from million-dollar Italian villa-style mansions on North Woodland Court to colonials on West Hudson Avenue to Cape Cod starter homes off Lafayette Place. There is also a luxury condominium complex, Cross Creek, built on the former site of the Englewood Golf Course near Route 80.

TRANSPORTATION

New Jersey Transit bus No. 166 leaves every 20 minutes bound for Port Authority in Manhattan. Buses run from 5 a.m. to 12:30 a.m. Several other NJ Transit lines run to the George Washington Bridge in Manhattan. Train service is available to Hoboken, with PATH connections to New York City, Newark, and Jersey City.

Recreation

The city is in the midst of a $1 million renovation of Mackay Park, the largest of the 14 public recreation facilities in town. The park offers new basketball and tennis courts, new soccer, baseball, and basketball fields, a swimming pool, jogging trails, and a park for children. The city hosts a semi-pro football team, the N.J. Colts, who play their home games at Winton White Stadium.

Englewood also sponsors a summer day camp, youth soccer, and Little League baseball for boys and girls. Mackay Park has an indoor ice skating rink and municipal pool.

Arts and culture

The John Harms Center for the Performing Arts is a showcase for all kinds of entertainment, from pop singers such as Tom Jones to the New Jersey Ballet. Harms also regularly presents theater, as well as gospel, folk, jazz, and blues concerts. Englewood is also home to the Williams Center for the Arts, a multi-disciplinary performing and fine arts complex. There are three live performance theaters, two cinemas, and an art gallery. Children and adult theater classes are held.

Child care services

The public schools offer the Quarles Early Childhood Learning Center. There are also 15 private child care facilities in town.

Senior services

The Englewood Housing Authority offers senior housing for low- and moderate-income residents. The Southeast Center for Independent Living on Engle Street offers a range of medical services at little or no cost. The Social Service Federation on Armory Street offers nutrition and day care for seniors, as well as a program for the blind, Shining Light.

Recent developments

The city has begun to lure private development to the western side of Palisade Avenue. The result is the new Palisade Court complex, a $30 million retail complex anchored by ShopRite supermarket and several national chains, including a Kay-Bee Toys and Sam Goody music store.

DRAWBACKS

Englewood still feels very much like a racially divided town. That feeling is reflected in the downtown and in many of the neighborhoods. Some are integrated, but other sections are almost entirely white or entirely black. The situation is most pronounced in the high school. Most white parents enroll their children in private schools.

PROMINENT RESIDENTS

Because of its proximity to New York City, Englewood has been a home base for many people in show business. Current residents include comedian Eddie Murphy and rock-and-roll legend Wilson Pickett. Actor John Travolta grew up in the city. Legendary Green Bay Packer Coach Vince Lombardi learned his "x's" and "o's" at St. Cecelia's School. Malcolm Borg, chairman of the Board of the Record, resides in Englewood.

PHONE NUMBERS

Township clerk (201) 871-6611
School district (201) 833-6060
Public library (201) 568-2215

— *Richard Cowen*

DEMOGRAPHICS

County: Bergen
Size: 4.9 square miles
Population: 24,850
Density: 5,046/square mile
Median age: 36.3
White: 49.1 percent
Asian: 4.9 percent
Black: 39.5 percent
Median house value: $221,100
Upper 25 percent: $383,300
Lower 25 percent: $165,100
Median year built: 1949
Median rent: $528
Single-family homes: 4,419
Condominiums: Not available
Median property taxes per household (1994): $5,826
Median household income: $46,758
Industrial property: 136 parcels
Sewers: Public
Library: 122,688 volumes
Media: The Record covers the town, as do the Englewood Press-Journal and the Suburbanite, both weeklies. Time Warner Cable provides cable service.
Fire and ambulance: Paid
Police: Paid
Crime rate per 1,000 (1994): 55.6
Violent crime rate per 1,000 (1994): 7.3

Englewood Cliffs

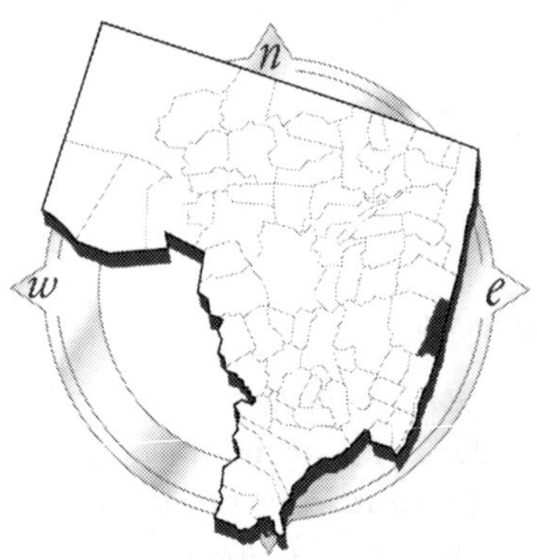

Despite its location a mile north of the congested area around the George Washington Bridge, the former farming community of Englewood Cliffs retains some of the flavor of its bygone days.

"There are no high-rises, very little commercial development; there's a country-like feeling," said town historian Russell Jehn. "Our forebears had the foresight, in planning, to keep the community as it was."

Shade Tree Commissioner Ruth Lustgarden remembers when builders began to develop large tracts of land in Englewood Cliffs in the Fifties.

"Englewood Cliffs was a tiny town with very little development," Lustgarden said. "All of a sudden, developers discovered us and began indiscriminately cutting down trees. We had to stop it." Lustgarden founded the Shade Tree Commission in 1957, which stopped the destruction and undertook a replanting program.

Today, Englewood Cliffs is a town of interesting contrasts. East of Sylvan Avenue, nicknamed the Billion Dollar Mile, are neighborhoods of narrow blocks where houses are crowded close together. Elsewhere are blocks of Sixties-style split-level and raised-ranch houses on larger-than-average lots. Sylvan itself is a quirky mix of convenience stores, upscale restaurants, car dealerships, and corporate buildings set back on acres of green lawn. These businesses are required to maintain their grounds according to strictly enforced zoning regulations. "It's a magnificently landscaped town, which helps keep land values up," Lustgarden said. Englewood Cliffs has received the Tree City U.S. Award for 15 consecutive years.

Noteworthy historical events

British Gen. Cornwallis climbed the Palisades and came up in Englewood Cliffs hoping to capture George Washington while he camped in neighboring Fort Lee. But Cornwallis was spotted by a farmer who alerted Washington, allowing the general to retreat with his army toward Hackensack.

Schools

Englewood Cliffs has two schools: North Cliff School for grades 1 through 3, and Upper School for grades 4 through 8. High school students are sent to Dwight Morrow High School in Englewood. (See Englewood entry for a description of the high school.)

The district constantly updates its curriculum. For example, science is now taught at every grade level, with an emphasis on laboratory work and practical applications. Daily journal writing is an English class requirement. Every classroom in the district has a computer, and both schools have a computer lab for group instruction. The district's computers are linked in a network that allows students and staff to communicate and access educational programs and software. All students in grades 3 through 8 study Spanish, and eighth-graders receive instruction in Latin. Other programs include developmental reading, English as a Second Language, and basic skills. Spending per pupil is high, $12,289 per year (1994-95).

Houses of worship

There are no houses of worship in Englewood Cliffs.

Houses

Englewood Cliffs is very affluent, but some small houses can be found at relatively modest prices.

Transportation

New Jersey Transit runs buses into Manhattan via the George Washington Bridge, a mile away, and the Lincoln Tunnel.

Recreation

The year-round recreation program includes tennis (four

courts); Little League, minor league, and Babe Ruth league baseball; basketball; girls' Ponytail Softball; and soccer. Fred Witty Field has several athletic fields, two lighted tennis courts, and a playground. The Bayview Avenue Park also has a playground.

Arts and culture

There are no museums or professional performing groups in town.

Child care services

There are no municipally run child care facilities.

Senior services

The Englewood Cliffs Senior Center Corp. meets monthly at its building at 7 West Bayview Ave. Built in 1982, the center has meeting rooms, a boccie court, and shuffleboard. The group takes frequent trips. Englewood Cliffs seniors can use the South East Senior Center in Englewood, which provides dental and vision care.

Recent developments

Developers have been tearing down older homes and replacing them with new ones.

Drawbacks

Many residents send their children to private high schools rather than Dwight Morrow High School in Englewood. School officials have for years tried to alter this arrangement to allow students to attend Tenafly High School. State officials are considering various regional solutions. The town also has no library of its own, but residents can use the Englewood Library without charge.

Phone numbers

Township clerk (201) 569-5252
School district (201) 567-7292

— *Marc Warren Watrel*

Demographics

County: Bergen
Size: 2.1 square miles
Population: 5,634
Density: 2,691/square mile
Median age: 43.6
White: 76.2 percent
Asian: 22.2 percent
Black: 1 percent
Median house value: $485,900
Upper 25 percent: $500,001
Lower 25 percent: $371,900
Median year built: 1964
Median rent: $1,001
Single-family homes: 1,799
Condominiums: None
Median property taxes per household (1994): $5,155
Median household income: $46,395
Industrial property: 1 parcel
Sewers: Public
Library: None
Media: The Record covers the town, as do the Englewood Press-Journal and the Suburbanite, both weeklies. Time Warner Cable provides cable service.
Fire and ambulance: Volunteer
Police: Paid
Crime rate per 1,000 (1994): 30.9
Violent crime rate per 1,000 (1994): 1.1

FAIR LAWN

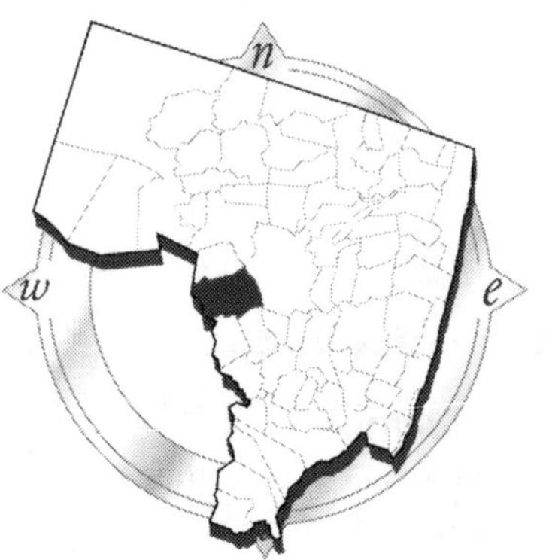

On an April day more than 70 years ago, about a thousand residents of what was then Saddle River voted for a town of their own. The residents wanted better school facilities and a better education for their children.

According to The Record's account of April 5, 1924, when the votes were counted and the measure had passed, the new borough of Fair Lawn was filled with the sounds of "singing and cheering and honking horns."

Today, the former spinach farming community can be proud of its progressive roots. The school system is ranked among the best in the state, and the community has grown into a multi-ethnic hub where Orthodox Jews from Russia, Koreans, Hispanics, and others share classrooms, community pools, and downtown shopping.

"We are not a melting pot, we are a wonderful mosaic," said Mayor Joseph Tedeschi, who has lived in the community for nearly 20 years. "More than 23 languages are spoken here, and that is a strength."

Fair Lawn is about 15 miles from Manhattan and is bordered on the north by Glen Rock and Hawthorne, and on the south by Saddle Brook and Elmwood Park. The land is about 99 percent developed.

Fair Lawn has three small shopping areas and many attractive neighborhoods. But it is probably best known for the section known as Radburn, one of the nation's first planned communities.

In 1928, the architects Clarence S. Stein and Henry Wright bought two square miles of Fair Lawn for what they called the "town for the motor age." They wanted to create a traffic-free community: a village of single-family row houses that would face 23 acres of interior parklands. Each moderately priced home would have dual access: footpaths for pedestrians through the common property and a road for cars.

Although the Depression would prevent the community from being fully developed, Radburn became internationally famous. "There are constantly people coming from all over the world," Tedeschi said. "People from England have built towns around the model." Today 3,000 residents live on Radburn's 149 acres. They pay extra taxes ($500 to $600, depending on an assessment) to maintain 23 acres of park, tennis courts, a pool, and a community center.

Noteworthy Historical Events

During the Revolution, River Road was an important military route and was guarded by the Continental Army's advance corps. Local farmers were often caught between British troops and Continental Army soldiers looking for provisions. When the war ended, a committee was established to compensate residents for losses.

Schools

The district serves 4,284 students, with six primary schools, two middle schools, and Fairlawn High, which New Jersey Monthly magazine rated as No. 61 among the state's top 75 high schools in 1996. This year, Money magazine ranked the school among the top 100 in value for dollars spent. It has also twice been named a Blue Ribbon school, a national model for excellence.

The high school offers more than 100 courses and 17 advanced placement courses. It is one of 22 Bergen County schools in the interactive television network, which offers 30 televised classes ranging from advanced foreign-language courses to college-level physics and business classes. High school students can also participate in a community service program in town.

There are several special-needs programs, including a gifted and talented program that begins at the elementary level.

About 67 percent of Fair Lawn High School graduates attend four-year colleges; 21 percent enroll in two-year schools. About 83 percent of the high school students take the Scholastic Assessment Test. The average SAT score was 440 verbal, 517 math in 1995.

Thirty-three percent of the students speak another language, according to Principal Elizabeth Panella, who described the high school as a microcosm of the larger world. "If it's out there, it's here in Fair Lawn," she said.

Fair Lawn also offers adult education programs.

Houses of Worship

Ahavat Achim Orthodox Congregation; Bethel Evangelical Free Church; Bris Avroham Russian/Jewish Community Center; Church in Radburn; Church of the Atonement Episcopal; Church of Christ; Congregation B'nai Israel; Congregation Shomrei Torah Orthodox, The Orthodox Congregation of Fair Lawn; Fair Lawn Bible Church; Fair Lawn Jewish Center; Grace Orthodox Presbyterian Church; Mikvah Fair Lawn; Our Saviour Lutheran Church; Pal Bok Presbyterian Church; The Peace Korean Reform Church; St. Anne's Roman Catholic Church; St. Leon's Armenian Church; Shomrei Torah; The Taiwanese Reform Church; Temple Avoda; Temple Beth Sholom; Van-Riper-Ellis Broadway Baptist Church; and Warren Point Presbyterian Church.

Houses

Small ranch-style homes in Fair Lawn start at $175,000. Larger homes can cost up to $650,000. Apartments and condos are available in sizes ranging from one to four bedrooms.

Transportation

New Jersey Transit offers bus transportation to Manhattan via the Lincoln Tunnel. Fair Lawn has two train stations. Both offer 20- to 30-minute service into Hoboken and PATH connections to Manhattan.

Recreation

Fair Lawn has more than 14 neighborhood parks and a community pool. The pool complex also has tennis courts and a walking path. In addition, there are tennis courts and ball fields in the Columbia Terrace recreation area.

During the summer, the borough runs an all-day recreational program for children that includes trips, games, and crafts.

The recreation department offers adult team sports year-round in volleyball, basketball, hockey, and soccer. The borough also offers exercise classes for adults.

For the borough's younger citizens, a town-run youth center is open Mondays through Saturdays from 7 to 9:30 p.m.

Arts and culture

The Maurice Pine Library is known for its art exhibits and lecture programs. The Fair Lawn Summer Festival includes ten free outdoor concerts including opera, jazz, and Dixieland.

Child care services

Fair Lawn operates before- and after-school programs. Several houses of worship, including Saint Anne's and the Fair Lawn Jewish Center, offer child care services. There are ten other private child care facilities in town.

Senior services

There is an active senior citizen center, used by about 700 to 800 seniors a week. Free minibuses take seniors to stores and other local destinations.

Recent developments

There are plans for 350 apartments to be constructed on 20 acres along Route 208. The town is considering building a more elaborate pool complex with water slides.

Drawbacks

Residents say local streets are sometimes congested by traffic from Route 208.

Phone numbers

Township clerk (201) 796-1700
School district (201) 794-5511
Public library (201) 796-3400

— *Emily Wax*

Demographics

County: Bergen
Size: 5.2 square miles
Population: 30,548
Density: 5,908/square mile
Median age: 40.6
White: 96 percent
Asian: 2.9 percent
Black: 0.6 percent
Median house value: $199,000
Upper 25 percent: $242,000
Lower 25 percent: $177,400
Median year built: 1949
Median rent: $539
Single-family homes: 9,216
Condominiums: 433 units
Median property taxes per household (1994): $4,493
Median household income: $56,569
Industrial property: 6 parcels
Sewers: Public
Library: 184,706 volumes
Media: The Record covers the town, as does the Shopper News, a weekly. Cablevision provides cable service.
Fire and ambulance: Volunteer
Police: Paid; there is also a volunteer force of more than 30
Crime rate per 1,000 (1994): 20
Violent crime rate per 1,000 (1994): 1.6

FAIRVIEW

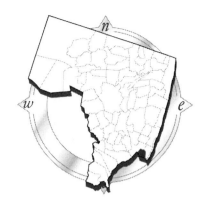

Fairview is a close-knit blue-collar town that takes pride in its ethnic diversity and its vast variety of programs for residents of all ages.

"We've a very diverse community made up of many different cultures," said Mayor Vincent Bellucci.

While its raucous politics and feuding are legendary, Fairview is also a place where people of all backgrounds and persuasions come together to help out in times of need or tragedy.

In recent years, the town's predominantly first- and second-generation Italian immigrants have been joined by an influx of newcomers from El Salvador, Guatemala, the Dominican Republic, the former Yugoslavia, and the Middle East.

Once a hub of the textile and embroidery industries, Fairview is struggling to revitalize its business district, upgrade its schools, and stabilize property taxes, which saw the biggest increase in Bergen County in 1996 — hardly a welcome prospect in a town where the per capita income is the county's lowest.

From the edge of the Meadowlands east to the top of the Palisades, the borough occupies just under a square mile in southeastern Bergen County, on the Hudson County border. About a quarter of its land is covered by churches, mausoleums, and two large cemeteries, all tax-exempt.

Modest homes crowd the narrow streets that run between Bergen Boulevard, Anderson Avenue, and Palisade Avenue, the town's main thoroughfares.

Anderson Avenue is a throwback to the turn of the century, an ethnic enclave where Italian, Spanish, and Serbo-Croatian are spoken on street corners and in gelaterias, bakeries, coffee shops, and storefront social clubs.

NOTEWORTHY HISTORICAL EVENTS

Fairview was home to Simon Douglas, one of the oldest living former slaves when he died in 1950. Born in 1843, Douglas left South Carolina with Sherman's army and settled in Fairview in 1866. In 1874 he built a blacksmith shop, which remained open until 1939, when he went blind. The town foreclosed on Douglas' home in the late 1940s for non-payment of taxes; however, residents of Fairview and surrounding communities set up a fund to raise the $3,000 needed to regain title to his house. He died at the age of 107.

SCHOOLS

Once the county's most troubled district, Fairview has made strides in recent years to rebuild its school system. In 1990, the state imposed Level II monitoring, one step away from a takeover, for failure to meet state standards. Among the problems were educational goals that had not been revised since 1977; no maintenance plan for facilities; and lack of formal curricula for many subjects. More seriously, students were crowded into turn-of-the-century buildings that did not meet health and safety codes. The crowding was compounded by the demolition of the English Neighborhood School, declared structurally unsound in 1991 after years of neglect.

In 1993, however, after finding marked progress in upgrading curricula, test scores, books, and facilities, the state lifted the district's probationary status. Its two elementary schools, the Lincoln School (kindergarten through grade 8) and No. 3 School (pre-K-5), have been refurbished, and a $3.4 million school annex, with new classrooms and administrative offices, is being constructed.

Fairview sends its high school students to neighboring Cliffside Park. (See Cliffside Park for details on the high school.)

Parochial schools include St. Elizabeth Seton School and Our Lady of Grace School.

HOUSES OF WORSHIP

Fairview Gospel Church; Greek Orthodox Church of the

Ascension; Jehovah's Witnesses Kingdom Hall; Our Lady of Grace Roman Catholic (R.C.) Church; St. John the Baptist R.C. Church; and Trinity Evangelical Lutheran Church.

Houses

The borough's housing is composed of one- to four-family dwellings; small apartment buildings, many of them aging and in need of repair; and fewer than a dozen condominium complexes. The Eastview Tower, an 18-story senior citizen residence, and the recently completed 12-story Fairview Apartments are the borough's largest residential structures.

Transportation

New Jersey Transit provides several bus routes along Fairview, Palisade, and Anderson avenues that link commuters with Port Authority in Manhattan and the George Washington Bridge. Another route terminates at the Bergen Mall in Paramus.

Recreation

Short on open space, Fairview concentrates its main recreation facilities at Columbus Park. These include a Little League field with lights, dugout, bleachers, and clubhouse; basketball and tennis courts; a roller hockey rink, a boccie court, and playground equipment.

The larger Babe Ruth Field, built on school property, is also lighted and doubles as the football field.

Staffed largely by volunteers, the town's six-week, all-day summer recreation program offers organized games, day trips to museums, zoos, and amusement parks, swim trips to beaches, and arts and crafts.

Arts and culture

There are no museums or theater groups in Fairview.

Child care services

There are two licensed child-care facilities in the borough of Fairview.

Senior services

The borough's Senior Citizens Center is open daily, offering hot lunches for a nominal fee, participating in a federal food-distribution program, and providing a range of social activities. The Fairview Senior Citizens Club, formed in the early Sixties and subsidized by the borough, has been active for three decades, hosting social functions, parties, shows, bingo, and bus trips.

The Bergen Pines Outreach Clinic provides services at the Fairview Health Center for resident seniors. The borough also runs buses for seniors and disabled residents; a new county-funded van takes residents on shopping trips. Federally subsidized housing is available at the Eastview Tower.

Recent developments

The town is building a $1 million library at the site of a former embroidery factory. It is using a $400,000 county grant to enlarge the storm sewer system to alleviate flooding in the Heights district.

In a bid to revitalize its business district, the town is seeking legislative approval to become an Urban Enterprise Zone, a designation that would allow businesses to charge a reduced sales tax and make that revenue available for improvements in the zone. It is also seeking federal grants to spruce up Anderson and Fairview avenues with new curbs, sidewalks, resurfacing, and lighting.

Drawbacks

Traffic, overcrowding, deteriorated housing, no municipal parking, and a limited commercial tax base are some of the problems. Fueled by school spending, property taxes rose 18 percent in 1996, the largest increase in Bergen County.

Phone numbers

Borough clerk (201) 943-3300
School district (201) 943-0564
Public library (201) 943-6244

— Peter Sampson

DEMOGRAPHICS

County: Bergen
Size: 0.8 square miles
Population: 10,733
Density: 12,720/square mile
Median age: 35 years
White: 90.5 percent
Asian: 3.3 percent
Black: 1.4 percent
Median house value: $184,000
Upper 25 percent: $225,300
Lower 25 percent: $153,2000
Median year built: 1953
Median rent: $613
Single-family homes: 841
Condominiums: 210 units
Median property taxes per household: (1994): $4,759
Median household income: $32,846
Industrial property: 127 parcels
Sewers: Public and private
Library: 20,000 volumes, 125 periodicals plus Magazine Express data base, 800 videos, and 600 music cassettes and books on tape
Media: The Record covers the town, as do the Sun Bulletin, Bergen News, and Jersey Journal. Time Warner provides cable service.
Fire and ambulance: Volunteer
Police: Paid
Crime rate per 1,000 (1994): 36.6
Violent crime rate per 1,000 (1994): 3.3

Fort Lee

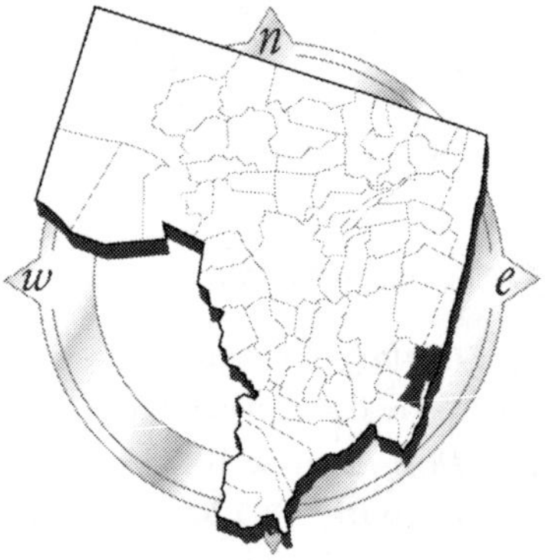

On a chilly spring morning in 1961, a team of construction workers with earth movers and bulldozers dug into the ground just off Main Street, inaugurating a new era not just for Fort Lee, but for all North Jersey. About a year later, work was completed on Horizon House, a 30-story condominium that set the pattern for dozens of similar apartment houses atop the Palisades from Fort Lee to Hoboken.

"New Jersey's Gold Coast began right here," said Fort Lee Mayor Jack Alter. "We're a breath of fresh air just five minutes from the city. That has made all the difference."

Today, 35 years after Horizon House was built, Fort Lee is called home by thousands of people who work in Manhattan and commute daily across the George Washington Bridge. It is also home to such businesses as Chase Securities, Kwasha Lipton, Sun Chemical, and the CNBC broadcast center.

The town, just two square miles, boasts some of the most expensive and sought-after real estate in New Jersey. Developers from hotel tycoon Harry Helmsley to real estate and pet food king Leonard Stern of Hartz Mountain continue to back major projects in the borough.

In recent years, Fort Lee also has become home to thousands of Asian immigrants and visiting Japanese businessmen and their families. The mix of Manhattan professionals and Asian culture makes Fort Lee's business district one of the most diverse and vibrant in Bergen County, with dozens of boutiques, delis, antique stores, coffee houses, and restaurants.

When a Russian radio station decided to set up shop in North

Jersey a few years ago, Fort Lee was the natural choice. Today, the station broadcasts in Russian, English, and Chinese.

"We are not New York, but we've got that undeniable cosmopolitan feel," said Debra Romano, an official with the Greater Fort Lee Chamber of Commerce. "Every time I walk downtown, I see something different. It's exciting just trying to absorb it all."

Noteworthy Historical Events

In 1609, Henry Hudson made a voyage up the river that now bears his name. Catching his first view of the Palisades north of what is now Hoboken, he called the area around Fort Lee, Englewood Cliffs, and Alpine "the good land." About 150 years later, Fort Lee, or Fort Constitution as it was known then, was the infamous starting site of George Washington's headlong retreat across New Jersey in the disastrous fall and winter of 1776. Throughout the summer, the revolutionaries had played havoc with British commerce and troop movements on the river by lobbing mortar shells from their new garrison in Fort Constitution. But when the Redcoats took Washington Heights and started heading west across the Hudson, Washington began an orderly, if ignominious, retreat. It was the low point of the war for the Americans.

Fort Lee was also home to many early motion picture companies. The "Perils of Pauline" serial, starring Pearl White, was filmed there. Universal Film Manufacturing Co. Studio is the best-preserved motion picture studio and lab extant in Fort Lee. The site, which housed the Universal company — now Universal Studios — was used by Samuel J. Goldwyn, David O. Selznick, and the Consolidated Film Corp.

Schools

With nearly half its enrollment composed of Japanese and Korean immigrants, the Fort Lee school district provides a true multicultural setting and an atmosphere of involvement for students and parents. Fort Lee's music program, for example, is among the most active in Bergen County. Hundreds of students play in the school band every year at a time when band programs in many other schools are floundering.

The school district, comprising 3,471 students in 1996, has four elementary schools, one middle school, and a high school. The district is growing rapidly, with 168 new students enrolled this year. About 95 percent of Fort Lee High School seniors go on to some institution of higher learning. The academic program reflects the diversity of the student body: Foreign language instruction includes courses in French, Spanish, Italian, Latin, Greek, and Japanese.

Fort Lee High School is one of only two in the United States to have been recognized twice by the U.S. Department of Education as a drug-free school. Since 1984, juniors and seniors have been able to earn college credit for work in 25 advanced courses.

In addition to their academic accomplishments, Fort Lee students have been recognized for their community service work, peer counseling, and mentorship work.

One unique aspect of the Fort Lee school system is the student body itself: 48 percent of the students speak a language other than English at home. "That is probably our greatest strength," said Superintendent Alan W. Sugarman.

Houses of Worship

Advent Lutheran Church; Church of the Good Shepherd Episcopal Parish; Church of the Madonna Roman Catholic (R.C.) Church; Eden Presbyterian Church; First Reformed Church of the Palisades; Fort Lee Gospel Church & Missionary Alliance; Fort Lee Jewish Community Center (Conservative); Gateway Community Church Assembly of God; Holy Trinity R.C. Church of Fort Lee; New Synagogue of Fort Lee; Sephardic Congregation of Fort Lee; United Methodist Church; and Young Israel of Fort Lee (Orthodox).

Houses

While a handful of Fort Lee homes date back to the American Revolution, the borough is better known for some three dozen high-rise condominiums and cooperative apartments. House-hunters have a range of choices, from garden apartments to luxury dwellings such as the Mediterranean complex, Horizon House, and the Plaza. Many of the apartments offer stunning views of Manhattan. Fort Lee's older residential neighborhoods are a mix of duplexes and newer, single-family homes close to shopping and transportation.

Transportation

Six bus lines offer service to and from New York City. Several cab companies also serve the town. Residents can get to Newark International Airport in a matter of minutes. The borough is five minutes from Manhattan via the George Washington Bridge. Ferries to the city leave all day from West New York, about 15 minutes south of Fort Lee. New Jersey Transit's PATH train across the Hudson is also available from the Hoboken terminal, about 25 minutes south of the borough. The New Jersey Turnpike, Palisades Parkway, and Garden State Parkway are just minutes away.

Recreation

Fort Lee is at the southernmost point of Palisades Interstate Park, a strip of green running along the river to Alpine and into New York. The park offers scenic bike trails, walking routes, and facilities for docking boats. The park is a favorite meeting place for cross-country skiers, anglers, in-line skaters, hikers, and picnickers. The national Fort Lee Historic Park has 33 wooded acres overlooking the George Washington Bridge and upper Manhattan skyline.

The department of recreation runs the recreation complex, youth center, eight borough parks, and five borough wading pools. Programs include preschool playgroups, creative crafts, basketball, karate, ballroom dancing, tennis, and ballet, among others. During the summer, the department runs a six-week day-camp program for children ages 3 to 13. The department also sponsors dances, ski trips, a tree-lighting ceremony, Ragamuffin Parade, and other outings. Youth center membership costs $1 per year and provides a supervised program weekdays after school and weekends.

Arts and Culture

Fort Lee Historic Park features a Visitors Center that sponsors exhibits detailing Fort Lee's role in the American Revolution. The Fort Lee Memorial Library on Main Street offers concerts, readings, lectures, and art exhibits.

Child care services

Fort Lee runs several child care programs, including morning and afternoon preschool playgroups for ages 3 and 4. There is also a latchkey program run by the elementary schools during the school year, and by the department of recreation in the summer. There are also eight private child care facilities in town.

Senior services

There are six senior citizens organizations, including Fort Lee Senior Citizens Club, 505 Club, 475 Club, Holy Trinity Senior Citizens Club, Leisure Club (Jewish Community Center), and Main Street Senior Citizens. The senior center on Main Street offers dozens of programs for the elderly, ranging from computer training to ballroom dancing.

Recent developments

Fort Lee's commercial center has been transformed in recent years by Asian immigrants who have breathed new life into Main Street in the form of delis, coffee shops, travel bureaus, and upscale clothing stores. Many of the shops cater to visiting Japanese businessmen, who make Fort Lee their home for five-year stints. Elected officials in Fort Lee are designing a special improvement district that would remake storefronts along a large part of Main Street and Lemoine Avenue. Another project about to get under way is the expansion and renovation of the library, which will add nearly 10,000 square feet of space.

Drawbacks

Seven major highways merge at the George Washington Bridge, often causing local roads to back up. It can sometimes take 30 minutes or more to cross town during rush hour, although the recent opening of a new connector road near the bridge has made rush hour less hectic. The pollution from auto emissions spurs periodic complaints. About 100 million cars and trucks every year pass over the bridge, the world's busiest. Residents of Fort Lee also complain about property taxes and the rising costs of municipal services and public schooling. Over the past three years, Fort Lee has lost $2.7

million in aid from the state. As a result, property owners face a heavier tax burden to pay for public education and municipal services.

PROMINENT RESIDENTS

Dozens of the famous and infamous have made Fort Lee their home, from mob boss Tony Strollo and Murder Inc. mastermind Albert Anastasia (gunned down in a barber chair) to comedians Buddy Hackett and Charlie Callas. Singer Whitney Houston once lived in the borough and still keeps a studio there. Mickey Mantle lived in Fort Lee during the Yankees' heyday in the Fifties and early Sixties. Dave Winfield became a Fort Lee resident in another era of Yankee history. More recently, New York Knicks center Patrick Ewing took up residence in a condominium on the north side of town. Other famous residents include psychologists Joyce Brothers and Ruth Westheimer.

PHONE NUMBERS

Township clerk (201) 592-3570
School district (201) 585-4612
Public library (201) 592-3614

— Jeff Pillets

Demographics

County: Bergen
Size: 2.5 square miles
Population: 31,997
Density: 12,652/square mile
Median age: 40.4 years
White: 77.2 percent
Asian: 20.3 percent
Black: 1.3 percent
Median house value: $283,000
Upper 25 percent: $372,200
Lower 25 percent: $218,300
Median year built: 1965
Median rent: $702
Single-family homes: 2,295
Condominiums: 8,904 units
Median property taxes per household (1994): $7,276
Median household income: $46,395
Industrial property: 12 parcels
Sewers: Mostly public; small number of septic systems
Library: The library offers 101,000 books, 276 periodicals, and more than 5,000 music recordings. The library is linked by computer to 65 others in Bergen County.
Media: The Record covers the town, as do the Bergen News, Palisadian, and Sun Bulletin. Time Warner Cable provides cable service.
Fire and ambulance: Volunteer
Police: Paid
Crime rate per 1,000 (1994): 33
Violent crime rate per 1,000 (1994): 3

FRANKLIN LAKES

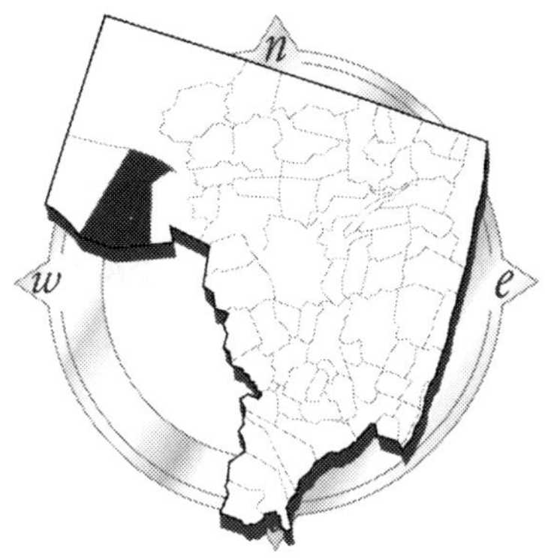

One of the quieter and more rustic areas in North Jersey, Franklin Lakes is also a thriving suburban hub known for its abundant, dew-dropped greenery and rapid population growth.

Originally settled by the Mensi, a Native-American tribe of the independent Lenni Lenape nation, it is also one of the oldest townships in Bergen County, having been founded in 1772 in the name of William Franklin — one of New Jersey's first (and youngest) governors, and Benjamin Franklin's son.

Today, though many of its historic mills and homesteads are being turned into shopping malls as development continues to encroach on North Jersey, Franklin Lakes is still hailed by residents and municipal officials as a beautiful, wooded suburb that has managed to keep its ties with its agricultural heritage.

Residents' appreciation for history and community, as well as good zoning plans, have been important, said Mayor Thomas Donch, but he stressed that what makes the town stand out among its neighbors is its commitment to volunteerism.

"The town still retains its bucolic, open-space setting," Donch said. "But if you don't have the resources or the people to help, it doesn't quite work." Franklin Lakes, with its tradition of volunteerism, makes the sense of community look easy.

The township mixes many of its original houses, built in the 1700s, with some of its most modern luxury homes. Local Realtors say it's this, and the town's location, that make it attractive to both senior citizens and young couples starting a family. "It's got a country feel, even though it's practically next to the city," said Pat Kelly, manager of McBride Realtors in town. "And like any lake community, it's a relaxing atmosphere to be in."

Noteworthy historical events

Franklin Lakes was Indian turf until 1694, when the Mensi tribe handed over 5,500 acres of rich and fertile farmland to Dutch settlers Arent Schuyler and Anthony Brockholes.

Schools

Franklin Lakes is recognized for excellence in education. The district serves 1,091 students, with three primary schools and one middle school. High school students are split between Ramapo High School and Indian Hills Regional High School, which were named 9th and 52nd best in the state, respectively, by New Jersey Monthly magazine in 1996.

Ramapo High School has 15 advanced placement classes, including chemistry and several foreign languages. In 1994-95, the average SAT scores were: verbal 558, math 579. Ninety-three percent of graduating seniors go on to four-year colleges.

The school system, however, has been the focus of some heated debate in recent years, as board members began hashing out proposals regarding what has become known as the Franklin Lakes split. The split refers to a 24-year-old arrangement in which Oakland students attend Indian Hills High School in Oakland, Wyckoff students attend Ramapo High School in Franklin Lakes, and students from Franklin Lakes are split between the two.

The arrangement, naturally, has affected friends and neighbors in Franklin Lakes; some parents have objected to sending their children to Ramapo, while others react similarly to Indian Hills. While the Board of Education recently rejected a proposal to unify Franklin Lakes by sending all its students to Indian Hills, debate over the split rages on.

Houses of worship

Barnert Memorial Temple; Ebenezer Netherland Reformed Church; Franklin Lakes Baptist Church; Franklin Lakes Christian Reformed; Franklin Lakes United Methodist Church; Grace

Community Church; Most Blessed Sacrament Roman Catholic Church; Presbyterian Church at Franklin Lakes; St. Alban's Episcopal Church; and Union Reformed Church.

Houses

Housing ranges from 1700s period colonials to small cottages to modern luxury homes.

Transportation

There is no direct bus or train line out of town. The nearest direct line of transportation is the Short Line bus service out of nearby Mahwah to Port Authority in Manhattan — about a 60-minute trip. The same bus line offers trips to Atlantic City.

Recreation

Outdoor activity is popular in this region and is especially enticing during the fall, as the leaves change and the air cools. The New Jersey Audubon Society headquarters, with its Lorrimer Sanctuary and Nature Center, provides some good observation points for spotting hawks and migratory birds. The center also has permanent and seasonal exhibits, as well as nature trails.

The Saddle Brook horseback riding area on Pulis Avenue offers riding lessons Tuesdays through Sundays. The area, a former missile site, adjoins the Campgaw Reservation in Mahwah.

Arts and culture

There are no museums or professional performing groups.

Child care services

Franklin Lakes has two private child care facilities.

Senior services

None located in the township.

Recent developments

The normally quiet community recently found itself at the center of a controversy when a Maryland-based company proposed building a self-contained, quarter-billion-dollar senior citizen "city" in the center of town. The senior campus layout, which was slated to be built at the site of the former IBM Corp., was a double-edged sword for residents, who approved of its prospects for raising money but expressed concern over a potential 25 percent increase in the town's population. Eventually, the plan was rejected in favor of letting a Ramsey-based insurance firm use space at the site.

Drawbacks

Franklin Lake is not the most accessible of towns. Hilly countryside can prove somewhat treacherous in winter, with an abundance of snow and ice.

Prominent residents

Phil Simms, former New York Giants quarterback.

Phone numbers

Township clerk (201) 891-0048
School district (201) 891-1856
Public library (201) 891-2224

— *Kevin Bryne*

Demographics

County: Bergen
Size: 9.5 square miles
Population: 9,873
Density: 1,044/square mile
Median age: 39.0 years
White: 93.2 percent
Asian: 6 percent
Black: 0.4 percent
Median house value: $500,001
Upper 25 percent: $500,001
Lower 25 percent: $379,300
Median year built: 1968
Median rent: $974
Single-family homes: 3,045
Condominiums: Not available
Median property taxes per household (1994): $7,468
Median household income: $100,992
Industrial property: 16 parcels
Sewers: Mostly private, some public
Library: 75,500 volumes and 26,000 audiovisuals
Media: The Record covers the town, as do the Villadom Times and the Rockland Journal, both weeklies. TCI provides cable service.
Fire and ambulance: Volunteer
Police: Paid
Crime rate per 1,000 (1994): 14.5
Violent crime rate per 1,000 (1994): 0.5

GARFIELD

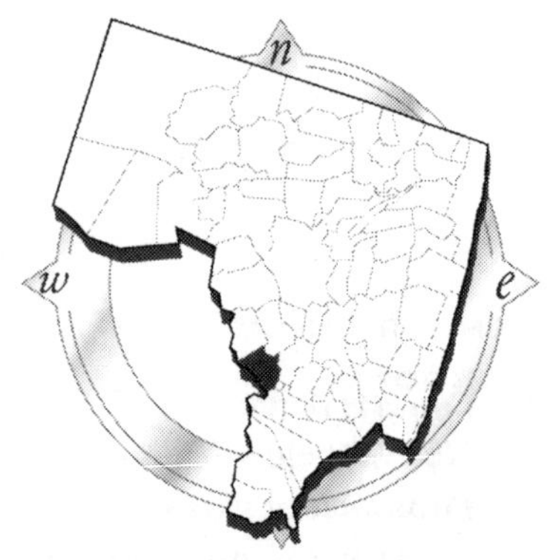

Historically, European immigrants were attracted to Garfield for its ample employment opportunities in the textile industry, which burgeoned there at the turn of the century. Workers established their families in Garfield and, generation after generation, struggled to build a stable, working-class community.

Modern-day immigrants seem to be following this lead — mainly because, in addition to its continuing easy access to employment, Garfield offers relatively inexpensive housing. Although in recent years major companies have moved out of the city, it is working on a master plan to revitalize its industrial base, favoring the cultivation of minor industry over the larger enterprises that traditionally were located there. Garfield has the added advantage of being close to several major highways. Even if residents cannot find work within the community, it is never out of reach.

Like their predecessors, the latest waves of newcomers have been rapidly absorbed into the community.

The city's crime rate is comparable to — or lower than — the levels in other New Jersey towns of greater size.

Garfield is "a better melting pot than the City of New York," declared Councilwoman Lucy Matijackovich. "There is a great respect for nationality," she said, while "no one culture has disrupted the peace and security of the community."

Noteworthy historical events

With its large wool and worsted mills, Garfield was a major contributor to North Jersey's thriving textile industry during the early part of this century. Historian Elizabeth Grey reported that most of the U.S. military uniforms used in both world wars were produced in Garfield.

Wax paper was invented in Garfield — albeit as the result of an accident in a local paper factory.

Schools

The Garfield school district has five elementary schools, kindergarten through grade 6. Two of these schools have special education classes. Seventh- and eighth-graders attend Thomas Jefferson Middle School, then go on to Garfield High School.

The school system is notable for its extensive English as a Second Language (ESL) program. Of the 900 students attending high school, 26 percent are ESL students, typically coming from Polish- or Spanish-speaking homes.

Garfield High also offers a selection of advanced placement classes in subjects including U.S. history, calculus, biology, and Spanish.

Average standardized test scores among Garfield's high school students are somewhat low. While for 1994-95 the percentage of students passing the statewide High School Proficiency Test hovered at or slightly above the state levels for the individual reading, writing, and mathematics sections, the percentage who passed all three sections — 71.2 — was below the state's overall rate of 73.2 percent. Among the 61 percent of Garfield High students who took the SATs in 1995, the average scores — 354 verbal, 399 math — were also well below the state averages.

Garfield's parochial schools include Heritage Christian School, Holy Trinity Lutheran School, Northeast Christian Academy, Our Lady of Fatima Roman Catholic (R.C.) Interparochial School, and St. Stanislaus Kostka R.C. School.

Houses of worship

Albanian American Islamic Center; Beth Israel Messianic Congregation; Bible Church International (Southern Baptist); Calvary Baptist Church; Community Baptist Church; First Presbyterian Church of Garfield; Friendship Baptist Church; Full Gospel Church; Hindu Community Center; Holy Name Roman

Catholic (R.C.) Church; Holy Trinity Lutheran Church; Our Lady of Mt. Virgin R.C. Church; Our Lady of Sorrows R.C. Church; Praise Assembly of God; St. Stanislaus Kostka R.C. Church; Three Saints Russian Orthodox Church; and Zion Lutheran Church.

Houses

Houses are mainly two-family structures, although a scattering of colonials, split-levels, and Cape Cods can also be found.

Transportation

New Jersey Transit provides bus service from Garfield to Port Authority in Manhattan. NJ Transit also provides train service to Hoboken, where connections can be made to Newark and points south, as well as to the PATH system and ferries to Lower Manhattan. Additionally, NJ Transit offers bus service within Garfield and to nearby communities, including Passaic and Paterson.

Recreation

While the city sponsors a basketball league for ages 6 to 12, numerous private leagues are allowed access to its fields, parks, and other recreational facilities. Private leagues include children's baseball, T-ball, football, softball, and adult softball, as well as a cheerleading program. The city also sponsors an annual Christmas party, Halloween parade, and Easter egg hunt.

Arts and culture

The Garfield Historical Society is at work on a three-year project to update the city's written history and find space for its collection of artifacts.

Child care services

After-school programs for children from kindergarten up are available weekdays, for a fee, through the Garfield department of recreation, the Garfield YMCA, and the Garfield Boys' and Girls' Club. These programs provide transportation from local schools to the after-school facilities.

There is also a private child care center in the borough.

Senior services

Garfield offers an extensive program for its senior citizens. The Garfield Senior Center, a county facility located on city property, is open Mondays through Fridays from 8 a.m. to 3:30 p.m. and offers its own transportation, breakfast, and a hot lunch. The center makes referrals for seniors who need assistance with any number of problems and issues. On-site medical care, including blood-pressure checks, mammograms, and general medical education, is also provided. Recreational activities include bingo, billiards, ceramics, a film series, a choir, and arts and crafts. There are dinner-dances and monthly trips to Atlantic City. AARP and the Golden Age Club have chapters in Garfield.

Recent developments

Mayor Louis Aloia reports that the city, in conjunction with the Passaic River Coalition, is developing a five-acre walking park along River Drive on what is currently business and industrial property.

Drawbacks

Garfield experienced a sizable drop in its ratables in recent years when tenants moved out of some factory properties. The largest drop occurred three years ago.

Phone numbers

Township clerk (201) 340-2001
School district (201) 340-5000
Public library (201) 478-3800

— Maria C. Zingaro

DEMOGRAPHICS

County: Bergen
Size: 2.1 square miles
Population: 26,727
Density: 12,548/square mile
Median age: 34.9 years
White: 93.7 percent
Black: 2.2 percent
Asian: 1.7 percent
Median house value: $172,900
Upper 25 percent: $199,100
Lower 25 percent: $147,100
Median year built: 1941
Median rent: $544
Single-family homes: 2,069
Condominiums: Approximately 75 units
Median property taxes per household (1994): $4,836
Median household income: $31,649
Industrial property: 89 parcels
Sewers: 11,346 public, 63 septic
Library: 83,855 volumes
Media: The Record covers the town, as do the Messenger and the Shopper News, both weeklies. Cable service is provided by TCI.
Fire and ambulance: Volunteer
Police: Paid
Crime rate per 1,000 (1994): 33.8
Violent crime rate per 1,000 (1994): 2.7

GLEN ROCK

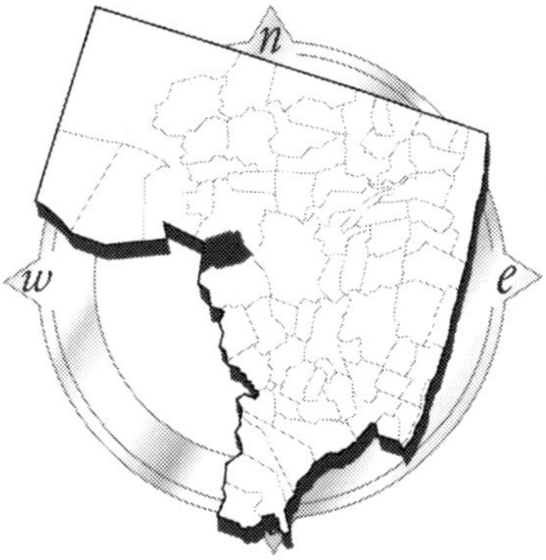

Glen Rock has never been known as a party town. Its image is that of a laidback bedroom community with tree-lined streets, well-maintained homes, and superior schools.

In recent years, however, this normally sedate community in northwestern Bergen County has had much to celebrate, and its more than 11,000 residents have often found themselves gathering for festivities with a distinctly community flavor.

To mark Glen Rock's 100th anniversary in 1994, the borough sponsored a year of centennial events, highlighted by a winter carnival and a Fourth of July fair. Those, in turn, created an appetite for more celebrations, which climaxed in the fall of 1996 with a street fair billed as "Paris in the Parc."

Long before the centennial, however, Glen Rock residents had shared a feeling of community. John and Judy Hawes recognized that bond when they settled in the borough in 1941; it was among the most compelling reasons why they moved to Bergen County from Forest Hills, N.Y.

"Forest Hills seemed like a place where you just went home to sleep," Judy Hawes said. "Glen Rock, on the other hand, seemed like a little village, and it still has that homey, community feeling."

Convenience was another major selling point. Until his retirement in 1976, John Hawes commuted six days a week (Monday through Saturday) to Manhattan, where he headed the foreign-exchange department at Bankers Trust Co. His home is a few blocks from the Borough Hall train station in Glen Rock, a regular stop on New Jersey Transit's Bergen County Line. From there, it was a half-hour train ride to Hoboken, then a short ferry ride to New York.

Parents in Glen Rock are deeply involved with school activities. Each year, for example, parents of graduating seniors plan, stage, and host an elaborate ball. John and Judy Hawes chaired the committee in 1961, when one of their four children was a senior.

"We enjoy being involved in community activities," John Hawes said, "and there are so many different ones here in Glen Rock. This town has a real sense of community."

Across Rock Road from the library stands Kilroy's Wonder Market, a local institution for three-quarters of a century. It's a cozy, scaled-down version of a supermarket, just as Glen Rock itself is sometimes described as a smaller-scale version of Ridgewood.

Backyard trash pickup is provided by municipal employees. Residents have access to a borough recycling and compost center that's open daily. The Rock Road business district, while relatively small, is quite diverse, comprising restaurants, pizza parlors, luncheonettes, drugstores, beauty shops, dry-cleaning stores, and banks. The long-established Glen Rock Inn, a popular dining spot, helps anchor the district. For shopping on a grander scale, residents can venture to the upscale Ridgewood business district and the sprawling Paramus malls, both within a few minutes' drive.

In at least one respect, however, Glen Rock is very different from the community John and Judy Hawes joined 50 years ago: They paid just $6,200 for their home, while today, a typical Glen Rock home sells for upwards of a quarter-million dollars.

Noteworthy historical events

Glen Rock was part of Ridgewood until 1894, when residents of the community, then primarily farmers, became alarmed at a plan for a new Ridgewood school that would cost $50,000 — an unheard-of sum at the time — to supplant the district's rural schools. The residents decided to incorporate their lands and founded the Borough of Glen Rock.

A block from the train station at Rock Road and Doremus Avenue is the 570-ton boulder for which the borough is named. The granite rock, believed to have been deposited by glacial activity 10,000 years ago, served in bygone days as a base for Indian signal fires and later as a reference point in establishing property lines.

Schools

Schools and education are high-priority matters in Glen Rock. Residents take justifiable pride in the quality of their school system, which consists of about 1,800 students in three elementary schools and a combined junior-senior high school. New Jersey Monthly Magazine, in its 1996 survey, selected the high school as No. 26 among the best 75 in the state, stating: "Small, suburban Glen Rock High School outperforms many competitive upper-middle-class schools." The ratio of students to teachers is 14.6 to 1. The median teacher salary is $57,751. Glen Rock sends 86 percent of its students to four-year colleges and another seven percent to two-year colleges. About 94 percent of students take the Scholastic Assessment Test, scoring an average of 468 verbal, 532 math in 1995.

The Barnstable Academy and St. Catharine's Interparochial School are located in Glen Rock.

Houses of Worship

All Saints Episcopal Church; Community Church of Glen Rock; Glen Rock Jewish Center; Lutheran Church of the Good Shepherd; St. Catharine's Roman Catholic Church; and Shri Guru Singh Sabha.

Houses

Colonial and Tudor-style homes predominate, and on many blocks it would be hard to find two homes that look the same.

Transportation

Glen Rock is the only Bergen County community with two train stations served by different rail lines. New Jersey Transit's Main Line trains stop about a quarter-mile from the Bergen County Line; the two sets of railroad tracks frame the central business district. Both rail lines terminate in Hoboken, where commuters can catch PATH trains into Manhattan. Several bus lines also make regular runs through Glen Rock on their way to Manhattan, the shopping malls, and other destinations in the region.

Recreation

Organized activities for children include softball, basketball, football, and soccer leagues for boys and girls, along with a recently established in-line skating hockey program. For adults, there are tennis courts, basketball and volleyball courts, and baseball fields.

For simply relaxing, there's the municipal swimming pool on Doremus Avenue, the adjacent arboretum with its well-stocked fishing pond, the bucolic Saddle River County Park, and several smaller parks and other recreation sites sprinkled throughout the borough.

Arts and Culture

The Glen Rock Arts Council was formed two years ago as an outgrowth of the borough's centennial celebration. Since then, it has held two film festivals at the high school, a concert and, most impressively, the street fair dubbed "Paris in the Parc." The well-stocked library is a focal point of community life.

Child Care Services

Glen Rock has several private child care facilities.

Senior Services

The non-profit Glen Rock Senior Citizen Housing Corp. operates Glen Court, a three-story, 81-unit complex for seniors.

Recent Developments

In 1995, voters approved a $6.8 million bond issue to finance school renovations. The improvements are currently being made.

Drawbacks

Parking is inadequate in the central business district; municipal officials are considering solutions. Despite the many organized activities, young people complain about the lack of informal social outlets, notably the absence of a movie house in the borough.

Phone Numbers

Township clerk (201) 670-3956
School district (201) 445-7700
Public library (201) 670-3970

— *Ed Reiter*

Demographics

County: Bergen
Size: 2.8 square miles
Population: 10,883
Density: 4,204/square mile
Median age: 38.7 years
White: 91.7 percent
Asian: 6 percent
Black: 2.4 percent
Median house value: $255,500
Upper 25 percent: $302,600
Lower 25 percent: $213,600
Median year built: 1950
Median rent: $930
Single-family homes: 3,662
Condominiums: Not available
Median property taxes per household (1994): $5,876
Median household income: $65,976
Industrial properties: A small area along Broad Street
Sewers: Public
Library: 83,000 volumes, 200 periodicals, 700 videos, 900 audiobooks, and 700 compact discs
Media: The Record covers the town, as do the weeklies the Ridgewood News, the Suburban News, and the Villadom Times. The Glen Rock Gazette, a weekly newspaper established in 1994, is mailed at no charge to borough residents. TCI provides cable service.
Fire and ambulance: Volunteer
Police: Paid
Crime rate per 1,000 (1994): 13.8
Violent crime rate per 1,000 (1994): 0.5

HACKENSACK

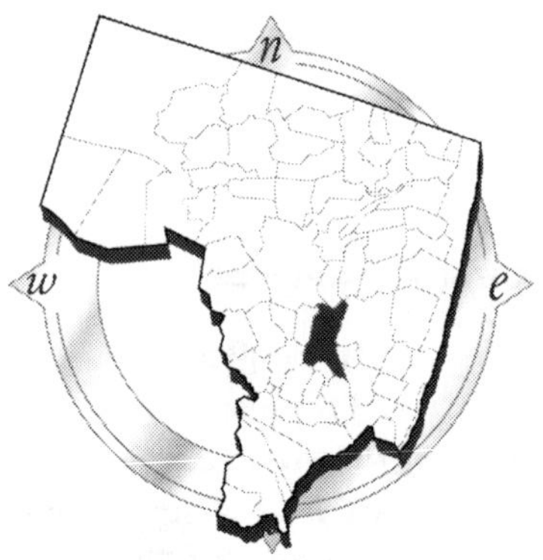

If you think of Bergen County as an urban area unto itself, then Hackensack is its downtown. The hub of county government — the courthouse, Board of Freeholders, prosecutor's office, and other county agencies — is based here, adding to the city's bustling urban style, with many of the attractions and drawbacks that designation implies.

This is a gateway city, very much defined these days by its diversity and openness to newcomers.

With a healthy inventory of moderately priced homes and affordable apartments, Hackensack attracts settlers from around the region and, increasingly, from other countries.

The ethnic diversity is manifest in its annual Colombia Independence Day celebration, held at 21-acre Foschini Park and featuring food stands, music, and cultural displays.

The city's schools have risen to the challenge of educating a changing population drawn from a broad range of cultures and economic backgrounds.

Hackensack's business district was once the commercial magnet of Bergen County, a two-mile shopping strip that stretched from the courthouse green to the Sears department store. But Main Street merchants have waged a losing battle with the nearby malls for decades, and many have simply surrendered. Empty storefronts are a familiar sight, though some longstanding businesses continue to hang in there. Parking, as always, is in short supply.

Despite the gaps, Main Street is a surprisingly enticing place, with an array of new stores and ethnic restaurants, such as Thai and Central American, that reflect the city's international flavor.

Hackensack shows its best face in its residential neighborhoods. Attractive, well-kept homes, towering shade trees, and an abundance of parks and ball fields contribute to a small-town way of life that is as appealing as it is unexpected in such a busy place. And the stylish apartment towers that line Prospect Street make for an urban corridor that can rival parts of Manhattan.

The Johnson Public Library on Main Street is a downtown anchor, with an impressive collection of books and research materials, a well-stocked children's room, and a broad range of cultural offerings. In Hackensack University Medical Center, the city boasts a hospital of rapidly growing prestige, with widely respected specialties in coronary care and pediatrics.

Noteworthy Historical Events

In 1639, the Dutch settled the area as a trading post, carrying on business with the Acensack Indians, from whom the city takes its name. During the next five decades small businesses sprang up, and in 1696 the settlers erected the First Dutch Reformed Church. The church, rebuilt in 1791, still stands as a national historic landmark.

Hackensack was an important Colonial settlement in the mid-1700s, when trade flourished along the Hackensack River. During this time, immigrants flocked to Hackensack to enjoy the thriving job market, which included mining clay and other resources from the riverbanks and harvesting crops of strawberries and melons. During the Revolution, George Washington headquartered in Hackensack while surveying local roads and bridges. In November 1776, he and his troops camped on The Green, where Washington decided to continue the retreat from British and Hessian forces. This paved the way for the first American victory in December 1776 at the Battle of Trenton. Many Revolutionary soldiers, including Gen. Enoch Poor, are buried in the graveyard of the First Reformed Church, directly across from Hackensack's impressive courthouse.

Schools

Superintendent of Schools Joseph Montesano referred to Hackensack's public school system — composed of four elementary schools, one middle school, and one high school — as a "microcosm of the real world, enhanced by the intermixing of different cultures and ethnic groups." A wide variety of courses are offered: College prep programs, business, technical, and trade courses serve the more than 4,000 students. Hackensack High sent 55 percent of the 1996 graduating class to four-year colleges (three to Ivy League schools), and 30 percent continued at two-year colleges.

About 80 percent of Hackensack students take the SAT tests. The 1995 SAT averages were 391 verbal, 473 math.

Hackensack has been chosen as the pilot school system to bring Odyssey of the Mind, an interscholastic program that fosters problem-solving ability and creativity, into the classroom.

Hackensack has scored consistently high in the Odyssey of the Mind international competition: In 1995, two of the town's 10 teams went to the world finals.

More sports programs are offered in Hackensack than in any other school system in the county, and the high school football team has been state champion for the last four consecutive years.

The city also is home to Hackensack Christian Schools, Holy Trinity Elementary School, Kings Kids Academy, and to Bergen County Vocational-Technical High School.

Houses of worship

Bergen Christian Fellowship; Bergen Korean Baptist Church; Beth Ha Kerem Messianic Congregation; Bethel Church of God in Christ; Bethel Gospel Church; Calvary Baptist ABC; Christ Episcopal Church; Church on the Green; Emmanuel Fellowship Church of the Nazarene; Faith Revival Center Inc.; First Baptist of Hackensack; First Congregational Church; First Presbyterian Church of Hackensack; First Reformed Church; Hackensack United Methodist Church; Holy Trinity Roman Catholic (R.C.) Church; Iglesia Bautista Calvario; Immaculate Conception (St. Mary's) R.C. Church; Jehovah's Witnesses Kingdom Hall; King of Kings Full Gospel Tabernacle; Korean Presbyterian Garden Church; Little Bethel Holiness Church; Mt. Holiness Temple; Mt. Olive Baptist Church; New Hope Baptist; New Life Assembly of God; St. Anthony of Padua Episcopal; St. Cyprian's Episcopal Church; St. Francis of Assisi R.C. Church; St. Gabriel's Syrian Orthodox Church; St. Joseph's R.C. Church; St.

Mark's Lutheran Church; Salvation Army Chapel; Second Reformed Church; Seventh Day Adventist; Temple Beth-El; Third Reformed Church of Hackensack; Trinity Baptist of Hackensack; Universal Hager's Spiritual Church; and Varick Memorial AME Zion Church.

Houses

Hackensack has one- and two-family houses of various sizes, as well as sprawling garden apartment complexes and luxury high-rise apartments and condos.

Transportation

The New York-Susquehanna & Western carries freight, while New Jersey Transit supplies morning and evening train service on weekdays. About 26 bus routes stop in Hackensack.

Recreation

Hackensack has one of the area's largest youth baseball programs, held at the baseball fields at Foschini Park. New lighted tennis courts have been built at Johnson Park. The city offers low-cost tennis lessons with pros from the nearby Oritani Field Club.

The Hackensack YMCA at Main and Passaic streets has been a mecca for area kids for decades, and today the pool still swarms with children taking swim lessons and adults swimming laps. The Y recently rebuilt its fitness center and locker rooms, and it is as well-equipped and attractive as many private fitness clubs. It also offers aerobics, dance, gymnastics, karate, and dozens of other classes.

The city's M&M Recreation Center sponsors adult and youth basketball leagues and offers lots of programs for kids, including low-cost karate classes.

The USS Ling, a diesel-powered World War II submarine commissioned in 1945, has been moored in the Hackensack River since 1973. The city organizes Fourth of July fireworks and the Columbus Day Parade with support from business groups.

Arts and Culture

The Orrie de Nooyer Auditorium at Bergen Technical High School hosts all kinds of performances, including Fifties revival shows, concerts, and the Irene Fokine Ballet production of "The Nutcracker" every year. The Center for Modern Dance Education offers dance and movement classes for everyone from infants to senior citizens and from up-and-coming stars to those with emotional, neurological, and physical disabilities.

Child care services

There are six privately run child care facilities in Hackensack, including Hackensack University Medical Center, which sponsors one of the largest day-care centers in the county.

Senior services

The city boasts 19 senior activity centers, including Martin Luther King Jr. Senior Center of Varick AME Zion Church and Senior Nutrition Program, which offers free programs including senior employment, Meals on Wheels, legal services, recreation, and nutrition. Literature is available in English, Spanish, and Korean.

Recent developments

In 1992, a $4 million flood control project, focused at River Street, was completed, and in 1993 the city began a $1 million project to revamp and improve its parks. The city plans to renew Hackensack's riverfront properties by constructing a walkway along the river. To better serve Main Street, a trackless trolley car system from one end of the district to the other is being planned.

Drawbacks

Downtown streets and main arteries such as River Street and Summit Avenue can become congested on weekdays, especially during rush hour. Essex Street can be an obstacle course for drivers and pedestrians alike.

Phone numbers

City clerk (201) 646-3980
School district (201) 646-7830
Public library (201) 343-4169

— *David Schaublin*

Demographics

County: Bergen
Size: 4.1 square miles
Population: 37,049
Density: 8,997/square mile
Median age: 35.1
White: 66.4 percent
Black: 24.8 percent
Asian: 3.7 percent
Median house value: $186,300
Upper 25 percent: $226,500
Lower 25 percent: $156,500
Median year built: 1962
Median rent: $639
Single-family homes: 3,384
Condominiums: 3,400 units
Median property taxes per household (1994): $5,594
Median household income: $38,976
Industrial property: 250 parcels
Sewers: Public and private
Library: 146,167 volumes
Media: The Record covers the town. Cable service is provided by TCI.
Fire and ambulance: Paid
Police: Paid
Crime rate per 1,000 (1994): 57.1
Violent crime rate per 1,000 (1994): 6.3

HALEDON

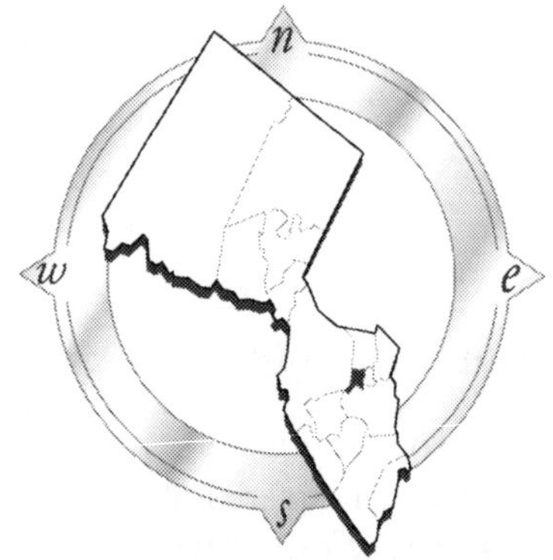

The borough of Haledon is known for its intimate charm and sense of community. "It's just a great small town," said Realtor Manny Carabello, who owned a retail store in Haledon for 27 years before becoming a real estate agent in the borough ten years ago. "You still have your neighborhoods; your kids can walk to school. People get to know each other."

Located in south-central Passaic County, Haledon is bordered by similarly blue-collar Prospect Park as well as North Haledon and Hawthorne. While it is close to urban centers such as Paterson and Hackensack, it doesn't share their problems, Carabello said. Most of the town is residential, but shops, luncheonettes and deli-style restaurants line Belmont Avenue, the main drag.

Mayor Jim Van Sickle cited the borough's stable tax rate, top-notch services, and community spirit as reasons to live in Haledon.

"We have a shopping area right in town," Van Sickle noted. "We really have a well-maintained town."

One of the borough's most popular assets is the Tilt Street Spring, where Haledon residents can get cold spring water at no charge. Mayor Van Sickle likes the spring so much, he mentioned it twice when asked about the borough's biggest selling points.

NOTEWORTHY HISTORICAL EVENTS

During the silk workers' strike of 1913 in Paterson, police forbade union leaders to meet in the city. Pietro Botto, who lived on Norwood Street in Haledon, offered his home as a meeting place. The Botto House is now home to the American Labor Museum, commemorating milestones in the American labor movement.

Schools

Haledon's school district serves about 740 students in grades kindergarten through 8, all in one building. In addition to a program for gifted and talented students, the district offers a variety of special-needs classes, including some for autistic and for multiple-handicapped children. In 1996, the district started a before-school breakfast program and began a tutoring program before and after school.

High school students from Haledon join those from nearby Prospect Park and North Haledon in attending Manchester Regional High School, located in Haledon and serving about 660 students. The high school offers more than 70 courses, including honors classes in math and literature, and recently opened a technology lab that provides training in computer-assisted drafting. The school has a policy of mainstreaming its special-needs students whenever possible. More than 70 percent of Manchester Regional graduates attend a two- or four-year college. In 1995, Manchester graduates were awarded more than $300,000 in scholarship money. Average SAT scores for Manchester Regional students were not available.

Houses of worship

Cedar Cliff United Methodist Church; First Christian Reformed Church; Korean American Community Church; Living Word Fellowship of Haledon Inc.; and St. Mary's Episcopal Church.

Houses

Most of the homes in Haledon are multi-family dwellings. Single-family homes range from modified Cape Cods to colonials.

Transportation

New Jersey Transit offers bus service from Haledon to Paterson, Passaic, and other major eastern North Jersey communities. From those hubs, riders can make connections to New York City, Newark, and Trenton.

Recreation

Even though Haledon is a small town — just over a square mile — it has two parks, with benches, ball fields, and a playground.

There are year-round programs in baseball, softball, football, soccer, basketball, and indoor roller hockey, as well as cheerleading.

Arts and Culture

The Botto House, which is listed on the state and national registers of historic places, celebrates the history of immigrants and the American labor movement through visual and performing arts. The library and Haledon Police Action offer summer arts and crafts.

Child Care Services

The borough has no municipally run child care centers, but there are several privately run facilities, and a Head Start program.

Senior Services

The Haledon Senior Citizens Group meets weekly; the Haledon AARP chapter meets once a month. There are monthly trips to the mall, and grocery shopping trips are scheduled several times a week. The county provides Meals-on-Wheels services.

Recent Developments

An expanded drive-in recycling center recently opened.

Drawbacks

Residents who live near the Stone Industries Quarry, located on Central Avenue, have complained for years about noise and vibration damage to their homes from the blasting.

Prominent Residents

Olympic gold-medal wrestler Bruce Baumgartner grew up in Haledon; his family still lives there.

Phone Numbers

Township clerk (201) 595-7766
School district (201) 790-9000
Public library (201) 790-380

— Jennifer Van Doren and Marc Warren Watrel

Demographics

County: Passaic
Size: 1.15 square miles
Population: 6,951
Density: 6,018/square mile
Median age: 35.1 years
White: 92.2 percent
Black: 3.6 percent
Asian: 0.9 percent
Median house value: $171,000
Upper 25 percent: $200,000
Lower 25 percent: $95,000
Median year built: 1920-1930
Median rent: $614
Single-family homes: 855
Condominiums: 10 units
Median property taxes per household (1994): $4,618
Median household income: $36,076
Industrial property: 27 parcels
Sewers: Public
Library: 17,000 books, about 800 CD titles, and 800 videos
Media: The Record and the North Jersey Herald & News cover the town, as do the weekly Hawthorne Press and Shopper News. TCI provides cable service.
Fire and ambulance: Volunteer
Police: Paid
Crime rate per 1,000 (1994): 22.2
Violent crime rate per 1,000 (1994): 2.3

HASBROUCK HEIGHTS

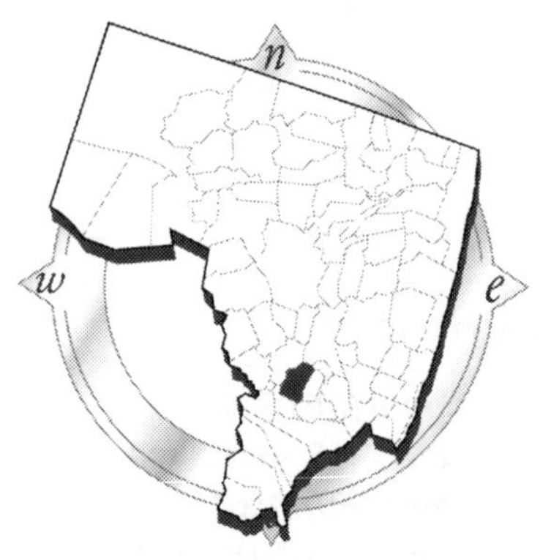

Entering Hasbrouck Heights, it's hard not to feel that time has stopped: that Eisenhower is still in the White House, Marlon Brando is still thin, and the Dodgers are still in Brooklyn. This southern Bergen County town harkens back to a less frantic, simpler time, and its 11,000 residents seem to like it that way.

Downtown, mothers with strollers move briskly in and out of the stores in the thriving shopping district. Students hang out after school in the diners and pizza places. The tree-lined streets are clean. There is a sense of permanence and stability, an atmosphere that is preserved even though the town's neighbors — Hackensack, Lodi, Wood-Ridge, and Teterboro — are far more commercially or industrially developed.

But Hasbrouck Heights combines convenience with its tranquility. A network of public roads — nearby Routes 80, 17, 46, and 3, the Garden State Parkway, and the New Jersey Turnpike — provides easy transportation for residents who commute elsewhere in New Jersey or to New York City.

"Our citizens thrive here," said Mayor Bill Torre. "Families with young children continually move into town, rejuvenating it. The enthusiasm of our youth and our senior citizens is remarkable."

Originally inhabited by the Lenni Lenape Indians, Hasbrouck Heights was farmed by Dutch settlers as early as 1633. By 1669 it was settled as a village, and it remained that way until the mid-1800s, when the arrival of the railroad transformed it into a thriving suburb. In 1894, it was incorporated as a borough. Today, many of its residents are descendants of Irish, Italian, German, and Polish immigrants who arrived in the 19th or early 20th century.

Noteworthy historical events

Originally named Corona, the borough's name was changed in 1889 in honor of Dillon Hasbrouck, general manager of the New Jersey and New York Railroad, who was responsible for building two train stations in town — and who residents hoped might be flattered into doing other favors.

Schools

Hasbrouck Heights has three schools: Lincoln and Euclid schools for kindergarten through grade 6, and Hasbrouck Heights Middle Level and Senior High School for grades 7 through 12. Both elementary schools encourage a strong home-school partnership. Enrichment programs include computer instruction, art, drama, and music. Lincoln School recently converted a classroom into a science lab.

Hasbrouck Heights Middle Level & Senior High School offers seven advanced placement classes, math and English labs, and cooperative AP physics-calculus. In the high school, students can opt for pre-college, business, or vocational classes. Freshmen complete a comprehensive academic cycle that includes ten-week courses in research process, public speaking, technology, and problem solving. Selected students can enroll in college-level courses, for credit, through a cooperative program with Fairleigh Dickinson University. SAT scores for 1995 were 392 verbal and 465 math. Ninety percent of the Class of 1995 went on to two- or four-year colleges.

There is a Roman Catholic elementary school, Corpus Christi, in town.

Houses of worship

All Faith Chapel; Bible Baptist Church; The Community United Church of Christ; Corpus Christi Roman Catholic Church; The Cross Korean UMC; Episcopal Church of St. John the Divine; First United Methodist Church; First Reformed Church; Holy Trinity Lutheran Church; and Temple Beth Elohim.

Houses

Brick and stone Cape Cods and Tudors are common, as are

some lovely turn-of-the-century Victorians. Most of the houses sit on 50-by-100-foot lots. There are some two-family houses and garden apartments.

Transportation

New Jersey Transit runs two buses to Port Authority in Manhattan (about a 40-minute ride) every five minutes during rush hour. There is also train service to Hoboken, which connects with the PATH train to Manhattan, Newark, and Jersey City.

Recreation

Hasbrouck Heights has won 14 Bergen County awards in the last six years, for programs such as boys' and girls' basketball, wrestling, adult co-ed volleyball, and over-30 basketball. Senior citizens are encouraged to join the senior-citizen Olympic Team. There are self-defense classes for all ages. The summer camp program, Camp Rec-Trek, offers day trips, games, and other programming. The town maintains Myers Park and Woodland Park, which has several athletic fields and a playground. There is a community swim club for which families pay an annual membership fee.

Arts and Culture

There are no museums or professional performing groups in town.

Child Care Services

Hasbrouck Heights has no municipally run child care facilities. There are, however, several privately run facilities.

Senior Services

The Leisure Club meets monthly at Corpus Christi Church.

Recent Developments

Although there isn't much land left for development, the town is always renewing itself. Woodland Park, its largest recreational facility, is undergoing a face lift. A new ordinance permits restaurants to have outdoor, cafe-style dining. Plans are in the works for a new library and a combination youth and senior citizen center.

Drawbacks

Because of the network of highways, traffic sometimes spills over onto local streets.

Prominent residents

Frank Sinatra lived in Hasbrouck Heights during the 1930s and '40s.

Phone numbers

Township clerk (201) 288-0195
School district (201) 393-8145
Public library (201) 288-6653

— *Marc Warren Watrel*

DEMOGRAPHICS

County: Bergen
Size: 1.5 square miles
Population: 11,488
Density: 7,610/square mile
Median age: 38.6
White: 94.6 percent
Asian: 3.7 percent
Black: 0.8 percent
Median house value: $202,400
Upper 25 percent: $241,300
Lower 25 percent: $177,100
Median year built: 1948
Median rent: $621
Single-family homes: 2,982
Condominiums: None
Median property taxes per household (1994): $4,794
Median household income: $44,672
Industrial property: 11 parcels
Sewers: Public and private
Library: 48,325 volumes
Media: The Record covers the town, as do the Observer and the Shopper News, both weeklies. Cable service is provided by TCI.
Fire and ambulance: Paid
Police: Paid
Crime rate per 1,000 (1994): 29.7
Violent crime rate per 1,000 (1994): 0.5

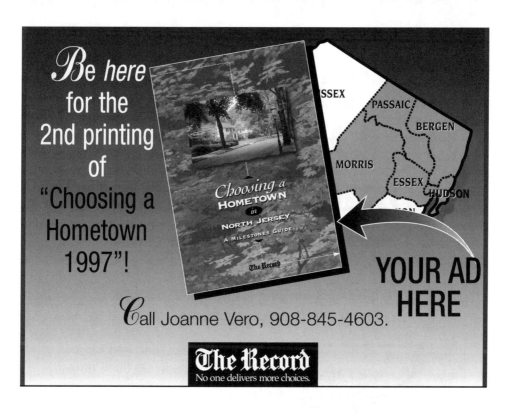

HAWTHORNE

Hawthorne is admired as a friendly, small-town community with all the benefits of a modern urban center. Minutes from downtown Paterson and Hackensack and less than an hour from Manhattan, the 3.4-square-mile borough is compact enough to retain its village atmosphere despite encroaching development.

"Everyone knows everyone else here," said the borough's mayor, Paul Englehardt. "I hate to say it, because it sounds cliched, but it's just like Mayberry, U.S.A."

"Hawthorne has a lot to offer for families with children, as well as for seniors," said Anthony J. Cali, of A.J. Cali Realtors. "There are parks, there's a community pool, a library with lots of events, and tons of sports programs for all ages."

"People move here and bring their families here, then the kids go away to college and move back home," Englehardt said.

NOTEWORTHY HISTORICAL EVENTS

It is believed that the Marquis de Lafayette camped in Hawthorne, along the Passaic River, in 1780.

SCHOOLS

The Hawthorne school district has 2,100 students in three elementary schools, one middle school, and one high school. The district is well-regarded and was listed in New Jersey Monthly magazine's 1995 survey of the state's top 45 school districts.

The elementary schools run preschool, handicapped, and gifted and talented programs in addition to the basic curriculum.

The high school offers 115 courses in many disciplines, including honors, advanced placement classes, work-study, and special needs. About 81 percent of Hawthorne High School graduates go on to two- or four-year colleges. Average SAT scores in 1995 were 390 verbal, 454 math.

St. Anthony Roman Catholic School is also in Hawthorne.

Houses of Worship

First Baptist Church; First Reformed Church of Hawthorne; Hawthorne Gospel Church; Hawthorne United Methodist Church; Jehovah's Witness Congregation of Fair Lawn; Rea Avenue Reformed Church; St. Anthony's Roman Catholic Church; and St. Clement's Episcopal Church.

Houses

The housing choices range from sprawling, palatial estates in The Heights, a section with an impressive view of High Mountain and the valley, to affordable apartments within walking distance of shopping centers.

Transportation

There is a station in town for New Jersey Transit's Main Line, which brings rail passengers to the PATH trains in Hoboken and from there to New York, Newark, and Jersey City.

Recreation

Hawthorne's recreation department offers team sports year-round, including football, wrestling, basketball, roller hockey, softball, baseball, and soccer, as well as a cheerleading program.

Six recreational complexes are spread throughout the borough. Among them, residents have access to a full-size swimming pool, football fields, tennis courts, soccer fields, a 1/4-mile track, basketball courts, volleyball courts, Little League baseball fields, picnic areas, and an in-line skating rink.

Arts and Culture

The Louis Bay 2nd Library offers cultural events and monthly art exhibits by local and regional artists, along with juried shows such as the annual Friends of the Library Art Show. The Hawthorne Symphony, composed of local musicians, presents several concerts throughout the year.

Child care services

There are three state-licensed child care centers and each elementary school offers after-school care from 3 to 6 p.m., for a fee.

Senior services

The borough Health Department offers year-round health services to senior citizens, including blood-pressure checks and flu shots.

Recent developments

The library, already known for its size, is planning a major expansion, including a 3,500-square-foot children's library.

Drawbacks

The Borough Council recently approved a plan for construction of a mix of condominiums, rental units, and town houses totaling 115 units. The development — the result of a state-mediated agreement under fair-housing laws — has been the subject of much debate. Some say it will bring too many people and too much traffic into the area. Others say the housing is sorely needed and the population growth won't hurt the schools.

Phone numbers

Township clerk (201) 427-1167
School district (201) 423-6401
Public library (201) 427-5745

— Jennifer Van Doren

DEMOGRAPHICS

County: Passaic
Size: 3.4 square miles
Population: 17,084
Density: 5,029/square mile
Median age: 36.8
White: 97.9 percent
Asian: 1 percent
Black: 0.4 percent
Median house value: $191,000
Upper 25 percent: $236,700
Lower 25 percent: $165,200
Median year built: 1947
Median rent: $667
Single-family homes: 3,716
Condominiums: 153 units
Median property taxes per household (1994): $4,501
Median household income: $43,109
Industrial property: 109 parcels
Sewers: Public and private
Library: 77,167 volumes
Media: The Record covers the town, as do the Hawthorne Shopper and the Hawthorne Press, two weeklies. TCI provides cable service.
Fire and ambulance: Paid
Police: Paid
Crime rate per 1,000 (1994): 17.6
Violent crime rate per 1,000 (1994): 1.1

HILLSDALE

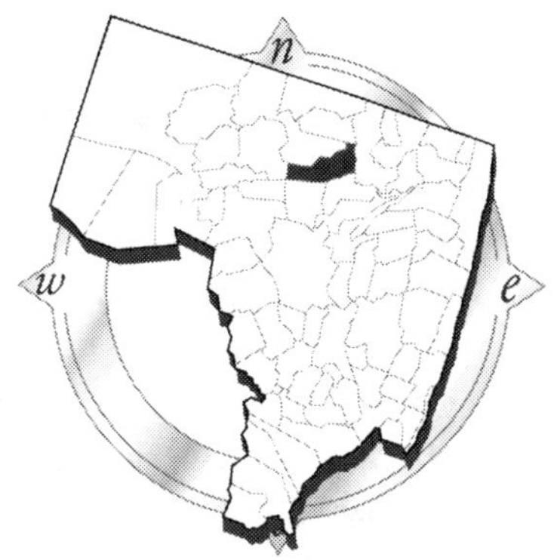

Hillsdale residents think of their borough as a village pretending to be a suburb. Just 30 minutes from the George Washington Bridge, and with a bustling train station and commuter parking lot, Hillsdale has all the conveniences of a suburb — including a walkable downtown where a visit to the bank, the hardware store, and the pizza place can be accomplished in less than 20 minutes. Nearby Westwood, to the south, offers more shopping in its larger downtown.

But those who live here say it's the community spirit that makes Hillsdale special. It's evident downtown, where residents frequently can be seen waving hello to one another as they pass on the street. And it's manifest in a sign at the main intersection that reads: "Folks: Our food pantry is almost bare. We again ask for your help."

The food pantry, started by a young boy as a Scouts project, has brought people closer together and elicited many acts of kindness and generosity. "At the food bank recently, our freezers broke," said Lois Kohan, the borough's public health nurse. "Within days, word got out and people donated freezers."

In 1995, when the town needed a new field house in Memorial Field, a group of local tradesmen and do-it-yourselfers got together for an old-fashioned barn-raising and constructed the two-story building — saving the borough hundreds of thousands of dollars. Another volunteer group helped refurbish Beechwood Park.

"What makes this feel like a village is that we worry about each other," said Max L. Arnowitz, a councilman for 12 years. "Everyone is expected to help out in collecting food for the needy or in getting a project up and running."

Noteworthy historical events

In 1873, the railroad extended from Hillsdale to Haverstraw, N.Y., and the borough's station became its headquarters. A four-story hotel was erected on the corner of what is now Hillsdale Avenue and Broadway. The local watering hole,The Hillsdale House (now Chicken Delight), was the downtown hub.

In 1922, a women's fire squad, part of the borough's fire department, was said to be the only one of its kind in the world. The story was picked up by the New York press and attracted nationwide attention.

Schools

The Hillsdale school district serves about 1,105 students, in three primary schools and one middle school.

There are also several special-needs programs, including a gifted and talented program that begins at the elementary level.

Starting in the fall of 1997, all high school students will attend the regional Pascack Valley High School in Hillsdale, along with students from River Vale. (Previously, some Hilsdale teens attended Pascack Hills High, in Montvale.) Pascack Valley offers more than 100 courses, five honors programs, and six advanced placement courses. About 91 percent of Pascack Valley High School graduates attend two- or four-year colleges. About 90 percent of the high school students take the Scholastic Assessment Test. The average verbal SAT score in 1995 was 505; average score in math was 509.

St. John's Academy, the Baptist Interparochial School for kindergarten through grade 8, is located in Hillsdale.

Houses of worship

Hillsdale United Methodist Church; Holy Trinity Episcopal Church; Pascack Bible Church; St. John the Baptist Roman Catholic Church.

Houses

The borough has several distinct neighborhoods. The most expensive housing can be found in Royal Park, where large homes are valued at $400,000 to $800,000. The Tandy Allen section, in the middle of town, was developed during the Sixties and has the classic ranches of that period. Downtown Beechwood Park has summer cottages that border on the Pascack Valley Brook.

"It's a middle-class neighborhood with everything from $130,000 homes to $800,000," said Bill Teubner, president of Prudential Higgins Realtors. "The commute into the city is easy, and the local shopping is nice."

Transportation

The Main Bergen line runs through Hillsdale to the Hoboken station, where commuters can take the PATH to Newark, Jersey City, and New York. Rockland Coach Bus Service provides service to Port Authority in Manhattan.

A new 100-space commuter parking lot provides for Hillsdale as well as outside residents.

Recreation

The Hillsdale recreation department offers men's basketball and volleyball. There is a walking club, which meets every Saturday at 9 a.m. There is also a chess club that meets at the library.

For children, the recreation department offers bowling, in-line hockey, basketball, and indoor soccer.

There are also three independent athletic associations that run basketball, football, and soccer teams for girls and boys.

The borough has well-maintained parks with fields for baseball, soccer, and football. There are also pocket parks — such as Veterans Park in the heart of the downtown district — that have swings and other play equipment for smaller children.

The high school has tennis courts that residents can use after school hours. Beechwood Park is the site of summer concerts.

The Stony Brook Swim Club, which has three pools, is popular with families. The facility is also used by a swim team and the borough-run day camp.

Arts and Culture

The Hillsdale library displays art work and photography throughout the year.

Child care services

There are five private child care facilities in the borough.

Senior services

More than 25 percent of the population is over 65. The Hillsdale 50 Plus Club is working with the Board of Education to build a senior center. The seniors hold a lunch at the library every Tuesday, and the borough subsidizes eight to ten trips a year. "We have wanted a senior center for years," said Mike Brizney, head of the 50 Plus club. "These days we are hopeful."

Recent developments

Forty-two condos were built by Stony Brook Swim Club, and a 14-house development was under construction in 1996.

Drawbacks

Flooding from the Pascack Brook is the biggest issue. Residents have organized a group called the Concerned Citizens of Hillsdale and Westwood to try to solve the problem.

Prominent residents

Jazz pianist Teddy Wilson lived in Hillsdale until his death.

Phone numbers

Township clerk (201) 666-4800
School district (201) 664-0282
Public library (201) 358-5072

— *Emily Wax*

Demographics

County: Bergen
Size: 2.98 square miles
Population: 9,750
Density: 3,271/per square mile
Median age: 38.1
White: 94.7 percent
Asian: 4.3 percent
Black: 0.6 percent
Median house value: $248,100
Upper 25 percent: $312,600
Lower 25 percent: $199,700
Median year built: 1956
Median rent: $640
Single-family homes: 3,087
Condominiums: 50 units
Median property taxes per household (1994): $5,448
Median household income: $62,039
Industrial property: 1 parcel
Sewers: Public
Library: 54,372 volumes, 180 periodicals, 2,300 music cassettes and books on tape, and 60 compact discs
Media: The Record covers the town, as does the weekly Community Life. TCI and Cablevision provide cable service.
Fire and ambulance: Volunteer
Police: Paid
Crime rate per 1,000 (1994): 12.7
Violent crime rate per 1,000 (1994): 0.3

HOBOKEN

Hoboken during the old days — as older residents of the mile-square city like to say — had more homegrown, streetwise moxie and ethnicity than Hell's Kitchen. It also had a shy, skinny kid named Francis Albert Sinatra, who often walked along Washington Street singing quietly to himself.

But Hoboken's more recent claim to fame isn't confined to pop music's Chairman of the Board. Now a hot locale for young artists, actors, rock bands, and twenty- and thirtysomething business types, Hoboken has become a sort of miniaturized Big Apple — a pleasant, upscale locale with a lower cost of living than Manhattan, safer neighborhoods, an equally fine selection of restaurants, an active nightlife, and a breathtaking nighttime view of the New York City skyline.

For Maureen Singleton, a real estate broker on Washington Street (or "The Avenue," as old-timers call it), the town is "a hot market" — not just because of the young singles who flock to its bars and eateries, but because of rising property values that are attracting more couples and families.

NOTEWORTHY HISTORICAL EVENTS

Hoboken introduced to the world the first game of organized baseball in 1846, when a group of locals played the game on cricket grounds called the Elysian Fields. The town is also home to the Maxwell House coffee plant on the Hudson River.

SCHOOLS

The quality of education in Hoboken's school district, which consists of three primary schools, three middle schools, and one high school, is a continuing source of concern for city residents. While school officials maintain that reading and math test scores for the city's 6,000 students are on a steady climb, parents who have enrolled their children in the schools say they are equally concerned about space constraints and disciplinary problems.

About 23 percent of the public school graduates go on to four-year colleges, and five percent to two-year colleges.

HOUSES OF WORSHIP

All Saints Episcopal Church; Christian Missionary Alliance; Church of God Prophesy; Community Church of Hoboken; Emmanuel Pentecostal Church; First Church of Christ Scientist; First Presbyterian Church of Hoboken; Hoboken Evangelical Free Church; The Hoboken Jewish Center; Igelesia Damasco Pentecostal Mizpa Inc.; Jehovah's Witnesses Kingdom Hall; Mt. Olive Baptist Church; Our Lady of Grace Roman Catholic (R.C.) Church; Plymouth Brethren Gospel Hall; St. Ann's R.C. Church; St. Francis Parish; St. John's Lutheran Church; St. Josephs' R.C. Church; St. Matthew-Trinity Lutheran Parish; St. Peter & Paul R.C. Chruch; Spanish Seventh Day Adventist Church; Temple B'nai Abraham; and United Synagogue of Hoboken.

HOUSES

While there are no free-standing single-family homes in town, apartments are readily available. Older, smaller apartments rent for between $600 and $800 a month, with newly renovated units bringing between $1,000 and $3,000 a month.

The city's brownstones, some of which date to the mid-19th century, are valued between $150,000 and $400,000.

TRANSPORTATION

Red Apple and New Jersey Transit offer all-day bus service to and from Port Authority in Manhattan — about a 15- to 20-minute trip. PATH trains off First Street provide fast transportation to downtown New York and the World Trade Center 24 hours a day. New Jersey Transit trains operate out of Hoboken to the Shore Points.

Recreation

Local gyms, including the YMCA and Powerhouse on Washington Street, coffee bars, and countless bars and restaurants provide pleasant, stress-free locales in which young singles can mix and mingle or unwind after a commute back from the city.

For outdoor exercise, the neighborhood has several parks, including two on Hudson Street and one neighboring the high school track and football fields off Clinton and Tenth streets. The track and a pair of nearby outdoor tennis courts are accessible to residents.

The Hudson Street Cinema often features mainstream movies paired with little-seen independent films — a dose of highbrow culture for ex-New Yorkers who may miss the arthouse films of Greenwich Village.

Hoboken's street fairs are annual highlights that attract locals and outsiders for their color, food, arts and crafts, and outdoor entertainment.

Arts and culture

By 1920, Hoboken had 20 active theater companies and had been dubbed "the last seacoast of Bohemia" by native artist Christopher Morley. That bohemian lifestyle is still very much alive.

The town offers poetry readings, theater, dance, and music programs, including the Hoboken Chamber Orchestra. Religious festivals and parades, such as Cinco de Mayo, Columbus Day, and St. Patrick's Day, are an enduring sign of the city's diverse ethnic makeup. Other events include The Hoboken Spring Art and Music Festival, a summer concert series at Church Square Park, and Movies Under the Stars at Erie-Lackawanna Plaza.

The campus of the Stevens Institute of Technology provides a spectacular skyline view of New York City. It's also one of the best places from which to see the annual Fourth of July fireworks display in the harbor.

Hoboken has become a favorite location for Hollywood filmmakers because of its mix of untouched turn-of-the-century architecture, gritty side streets, and picturesque views of Manhattan. Among the films shot in Hoboken were "On the Waterfront," "The

Age of Innocence," "The Professional," "The Basketball Diaries," "Sleepers," and "Picture Perfect."

Child Care Services

Hoboken has eight private child care facilities.

Senior Services

Senior care is provided by St. Matthews-Trinity Lutheran Parish Center on Washington Street and St. Mary's Hospital, in the heart of Hoboken off Willow Avenue.

Recent Developments

Demolition has begun on the waterfront for a multimillion-dollar, 17-acre, city-owned redevelopment project called South Waterfront. The master plan is for a 14-story office building on First Street east of River Street. The Second Street block would be a hotel and smaller office building, and adjacent to that, a ten-story, 425-unit residential building.

Drawbacks

Like any big, happening city, Hoboken is very crowded. Elderly residents, many of whom have lived in Hoboken since they came to America in the 1920s, have complained that the hyperactive bar scene has caused a lot of noise and rowdy behavior by out-of-towners who drive into the city to go bar hopping on Friday nights and weekends. Stricter police enforcement, however, seems to have quelled some of these problems.

Meanwhile, residents who own cars face the daunting task of locating a parking space in town, which after 7 on most weeknights is practically impossible.

Other irritations arise from the city's alternate-side-of-the-street parking rules for street cleaning. Failure to abide by these rules (especially if you are not a resident) results in parking tickets or vehicle towings — which generate significant revenue for the town.

Parking availability is further hindered in winter if blizzard conditions set in, even though the city's public works department has been hailed for its efficient snow clearing. On the upside, parking in town is less crowded during the summer, when many people head to the Jersey Shore.

In addition, crime in the town has dropped significantly in recent years. Occasional instances of yuppie bashing persist, in which juvenile gangs verbally or physically harass people on their way home from work late at night.

PROMINENT RESIDENTS

Frank Sinatra, legendary pop crooner/Academy Award-winning film actor/tough guy; John Sayles, independent filmmaker ("Lone Star," "Passion Fish," "City of Hope"), screenwriter ("Return of the Secaucus Seven"), and novelist; Mark Leyner, comedian and author ("Et Tu, Babe"); Tony Goldwyn, film and New York stage actor ("Ghost," "The Pelican Brief," "Holiday").

PHONE NUMBERS

Township clerk (201) 420-2026
School district (201) 420-2151
Public library (201) 420-2346

— *Kevin Byrne*

Demographics

County: Hudson
Size: 1.3 square miles
Population: 33,397
Density: 26,250/square mile
Median age: 30.8 years
White: 79 percent
Black: 5.4 percent
Asian: 4.5 percent
Median house value: $250,000
Upper 25 percent: $302,500
Lower 25 percent: $194,300
Median year built: 1939
Median rent: $511
Single-family homes: 178
Condominiums: 3,253 units
Median property taxes per household (1994): $7,973
Median household income: $34,873
Industrial property: 136 parcels
Sewers: Public
Library: 117,180 volumes; 3,258 audiovisual items; more than 1,000 CDs. In addition, the library keeps a collection of Sinatralia (including his birth certificate and sheet music for a locally penned tune called "Sing It Again, Frank") locked behind glass on the seond floor.
Media: The Star-Ledger, the Jersey Journal, and The Record are three Jersey-based dailies that cover the town, as do several New York City-based daily papers. The Hoboken Reporter is a free weekly publication hand-delivered to many residents. Cable service is provided by Cablevision.
Fire and ambulance: Paid and volunteer
Police: Paid
Crime rate per 1,000 (1994): 71.9
Violent crime rate per 1,000 (1994): 7.7

Ho-Ho-Kus

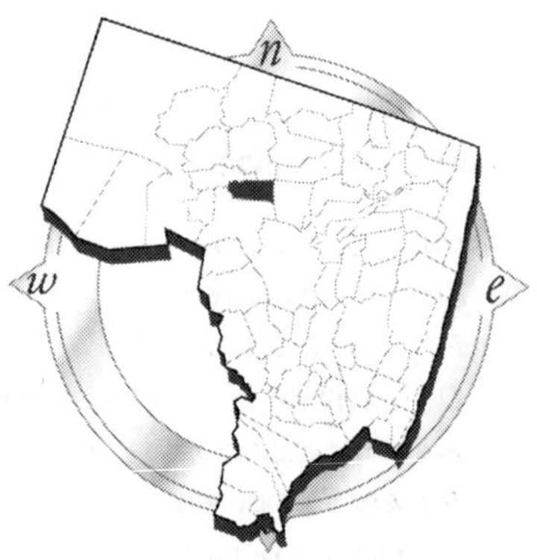

Roughly 20 miles from Manhattan and minutes from the superstores and shopping malls crammed along Route 17, the tiny borough of Ho-Ho-Kus remains stubbornly and charmingly true to its 19th-century roots.

That's just fine with the many Ho-Ho-Kus professionals who drive home from high-rise offices to spacious, turn-of-the-century homes, tidy yards, quiet streets, and friendly neighbors.

"It's a real steady town. Nothing changes too drastically," said Norma Rappaport, a resident and owner of Earthly Pleasures, one of the small shops in the center of town.

No chain stores, fast-food restaurants, or blinking neon signs jar the borough's old-fashioned tranquility. Instead, downtown — along Sheridan Avenue and Franklin Turnpike — consists of a handful of brick and Tudor buildings occupied by convenience stores, antique shops, a manicurist, a bakery, and other shops. Many homes are on the state and national registers of historic places. Classes are still held in the borough's only schoolhouse. And with its covered porch and upholstered reading chairs, the Worth-Pinkham Memorial Library feels more like a cozy den than a public building.

But that sleepy appearance masks the borough's responsive and efficient local government, residents say. True, most programs and offices, from the mayor's office to youth sports to the fire and ambulance corps, are staffed by volunteers. But that keeps taxes in check, residents point out; only 10 of the 70 Bergen County towns have lower rates.

"A lot of people have lived here for a long time. I don't think this is a town people rush away from," said resident Sue Maddison.

"We're located near everything. People are friendly, and our taxes are reasonable. We say, 'Where could we go and get as much?' "

Ho-Ho-Kus was once inhabited by the Lenni Lenape tribe. By the 1700s, the area was an established farming community; by the 1800s, it had become a center of industrial and commercial activity. By mid-20th century, Ho-Ho-Kus had transformed itself again, this time into a summer resort. Gradually, the families who had built spacious clapboard homes along the borough's hilly streets began to live in Ho-Ho-Kus year-round.

Ho-Ho-Kus was named for an Indian word that has been variously translated as cleft in the rock, running water, crackling of a tree, red cedar, or hollow rock.

But the hyphens came later. "We were Hohokus, one word," said Mayor Thompson. "And much, much too much mail went to Hoboken. So we had a campaign to put in the hyphens and the upper-case letters, so we would become very distinctive. We like to be known as the town with the hyphens and the ho's."

In 1996, the borough's name landed it in a new book: "Odd and Peculiar: The most unusual name of a town or village in each of the 50 states."

Noteworthy Historical Events

The Andrews Sisters put Ho-Ho-Kus on the map in 1948, when they came to visit and wrote their hit tune, "Ho-Ho-Kus, N.J." Soon, everyone knew the trio's vow to "sing until they choke us, about Ho-Ho-Kus."

Most New England towns boast that George Washington slept in their environs. In Ho-Ho-Kus, the nation's first president danced at The Hermitage, one of the borough's original homes, built in 1760. Alexander Hamilton also visited the gracious home during the American Revolution. At the time, the Hermitage was owned by Theodosia Prevost and her husband, Aaron Burr, son of the founder of Princeton. The Hermitage is now a state museum.

Schools

"Ho-Ho-Kus is a very small town with a very strong history of volunteer activity. That carries over into the school system," said

Board of Education President Bill Brightly. "Teachers are used to having parents involved in their children's education."

Children in kindergarten through eighth grade attend classes at the borough's original brick school. Built in 1936, the school, with its fireplaces, wallpaper, and wooden bookshelves, has an old-fashioned charm that typifies the borough. But the building needs renovations, and to pay for a new roof, windows, and better heating, Brightly said the district is planning to put a bond before voters.

Until 1996, high school students attended Midland Park High School; now they go to Northern Highlands Regional High School in Allendale, which is larger and has more course offerings. (See Allendale for more details on the high school.)

Third-graders take French or Spanish, and band starts the following year. Most classrooms have computers, thanks to the district's nearly completed five-year technology drive. Volunteers staff an arts program, including lectures on great painters and sculptors.

Ho-Ho-Kus is also home to ECLC of New Jersey, a private school for special-needs students ages 5 to 21. The school rents space from St. Luke's Church.

Houses of worship

Community Church of Ho-Ho-Kus; St. Bartholomew's Episcopal Church; and St. Luke's Roman Catholic Church.

Houses

The eastern portion of the borough has one-acre zoning, but across town, homes can sit on lots as small as 10,000 square feet.

Transportation

Short Line runs a bus route to Port Authority in Manhattan; it takes about 40 minutes. New Jersey Transit has daily train service to Hoboken, where commuters can connect to PATH trains to Manhattan, Newark, and Jersey Citiy.

Recreation

Ho-Ho-Kus has five parks, including the tiny Village Green in the borough center, with its wooden gazebo for brown-bag lunches.

Many people enjoy East Park, next to Saddle River Brook, where visitors picnic and walk along the park trails, and fishermen cast for trout and bass. The borough recreation commission, staffed by volunteers, organizes youth soccer, football, basketball, baseball, and softball. The Ho-Ho-Kus youth activities council hosts an annual dance. Children can attend the council's Saturday movies, an annual pet show, and bowling. There is an adult softball league, the borough garden club, and the Women's Club of Ho-Ho-Kus, which raises money for education grants and spearheads projects to beautify the borough.

ARTS AND CULTURE

The Hermitage museum has mystery story nights that draw on the history of the house and the area. Costume, furniture, and antique curiosity exhibits are held throughout the year.

The Village Players, an amateur theater group, performs spring and fall plays at the Ho-Ho-Kus schoolhouse.

CHILD CARE SERVICES

The Worth-Pinkham Memorial Library has an ongoing storytime for youngsters. Private child care facilities are available.

SENIOR SERVICES

Ho-Ho-Kus Seniors meets twice a month. The group organizes monthly bus outings to the Jersey Shore during the summer, as well as luncheons, big band and theater performances, and monthly lectures on varying topics. Members pay $10 a year.

Bergen County Special Transportation, based in Hackensack, shuttles elderly and handicapped residents to doctor's appointments and grocery stores. There is a suggested $1 round-trip fee.

RECENT DEVELOPMENTS

The borough would like to add recycling to its curbside services, which would involve additional taxes.

DRAWBACKS

Because the community is so small, volunteers are at a premium, especially for the local fire and ambulance squads, said Borough Administrator Catherine Henderson. Although recycling is mandatory, there is no curbside service, so residents must haul their newspapers, glass, and other recyclables to the public works department.

PROMINENT RESIDENTS

Former New York Giants Coach Dan Reeves lives in town. Past residents include Orville Victor, who created the dime-store novel while he worked at Beadle Publishing Co. in New York; and Arnold Gingrich, the founder and editor of Esquire magazine.

PHONE NUMBERS

Township clerk (201) 652-4400
School district (201) 652-4555
Public library (201) 445-8078

— *Leslie Haggin*

Demographics

County: Bergen
Size: 1.8 square miles
Population: 3,935
Density: 2,251/square mile
Median age: 39.5 years
White: 93.4 percent
Asian: 6 percent
Black: 0.3 percent
Median house value: $331,200
Upper 25 percent: $800,000
Lower 25 percent: $250,000
Median year built: 1953
Median rent: $1,001
Single-family homes: 1,397
Condominiums: 24 units
Industrial property: None
Median property taxes per household (1994): $5,176
Median household income: $89,961
Sewers: Public
Library: 21,551 volumes, 60 periodicals, 100 videos a month that rotate among 17 libraries, 130 audiobooks. The library belongs to the Bergen County Cooperative Library System.
Media: The Record covers the town, as do the weeklies the Villadom Times, the Suburban News, and the Town Journal. Cable service is provided by TCI.
Fire and ambulance: Volunteer
Police: Paid
Crime rate per 1,000 (1994): 8.4
Violent crime rate per 1,000 (1994): 0

KINNELON

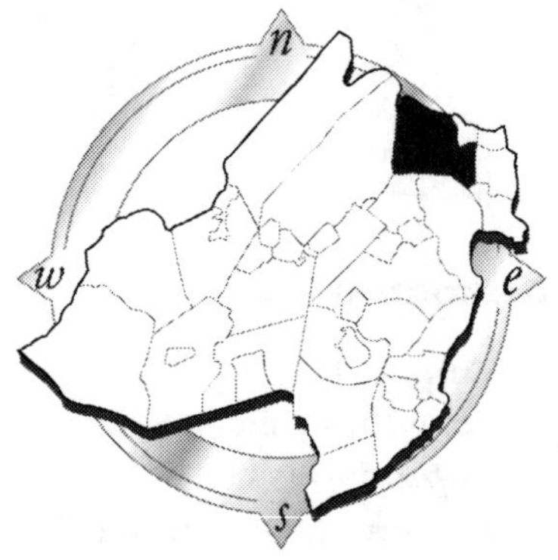

Thirty-nine percent of Kinnelon is undeveloped forest and wetlands, and most of the tiny borough's 8,500 residents like it that way. With a minimum lot size of 1 1/2 acres for single-family homes, there's plenty of room to spread out.

In a boroughwide survey undertaken last year, about 85 percent of respondents cited Kinnelon's rural atmosphere and open space — which includes 1,093 acres of reservoir properties as well as private lakes — as their top reason for living there.

The next most popular reason was quality of schools, residents said. Kinnelon's schools are regularly ranked among the best in the state.

The borough's lack of industry (only one business is classified as industrial), large lot sizes, commuter convenience, and lake communities were other top responses in the survey.

Kinnelon is also home to the gated private community Smoke Rise, and this, plus a median household income of more than $75,000, has given the borough a certain social cachet. Roz Pelcyger, director of the Kinnelon Library, said the borough is known for having "a set of interesting, exciting, successful, and enthusiastic people....It's the Chatauqua of New Jersey."

Kinnelon was settled by Dutch colonists in the late 1600s. In 1695, John Peter Meade and six other Dutchmen from Manhattan purchased the land grant known as the Pompton Patent, which encompassed more than 5,000 acres of land, including present-day Kinnelon. Pioneer farmers followed, settling throughout Kinnelon and other parts of the Pequannock Valley.

The borough was named in 1883 after Francis S. Kinney, a local landowner and president of the Sweet Caporal Cigarette Co., the first company to make cigarettes by machine.

Noteworthy historical events

In 1985, U.S. Air Force Lt. Col. William Pailes, a 1970 graduate of Kinnelon High School, traveled to space as a crew member of the space shuttle Atlantis. Pailes carried a Kinnelon High School banner with him on the trip and later presented it to the school.

Schools

Kinnelon's school system serves 1,519 students, with two elementary schools, a middle school, and Kinnelon High, which was rated 12th best high school in the state in New Jersey Monthly magazine's 1996 survey.

School officials said success stems from intense parent involvement and a motivated core of teachers at all grades who are willing to experiment with new teaching methods, including taking students outside the classroom to learn about science, nature, industry, and commerce.

The high school emphasizes college preparatory programs; advanced placement is offered in English, history, government, calculus, chemistry, biology, physics, French, Latin, and Spanish. Elective programs include physics/calculus robotics, telecommunications and networking, and advanced computer skills.

Kinnelon High School students in 1996 garnered a variety of awards and honors. The school had three National Merit Finalists, five Advanced Placement Scholars with Distinction, and eight Garden State Distinguished Scholars.

Ninety-four percent of Kinnelon High School students attend two- or four-year colleges. About 95 percent take the SAT; the average verbal score in 1996 was 532, the average math score was 554.

Our Lady of the Magnificat Roman Catholic School is located in Kinnelon.

Houses of worship

Christ Chapel; Church of God of Kinnelon; Jewish Congregation of Kinnelon; Kinnelon Church of God; Kinnelon Reformed Church;

Our Lady of the Magnificat Roman Catholic Church; St. David's Episcopal Church; Smoke Rise Community Church; and United Methodist Church of Kinnelon.

Houses

Zoning rules prohibit the construction of apartment buildings and condominiums because the borough has no public sewer or water supply. Single-family homes on large lots are the rule. There are two lakeside developments: Smoke Rise, a gated private community where many of the town's more expensive homes are located, and the Fayson Lakes section.

Transportation

New Jersey Transit buses to Port Authority in Manhattan stop at the Meadtown Shopping Center.

Recreation

The borough runs seasonal youth recreation leagues, including soccer, football, cheerleading, skiing (at Cragmeur, Vernon Valley, and Hidden Valley resorts), basketball, lacrosse, wrestling, baseball, tee-ball and softball.The county-owned Silas Condict park has about 20 acres of forest and draws hikers and picnickers. Boating, fishing, and ice skating are permitted on the park's small lake. In July, the borough runs a three-week youth recreation program that includes arts and crafts, sports, and field trips.

Arts and Culture

The Highlands Choral Society rehearses at the Pearl R. Miller School and performs concerts every Christmas and spring. The Friends of the Library sponsors theater groups, concerts, and an annual arts and crafts fair.

L'Ecole, a schoolhouse built in 1873, serves as the borough's official museum, and displays such artifacts as colonial farming implements. An annual celebration focuses on the culture of the Lenape tribe of Native Americans who once inhabited the area. The Center for Life Long Learning, based at the Kinnelon Library, offers adult education classes. The Italian American Cultural Society runs programs and trips related to Italian culture, including language courses, opera trips, and restaurant outings.

Child care services

There are no municipally run day care programs. There are four private child care facilities in town.

Senior services

A regional Dial-a-Ride system allows seniors and others to call for free rides within the five boroughs of Kinnelon, Butler, Bloomingdale, Riverdale, and Pequannock.

Senior Citizens of Kinnelon, which offers fellowship and entertainment, meets at the Kiel Avenue firehouse twice a month.

Recent developments

Fifty-four units of low- and moderate-income housing are planned for a wooded tract near Route 23. Borough officials also are considering doubling the size of Borough Hall, which was built 30 years ago. Recently, a former Kinnelon resident died in Florida and left more than $1 million to be invested and used for college scholarships for Kinnelon High School graduates.

Kinnelon Girl Scout Troop 48 will spend the next two years restoring the old Fredericks graveyard. And the students of Stoney Brook Elementary School are working on a campaign to save the 200-year-old butternut tree — the state's oldest and largest — that is the official symbol of Kinnelon.

Drawbacks

No apartment buildings; no existing low- or moderate-income housing; very little industry to offset property taxes; no public transportation in town.

Phone numbers

Township clerk (201) 838-5401
School district (201) 838-1921
Public library (201) 838-1321

— Tim May

Demographics

County: Morris
Size: 18.37 square miles
Population: 8,470
Density: 461/square mile
Median age: 37.8
White: 97 percent
Asian: 2.3 percent
Black: 0.4 percent
Median house value: $250,000
Upper 25 percent: $500,000
Lower 25 percent: $150,000
Median year built: Late 1950s to early 1960s
Median rent: $781
Single-family homes: 2,980
Condominiums: None
Median property taxes per household (1994): $6,097
Median household income: $75,481
Industrial property: 1 parcel
Sewers: Public and septic
Library: 57,307 volumes
Media: The Record, the North Jersey Herald & News, and the Daily Record of Morristown cover the town daily, as do the bi-weekly Suburban Trends and the weekly Suburban News. Cable service is provided by TCI.
Fire and ambulance: Volunteer
Police: Paid
Crime rate per 1,000 (1994): 13.2
Violent crime rate per 1,000 (1994): 0.6

LEONIA

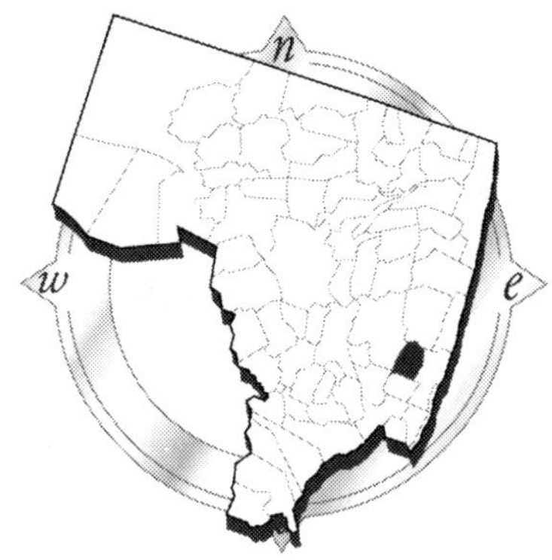

Only minutes from the George Washington Bridge, Leonia offers small-town living and an interesting cultural history, which makes it an attractive home to artists, writers, musicians, actors, and college professors, as well as the more typical Manhattan commuter.

Years ago, town leaders sought to ensure that Leonia would remain a quiet, happy enclave by enacting an ordinance outlawing bars, taverns, funeral parlors, and tattoo parlors — a ban that continues to this day. Except for a slice of meadowland in the westernmost corner of the community, commercial development is not allowed. Even Board Avenue, the main commercial strip lined with 50 stores, is free of fast-food outlets and taverns.

At the turn of the century, the lush green fields of Leonia attracted artists looking for housing close to Manhattan. One was illustrator Harvey Dunn, who opened a school of art on Grand Avenue. An artists' colony developed, helping to create Leonia's reputation as a bedroom community of artists and intellectuals.

A clever New York advertising man and land developer named Artemus Ward soon cashed in on this reputation by building an attractive neighborhood of individualized houses on irregular streets on the East Hill, and recruiting residents who were educated and culturally minded. Ward promoted it as the "Athens of New Jersey," and the name stuck, even as the educational levels of the surrounding communities have caught up to Leonia's.

Perhaps it is this reputation that has drawn so many famous people to Leonia over the years. The town has had four Nobel Prize winners — all Columbia physics professors. Sammy Davis Jr. and Pat

Boone used to live here, and Alan Alda lives in his house on Park Avenue when he's performing on Broadway. In addition to Dunn, well-known artist-illustrators have included Enos Comstock, Charles Chapman, and the sculptor Mahonri Young. Among writers, the best known is Robert Ludlum.

Although the town looks much the same as it did 50 years ago, Leonia is undergoing a dramatic demographic shift.

In the past 15 years, many Asian immigrants — mostly Japanese and Korean — have moved into the borough and now account for about one fifth of the town's population. Neighboring Palisades Park and Fort Lee have seen similar demographic shifts.

To help longtime residents and newcomers iron out the problems associated with such population changes, Leonia created the Human Relations Commission. It also has an active Environmental Commission. The Historic Preservation Commission is responsible for maintaining Leonia's historic sites — including a Civil War-era drill hall that is home to a local theater company.

Noteworthy Historical Events

In late November 1776, George Washington led the Continental Army in full retreat down Fort Lee Road to Englewood, where he narrowly escaped the British Army. During World War II, Leonia was home to Nobel Prize-winning physicists Enrico Fermi and Harold Urey, whose discoveries contributed to the development of the atomic bomb.

Schools

The borough's school system serves 1,610 students in one elementary, one middle, and one high school; that number also includes Edgewater students, who are sent to Leonia schools beginning in seventh grade. The schools pride themselves on their comprehensive curriculum, which stresses both basic and critical thinking skills; small class sizes; and a low student-teacher ratio.

The schools have a strong writing program, a gifted and talented program, and a middle-school portfolio program in which students work on extra-curricular projects in art, science, social studies, or language arts. It also offers a strong program for English as a

Second Language, reflecting Leonia's growing Asian populations.

The high school, which sends 84 percent of its graduates to four- or two-year colleges, also offers business subjects and industrial arts. Ninety percent of Leonia High School students took the SAT in 1995, scoring an average 425 verbal, 522 math.

St. John the Evangelist Roman Catholic School and East Bergen Regional Hebrew School are located in Leonia.

Houses of worship

All Saints Episcopal Church; Congregation Sons of Israel; Holy Spirit Lutheran Church; Korean Community Church; Leonia United Methodist Church; Mt. Zion Baptist Church; Presbyterian Church in Leonia; and St. John the Evangelist Roman Catholic Church.

Houses

A variety of large and small single-family homes can be found, in colonial and Victorian styles, with a sprinkling of newer split-levels and ranches. The last major housing development in Leonia occurred in the early 1980s, when 40 acres of a former golf course became a community of 128 large single-family homes called Vreeland Hills. Leonia has a number of older apartment buildings and some condominium complexes, but no high-rises.

Transportation

Both New Jersey Transit and the Red and Tan bus line run buses to Port Authority in Manhattan throughout the day and night. One-way fare costs between $2.55 and $3.25, depending on the bus line. Discount ticket books and passes are available.

Recreation

Wood Park, located behind the police department, has outdoor and indoor facilities including basketball, youth soccer, softball, and baseball. The recreation department also runs a summer program at Wood Park. Other team sports are played at Sylvan Field and Station Park. The municipal swimming pool is open from Memorial Day through Labor Day. Overpeck Park, a county-run expanse, features jogging paths, athletic fields, and a horse stable.

Arts and Culture

The Players Guild presents four plays and an outdoor summer performance in Wood Park. Leonia has two chamber orchestras: the Musicians Chamber Orchestra performs in the Second Sunday concert series at the Methodist Church, and the Leonia Symphonia performs at the Sons of Israel synagogue. One of the borough's strongest cultural resources is the library, which sponsors art exhibits, poetry readings, book club meetings, children's programs, and a lecture program called Leonians Talk.

Child Care Services

Each public school offers an after-school and summer day-care program, called Leonia School Age Child Care Program. Many of the churches also run preschool or nursery school programs.

Senior Services

A senior citizens club, located in the municipal annex on Grand Avenue, offers field trips and arts and crafts. A senior citizens housing complex is located on Glenwood Avenue.

Recent Developments

The public schools have embarked on a $5 million improvement plan that includes a new wing at Anna C. Scott School and new athletic fields at the high school.

Drawbacks

Leonia is surrounded by highways. Rush hour traffic often backs up on Fort Lee Road, the main east-west thoroughfare, sending frustrated commuters zigzagging through local streets in search of alternate routes.

Phone Numbers

Township clerk (201) 592-5742
School district (201) 461-9100
Public library (201) 592-5770

— Rich Cowen

Demographics

County: Bergen
Size: 1.5 square miles
Population: 8,365
Density: 5,546/square mile
Median age: 38.5
White: 81.5 percent
Asian: 14.1 percent
Black: 2.9 percent
Median house value: $256,200
Upper 25 percent: $338,000
Lower 25 percent: $202,700
Median year built: 1945
Median rent: $618
Single-family homes: 1,927
Condominiums: Not available
Median property taxes per household (1994): $7,186
Median household income: $51,735
Industrial property: 5 parcels
Sewers: Public
Library: 59,220 volumes
Media: The Record covers the town, as does the weekly Bergen News. Time Warner Cable provides cable service.
Fire and ambulance: Volunteer
Police: Paid
Crime rate per 1,000 (1994): 26.3
Violent crime rate per 1,000 (1994): 1.8

LYNDHURST

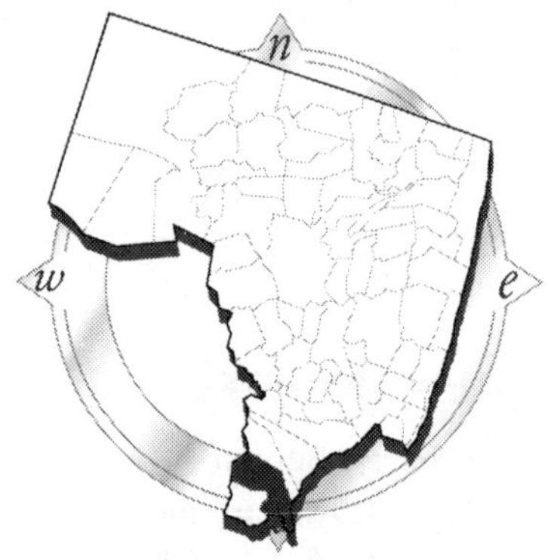

Situated in view of the New York City skyline, Lyndhurst maintains its small-town character, proud of the fact that schools are within walking distance for every child and that you can still walk into the supermarket and greet many of your neighbors by name.

"Lyndhurst is a family of 20,000 people," is how Mayor Louis Stellato Jr. described this township, bordered on the east by the Meadowlands and on the west by the meandering Passaic River, and near Nutley, Clifton, Rutherford, and North Arlington.

Industry in and around the township has grown steadily. In recent years, Lyndhurst has put the brakes on development to try to maintain the quality of residential life.

Many of the town's oldest families are still represented, according to historian Sylvia Kleff. Affordable housing and one of the five lowest municipal tax rates in Bergen County make Lyndhurst a popular choice for young families.

Like many North Jersey communities, Lyndhurst has attracted many immigrants. Longtime resident Elizabeth Hughes noted the addition of East Asian, Indian, and Middle Eastern immigrants to a predominantly Polish, Italian, and Irish population. "The flavor of the town is changing," she said. "New people are welcome." There is a diversity in social services as well, with extensive programs for people of all ages.

NOTEWORTHY HISTORICAL EVENTS

In January 1917, a blast now referred to as the Kingsland Explosion destroyed the Canadian Car Foundry, a Lyndhurst munitions factory. Sabotage by the German government, though never proved, has long been accepted as the cause of the disaster. The explosion was one in a series of similar incidents in North Jersey military-supply factories just before the United States became involved in World War I. No one was injured in the explosion, but the resulting fire burned for three days. Ammunition is still occasionally unearthed in the area. The site is being considered for designation as a national historic landmark.

Schools

Several initiatives are under way to improve the Lyndhurst school system, which serves about 1,900 students. The district has six schools for primary and middle-school students, and one high school. The newest of these buildings dates to 1920. "We are producing above-average test scores with below-average facilities," said Schools Superintendent Joseph Abate.

In an effort to keep taxes down, the district has established a donations-based Educational Fund, which is currently trying to raise $600,000 to add a gymnasium, auditorium, and several classrooms to one of the primary schools.

Standardized test scores have also been a concern. Although 77 percent of Lyndhurst students passed the High School Proficiency Test, exceeding the state average of 73 percent, Lyndhurst's average SAT scores were below the state average in both the verbal and math sections. Mayor Stellato said a major thrust is under way to improve the town's SAT scores.

The school system offers a gifted and talented program for grades 3 through 8, high school advanced placement and honors classes, and a Saturday enrichment program for all students, with offerings in science, drama, athletics, and other areas.

There are two parochial grammar schools in town. Lyndhurst also has an adult education program offering a variety of courses.

Houses of worship

Jehovah's Witness Congregation of Lyndhurst; Lyndhurst United Methodist; Our Lady of Mount Carmel Roman Catholic (R.C.) Church; Sacred Heart R.C. Church; St. Matthew's Evangelical

Lutheran Church; St. Michael the Archangel R.C. Church; St. Thomas Episcopal Church; United Presbyterian Church of Lyndhurst.

Houses

Houses are mostly medium-size colonials or Cape Cods. Older and newer houses are well interspersed. Prices can range from $139,000 for a two-bedroom fixer-upper to $200,000 for a four-bedroom colonial.

Transportation

New Jersey Transit and DeCamp provide bus service from Lyndhurst to Port Authority in Manhattan. New Jersey Transit provides train service to southern New Jersey, to PATH trains, and to Lower Manhattan ferries.

Recreation

The town sponsors leagues for baseball, basketball, soccer, football, T-ball, and roller hockey. Dancing, aerobics, and acrobatics are also offered. A recreational complex, including a baseball diamond, was built recently. Town Hall Park has been made accessible to the handicapped, and a gazebo recently installed there hosts musical performances and children's activities in the summer. Lyndhurst has sponsored an annual children's Halloween parade since the 1930s.

Arts and Culture

Lyndhurst's Little Red Schoolhouse is a one-room school that dates to 1804 and is maintained as a museum by the Lyndhurst Historical Society. A permanent exhibit depicts the one-room school as it may have looked circa 1912 and features authentic double desks and a potbelly stove. The museum mounts revolving exhibits on local history. A strawberry festival is held on the schoolhouse grounds every spring, and a harvest festival is held every autumn.

Child Care Services

The Lyndhurst school system offers before- and after-school programs. There are also eight private child care facilities in town.

SENIOR SERVICES

The township has an active and extensive program that includes local shuttle buses, medical and dental screenings, and recreational activities. Many activities are based at the municipal Senior Citizen Center. There are nine senior organizations in town. Additionally, the Joseph Corucci Complex, a HUD-sponsored, fully staffed apartment building, provides housing for the elderly.

RECENT DEVELOPMENTS

There is a proposal to extend Route 17 farther south, to intersect with Route 280. Because Route 17 currently ends at Ridge Road, the town's main street, Lyndhurst has heavy traffic running through the heart of town. Mayor Stellato said the diversion of this traffic will help the town by restoring small-town integrity while, paradoxically, bringing in additional ratables from large corporations along the new highway extension.

The township is renovating its library and town hall to ensure that they are handicapped-accessible.

The Meadowlands in Lyndhurst is frequently mentioned as a possible site for a professional baseball stadium.

DRAWBACKS

Traffic in town can be heavy, particularly at rush hour along the roads that feed into Route 3. While the extension of Route 17 might help to alleviate this traffic, there is concern that the highway will be built over the former site of the Canadian Car Foundry, a potential national historic site.

PHONE NUMBERS

Township clerk (201) 804-2457
School district (201) 438-5683
Public library (201) 804-2478

— *Maria C. Zingaro*

Demographics

County: Bergen
Size: 4.6 square miles
Population: 18,262
Density: 3,930/square mile
Median age: 38.7 years
White: 96.1 percent
Asian: 2.6 percent
Black: 0.4 percent
Median house value: $179,400
Upper 25 percent: $202,200
Lower 25 percent: $154,400
Median year built: 1947
Median rent: $559
Single-family homes: 3,220
Condominiums: 4,556 units
Property taxes per household (1994): $3,408
Median household income: $41,000
Industrial property: 111 parcels
Sewers: 7,699 public, 33 septic
Library: 49,122 volumes; the library also has children's reading and crafts programs
Media: The Record covers the town, as do the Commercial Leader and the South Bergenite, both weeklies. Comcast Cable provides cable service.
Fire and ambulance: Volunteer
Police: Paid
Crime rate per 1,000 (1994): 36.5
Violent crime rate per 1,000 (1994): 1.5

MAHWAH

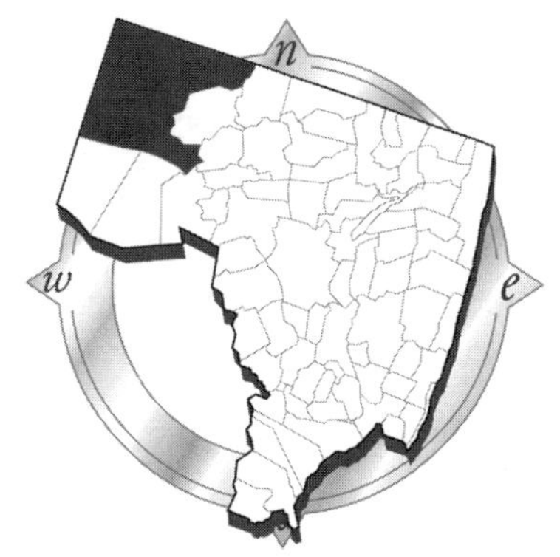

Hailed by residents for its small-town atmosphere amid 26 square miles of North Jersey's lush, rolling mountains and green valleys, Mahwah is one of Bergen County's largest and finest townships.

The township encompasses 16,450 acres in northern Bergen and is bordered by such other quality communities as Franklin Lakes, Oakland, Ramsey, Upper Saddle River, and Wyckoff. It is also neighbored by Rockland County, N.Y.

"We are close enough [to Manhattan], yet far enough away that it makes the commute a tolerable commute. We are within a few miles of everything," said Mayor David J. Dwork, who noted that the town's location puts it on the cusp of metropolitan culture without the threat of crime or overcrowding.

The town comprises five sections: Cragmere Park, which is mostly residential; West Mahwah, residential, but with some scattered business and industry; the town center; and Masonicus and Fardale, two former farming communities that have seen growth in residential properties and condominium developments, including Rio Vista and Society Hill at Kilmer Woods.

Still, people looking to buy in the township will find an abundance of open space — including 2,000 acres of state and county parks used for skiing, outdoor rafting, and camping, which have earned Mahwah the nickname "Bergen County's parkland."

"It's God's country up here," said real estate agent Helen Van Blarcom. "It's not congested, there are wonderful schools, and you can still afford to buy decent property here, whether you're a senior citizen or a young couple starting a family."

Noteworthy historical events

George Washington traveled through Mahwah four times during his military exploits in the late 1770s, at times staying with the Hopper family as he devised battle strategies. The French Army marched through Mahwah on the way to the Battle of Yorktown.

Schools

The Mahwah school system serves 2,276 students, with four primary schools, one middle school, and Mahwah High School — ranked as the 66th best in the state by New Jersey Monthly magazine in 1996.

The high school offers 130 courses, 22 honor programs, and ten advanced placement programs, with a language arts program recognized by the National Council of Teachers.

There are also special-needs programs, including a gifted and talented program that begins at the elementary level.

The high school is one of 22 Bergen County schools to have joined the interactive television network, which provides more than 30 televised classes ranging from advanced foreign language courses to college-level physics and business classes. A $10 million-plus school expansion program is under way to increase space and provide new technology.

Seventy-one percent of Mahwah High School graduates attend four-year colleges, with 15 percent attending two-year schools. Four percent enroll in Ivy League colleges. About 99 percent of the high schoolers take the Scholastic Assessment Test; the average combined score was 958 in 1995.

Mahwah is also home to Ramapo College of New Jersey, located on a 315-acre campus at the foot of the Ramapo Mountains. The college was built on the site of the historic Stephen Birch estate.

Houses of worship

Carmel Retreat; Church of Jesus Christ of Latter Day Saints; Fardale Chapel (non-denominational); Fardale Trinity Church; Grace and Truth Chapel of Mahwah; Holy Cross Lutheran Church; Holy Spirit Byzantine Catholic Church; Immaculate Conception Roman Catholic (R.C.) Church; Immaculate Heart of Mary R.C. Church;

Mahwah Full Gospel Church; Mt. Zion A.M.E. Church; Ramapo Hills Chapel; Ramapo Reformed Church; The Salvation Army Center; and Temple Beth Haverim.

Houses

There are diverse housing choices — everything from large stone mansions and sprawling ranches to Victorian-era homes, small cottages, and condominiums.

Transportation

Short Line Bus Co. provides all-day service from Mahwah to Port Authority in Manhattan, about a 60-minute trip. The line also runs to Atlantic City and other points south. New Jersey Transit provides train service from Mahwah to Hoboken via its Main Bergen line, with PATH connections to Newark, Jersey City, and New York.

Recreation

Mahwah has vast park areas, including the 1,350-acre Campgaw Mountain Reservation on Campgaw Road, which features hiking trails and nature workshops.

The Ramapo Valley Reservation off Route 202 and Ramapo Valley Road has a mountainside fishing pond and scenic preserve, with excellent nature trails.

Darlington County Park off Darlington Avenue has two lakes for swimming and one for fishing, as well as picnic areas, a snack bar, children's playgrounds, and tennis and handball courts.

The Campgaw Mountain Ski Center has a 1,650-foot slope with machine-made snow, two automated lifts, and a 600-foot beginner, or bunny, hill.

Summer recreation programs include arts and crafts workshops, outdoor activities, field trips, and nature hikes for preschoolers and elementary school students. The township also has one of the few year-round illuminated rinks for in-line skating, located in the Mahwah swimming pool complex.

Crossroads Corporate Center is the site of the A&P (formerly Pathmark) Tennis Classic in July.

Arts and Culture

The Small Town and Fancy Players present dramas, comedies, and musicals throughout the year. Ramapo College offers summer concerts, musicals, theater presentations, and art exhibits.

The "Old Station" railroad museum, which features a scale model of a Pacific-type locomotive and an Erie caboose, is open Sundays from 3 to 5 p.m.

Child Care Services

Mahwah has four private child care facilities.

Senior Services

The town boasts 75 senior-citizen rental units and free door-to-door van service inside and outside the municipality.

Recent Developments

Mahwah is building a 25,000-square-foot, $3 million library and is expanding its sanitary sewers for 200 families at a cost of $5 million.

Drawbacks

Inefficient snow removal caused difficulties during the winter of 1995-96, and the significant influx of new residents threatens overcrowding and traffic problems in town.

Prominent Residents

Les Paul, guitarist and folk singer.

Phone Numbers

Township clerk (201) 529-3730
School district (201) 529-5000, 5008
Public library (201) 529-2183

— *Kevin Byrne*

Demographics

County: Bergen
Size: 25.9 square miles
Population: 17,905
Density: 775/square mile
Median age: 32.9 years
White: 90.6 percent
Asian: 3.8 percent
Black: 3.6 percent
Median house value: $350,000
Upper 25 percent: $1,000,000
Lower 25 percent: $59,000 (affordable units)
Median year built: 1980
Median rent: $895
Single-family homes: 4,995
Condominiums: 2,800 units
Median property taxes per household: (1994): $4,034
Median household income: $56,468
Industrial property: 580 parcels
Sewers: Public and private
Library: 65,219 volumes, 300 periodicals, 900 videos, 2,300 music cassettes and books on tape, and 650 compact discs
Media: The Record covers the town, as do the Suburban News, Home and Store News (out of Ramsey), and Ramsey Reporter. TCI provides cable service.
Fire and ambulance: Volunteer
Police: Paid
Crime rate per 1,000 (1994): 21.6
Violent crime rate per 1,000 (1994): 0.6

MAYWOOD

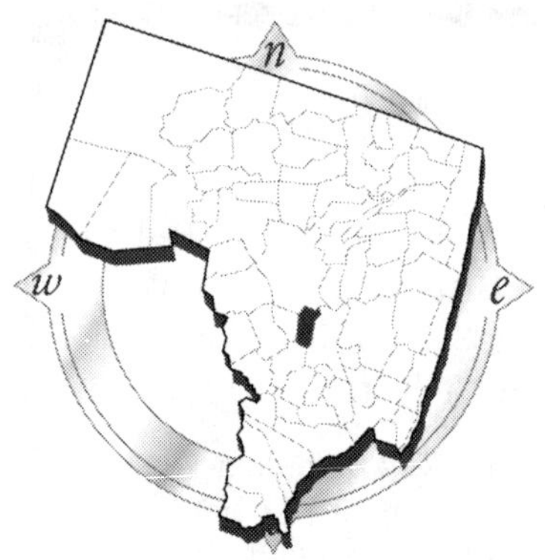

Amid the scramble and roar of Bergen County traffic, the small borough of Maywood provides unexpected respite and a charming touch of hometown feeling. Although it's just off the intersection of Routes 17 and 4, and close to Route 80 and several major shopping centers, Maywood is surprisingly quiet, yet not altogether isolated from the broader world.

Maywood's founders envisioned it as a commuter town, with a railroad connecting to ferry service that would shuttle businessmen across the Hudson River into Manhattan.

Longtime resident and Borough Hall staffer Jean Pelligra said Maywood is "like walking into the past ... like Mayberry." Part of this old-fashioned charm derives from the beauty of its tree-lined streets. Maywood has been designated a Tree City: Its trees have been catalogued, and the borough makes a continuous effort to preserve and replace them.

The small downtown shopping district has mostly small, independently owned businesses. Historian Betty Fetzer said the district is convenient for parking and walking. "Within three blocks you can find ... whatever you need for everyday life."

A strong volunteer and community spirit prevails. In times of crisis or disaster, the town rallies together for fund-raising.

Over the years, noteworthy people have visited Maywood. During World War II, Ed Sullivan, Bob Hope, and Joe Louis entertained troops at a temporary army base in town. Thomas Edison and Leon Trotsky are both rumored to have spent time in the borough. At one time, Gypsies were said to regularly pass through the town in covered wagons.

Noteworthy historical events

During the Revolution, George Washington used a course along what is now Maywood Avenue and Passaic Street for one of his retreats.

Schools

The Maywood school system operates an upper and a lower elementary school for 770 students in prekindergarten through eighth grade. An effort is under way to extend the length of the school day, said Schools Superintendent William Palmer. The upper school's program for the academically talented provides after-school enrichment for students gifted in art, science, or critical thinking. At no cost to parents, selected students can participate in any combination of the three disciplines through this teacher-staffed program. All sixth-, seventh- and eighth-graders can participate in a model Congress to learn about the legislative process. Each school has a computer lab, and regular and after-school instruction is available. Students requiring special assistance in academic areas attend the after-school extra-help club to receive aid without being pulled out of class. Special-needs students also are handled within the district.

Recently Maywood's schools have been recognized for their achievement. The lower school has received recognition from the New Jersey Association of School Administrators for two creative project initiatives: the Heritage Project, which stresses multicultural similarities and differences by tracing students' ancestries; and the Big Buddy/Little Buddy program, which teams up a third-grade student with a kindergartner to enhance cooperation and self-esteem. Upon completion of the eighth grade, Maywood students attend Hackensack High School. (See Hackensack for further details about the high school.)

Our Lady, Queen of Peace parochial school is located Maywood.

Houses of worship

First Presbyterian Church of Maywood; Japanese Christian Church of New Jersey; Lutheran Church of the Redeemer; Omega Mission United Methodist Church; Our Lady Queen of Peace Roman

Catholic Church; St. Martin's Episcopal Church; Temple Beth Israel; and Zion Lutheran Church.

Houses

Maywood houses are predominantly colonials and Cape Cods, with a sprinkling of bi-levels. Pre-World War II homes can be found along the winding streets of Maywood's Cedar Knolls section.

Transportation

New Jersey Transit provides bus service to Port Authority in Manhattan; buses run along Essex Avenue and Passaic Street. Transportation also is available from some parts of town to the Bergen Mall.

Recreation

In addition to its five parks and municipal swimming pool, Maywood offers extensive recreational activities. Adults can choose from aerobics, volleyball, basketball, softball (women only), and line dancing. Children can participate in arts and crafts, T-ball, baseball, softball, soccer, basketball, bowling, baton lessons, pompom lessons, gymnastics, or roller-skating.

Annual recreational activities include the Ragamuffin and Fourth of July parades. In December, a "Santa-cade," featuring Santa Claus and Frosty, travels from block to block, passing out candy and listening to youngsters' wish lists. During the summer, children from grades 4 through 8 can participate in an eight-week computer and music program, which culminates in an outdoor concert. Maywood's annual Youth Month gives high school students the opportunity to learn about municipal government by acting as counterparts to borough officials.

Arts and Culture

The Maywood Historical Society recently published a walking tour and map identifying ten historic homes in the borough. They include a chalet that was shipped, piece by piece, from Switzerland by the family of a Swiss lace maker; Temple Beth Israel, originally a church, unique for its clapboard and cobblestone construction; a turn-of-the-century residence on Oak Avenue notable for its colored-glass bow window; and a Dutch colonial home, circa 1700, built of red sandstone.

Child care services

Three private facilities offer child care.

Senior services

Maywood hosts two seniors' organizations, the Maywood Senior Citizens' Club and the Golden Age Club. The clubs sponsor ceramics and line dancing weekly, in addition to monthly trips and meetings. Lydecker Manor, a HUD-sponsored apartment complex, offers housing to borough seniors.

Recent developments

A proposal to build a bank building in the borough has just been approved. A proposal to build a strip mall, however, has met with opposition from residents who feared too much commercial development in town. Plans for a new municipal complex have been under discussion.

Drawbacks

The borough is undergoing a clean-up of thorium from its soil. Thorium, a chemical byproduct of industries operating in the area in the Thirties, has been removed from private properties. The cleaning of a storage site is under way.

Additionally, while property taxes have not been raised in a number of years, there is concern that the borough may not be able to maintain the same level of services in the face of increasing costs.

Phone numbers

Township clerk (201) 845-2900
School district (201) 845-9114
Public library (201) 845-2915

— Maria C. Zingaro

DEMOGRAPHICS

County: Bergen
Size: 1.3 square miles
Population: 9,473
Density: 7,360/square mile
Median age: 39.4 years
White: 93 percent
Asian: 4.2 percent
Black: 1.7 percent
Median house value: $194,800
Upper 25 percent: $$229,400
Lower 25 percent: $176,700
Median year built: 1947
Median rent: $638
Single-family homes: 2,488
Condominiums: None
Median property taxes per household: (1994): $4,387
Median household income: $45,600
Industrial property: 23 parcels
Sewers: 3,765 public, 6 septic
Library: 53,509 volumes in addition to the library's video and CD collection
Media: The Record covers the borough, as do Our Town and the Shopper News, both weeklies. Cable service is provided by TCI.
Fire and ambulance: Volunteer
Police: Paid
Crime rate per 1,000 (1994): 13.9
Violent crime rate per 1,000 (1994): 0.5

MONTCLAIR

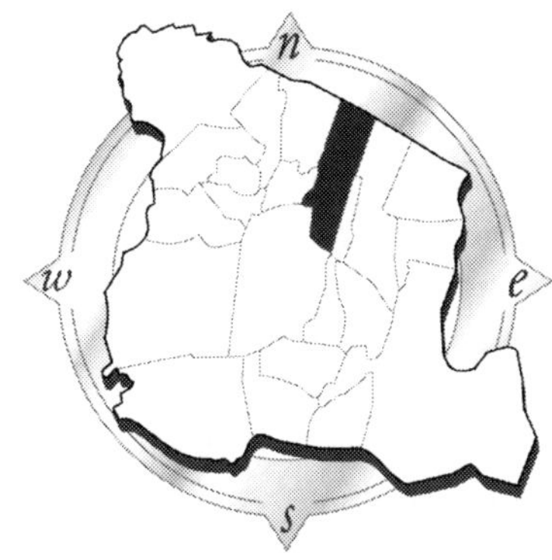

Montclair is a suburban community with an urban flair, a town with the sophistication — and some of the struggles — of a metropolis amid a setting akin to a collection of quaint villages.

"Think Upper West Side, think Columbus Avenue," one longtime resident commented. "It's a two-Starbucks town."

Downtown Montclair is home to some of the best restaurants in the region. The township is famous for its distinguished architecture, its support of the fine and performing arts, its three distinct shopping districts, and its nightlife. The magnet school system, organized in the Seventies, has justifiably been praised as a model of how to desegregate a school system while enriching the curriculum for all its students.

But despite its big-city sophistication, the landscape is dotted with English Tudor mansions, proud Victorians, and European village-style shopping areas. Bike paths and nature trails meander through the terrain. "Montclair has the feel of a turn-of-the-century community," said Burgdorf Realtors sales associate Eady Rickard. "It looks like a New England town, but, of course, it has a view of New York City."

While the town has a reputation for wealth, Montclair also has its share of middle- and working-class neighborhoods, some of them just a block or two from the fancy sections. Many of these areas are home to families who have lived in town for decades and who demonstrate their community pride through active neighborhood groups and less grandiose, but equally well-kept, houses.

Montclair sits on the first ridge of the Watchung Hills, 12 miles from Manhattan. New Yorkers first flocked to the town more than a century and a half ago for the quiet beauty and healthy air. A train line built in the mid-19th century made Montclair even more accessible to New York, transforming it from a rural to a suburban community by the turn of the century.

These transplanted New Yorkers, however, didn't leave their urban sensibilities behind. In addition to its amenities, the town revels in its diversity — of race, ethnicity, and sexual orientation — and prides itself on its reputation for tolerance.

That tolerance has its rough edges, as frank talk about race often surfaces in the community debates that are the town's hallmark. From arguments over multicultural programs in the schools to more furious battles over police protection, Montclairians never shy from pushing each other's buttons to get results. Progress isn't always pretty — but to many, that confrontational attitude, along with a determination to get things done, is part of the town's appeal.

Noteworthy historical events

In 1666, a group of Puritans left Connecticut to establish a town in the Colony of New Jersey, where "church and state were one," leading to the founding of Newark. Montclair is the original western boundary of that settlement. During the Revolution, Montclair saw little fighting, remaining a quiet farming community until the advent of the railroad, when it became a suburb of New York City.

Schools

Montclair's schools have received national attention as a model magnet system: The district's seven elementary schools and two middle schools specialize in areas of learning while reflecting the demographics of the students: 51 percent white and 49 percent black. Parents choose which school best fits the needs of their children: for example, one middle school focuses on science and technology, the other on the arts.

"The district created schools addressing certain issues," said Mt. Hebron School principal Dr. Bernadette Anand. "Parents shop around, which allows them freedom of choice." Bus transportation is provided to students who live more than a specific distance from their chosen school.

Montclair High School offers more than 200 college preparatory classes, including many advanced placement courses, business and industrial arts selections, and alternative programs in work/study, vocational education, and the performing arts. The district has come under some community fire in recent years for failing to remedy lagging achievement levels among black students, who now make up more than half the high school's enrollment. Average SAT scores were 426 verbal, 480 math. More than 80 percent of the high school graduates continue to a two- or four-year college, with a significant percent attending Ivy League schools.

There is a parochial primary and secondary school in town.

Montclair State University, located in town, offers bachelor and master degrees to 13,000 students. The college was designated by the state as a Center for Excellence for the Fine and Performing Arts.

Houses of worship

Valley Chapel (Assembly of God); Bright Hope Baptist Church; Community Baptist Church; Emanuel Hope Unified Baptist Church; First Baptist Church of Montclair; First Baptist Church; New Calvary Baptist Church; Rising Mt. Zion Baptist Church; St. Paul's Baptist Church; Temple of Unified Christians (Baptist); Union Baptist Church; First Church of Christ, Scientist; St. James Episcopal Church; St. John's Episcopal Church; St. Luke's Episcopal Church; Trinity Episcopal Church; The Living Church (Evangelical); The Salvation Army (Evangelical); Valley Road Covenant Church (Evangelical); B'nai Keshet Montclair; Congregation Shomrei Emunah; Jehovah's Witnesses Congregation; First Evangelical Lutheran Church; First United Methodist Church; St. Mark's United (Methodist); and Church of Redemption (Mormon).

Houses

Prices range from $150,000 to more than $3.5 million. The majority of homes date to the Twenties and Thirties. Charming wood-frame colonials and Tudors sit on smallish lots. Condominiums average $150,000.

Transportation

Fast access to the state's major highways puts New Jersey's business centers, as well, as its country and beach resorts, within easy reach. The Garden State Parkway, New Jersey Turnpike, Routes 3, 46, 80, 280, and other major arteries are minutes from downtown Montclair. Two rail lines connect with PATH trains in Hoboken, providing rapid transit to Manhattan, Newark, and Jersey City.

There are five train stations in town, but there are waiting lists for parking permits at all stations.

There are also two direct bus routes into Manhattan.

Recreation

Though Montclair is only six square miles, there are several large parks and 14 overall. Mills Reservation is a 157-acre facility with a wildlife preserve, lookout point, and several miles of trails. Presby Iris gardens has a late spring display of more than 4,000 irises. Montclair Hawk Lookout is a New Jersey Audubon Society sanctuary and a national landmark. Alonzo F. Bonzal wildlife preserve has 23 acres with nature trails. There are also public sports fields, playgrounds, bike paths, and public swimming pools.

Montclair sponsors weekly ski trips for students and has a comprehensive summer recreation program for ages 6 to 12 and a summer sports program for students through the 12th grade. Programs range from bowling to karate to football to softball. There is also a program for preschoolers.

Montclair recently launched a Friday night teenage social club, called Serendipity, that has become very popular.

Arts and Culture

The Montclair Art Museum houses a fine collection of American painting and sculpture from the mid-18th century to the present and includes American Indian art. Montclair State sponsors an annual independent filmmakers' festival and professional summer theater program. The college also houses two art galleries: Gallery One and the College Art Gallery. The New Jersey Symphony, N.J. Chamber Music Society, and The Orpheus Chamber Singers offer regular performances throughout the year. Montclair is also home to many theater and performing groups, including the Luna Stage Co., the Montclair Operetta Club, Barbershop Quartet, Montclair Community Band, and Montclair Dramatic Club.

The Montclair Public Library, which is undergoing a multimillion-dollar expansion, offers a film series.

CHILD CARE SERVICES

The district boasts one of the only all-day prekindergarten programs in the state, although it is in some jeopardy because of its expensive price tag. The town runs two day-care nurseries, and there are nine private day-care facilities. Montclair State University also runs a day-care center with half-day and full-day programs.

SENIOR SERVICES

The Montclair Office on Aging offers information on transportation, health care, and hot meals. The Sixty Plus Center of the YWCA offers activities including bus excursions and overnight trips. It also offers health insurance assistance, a hot midday meal and snacks, and crafts and games. The Senior Care and Activities Center is a non-profit, social adult day-care facility with a range of services and activities. There are specialized programs for those with Alzheimer's disease and other forms of dementia. Within Montclair, a free minibus provides seniors with transportation to shopping districts and other areas Mondays through Fridays.

RECENT DEVELOPMENTS

New Jersey Transit announced plans to build a direct train line to Manhattan through Montclair. Those plans, however, included tearing down 29 houses in a poor black section of town. The outcry was immediate. The plan is being reconsidered.

DRAWBACKS

Residents are still recovering from a recent heated debate over tracking students into classes by level of achievement. A multicultural World Literature program was introduced for ninth-grade students, and one of the middle schools was detracked. Though some enmity remains, the school board has fully backed the changes proposed by local educators.

The town's few poor neighborhoods also continue to struggle with crime and drugs. Taxes are another local issue. The taxes on a $300,000 home range from $9,000 to $11,000 per year. There are few business ratables in this 88 percent residential community.

PROMINENT RESIDENTS

Actors Olympia Dukakis, Frankie Faison, and Joe Morton; Jonathan Alter, the Newsweek commentator. Astronaut Buzz Aldrin grew up in Montclair. Former Sen. Bill Bradley lives in Montclair. The classic memoir "Cheaper by the Dozen," by Frank Gilbreth, was set mainly in Montclair.

PHONE NUMBERS

Township clerk (201) 509-4900
School district (201) 509-4010
Public library (201) 774-0500

— *Marc Warren Watrel*

DEMOGRAPHICS

County: Essex
Size: 6.3 square miles
Population: 37,729
Density: 5,985/square mile
Median age: 36.6
White: 65.5 percent
Black: 31 percent
Asian: 2.7 percent
Median house value: $271,700
Upper 25 percent: $371,800
Lower 25 percent: $208,200
Median year built: 1939
Median rent: $670
Single-family homes: 7,011
Condominiums: Not available
Median property taxes per household (1994): $8,104
Median household income: $52,442
Industrial property: 4 parcels
Sewers: Public and private
Library: 165,878 volumes
Media: The Record and the Star-Ledger of Newark cover the town, as does the weekly Montclair Times. Comcast provides cable service.
Fire and ambulance: Paid
Police: Paid
Crime rate per 1,000 (1994): 57
Violent crime rate per 1,000 (1994): 7.3

MONTVALE

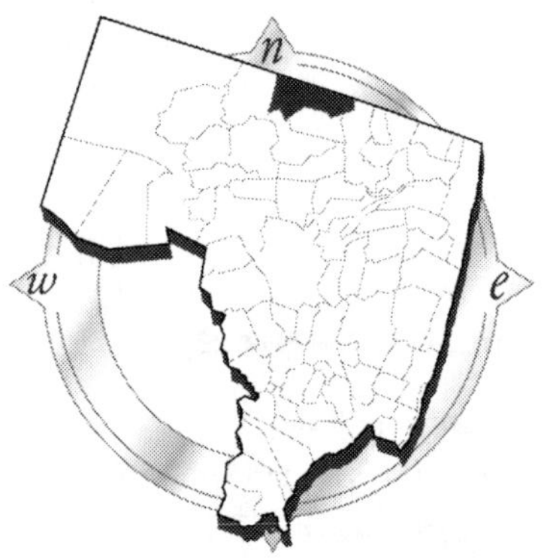

During the late Fifties, Montvale officials upset local farmers by approving 250 acres of rolling open space for light industry. At that time, Montvale was famous for its plump strawberries and sweet corn.

Now, about all that survives of that bucolic idyll is the DePiero family farm at 300 Grand Ave., 52 acres of farmland in a sea of several million square feet of corporate office space. Some of the land now devoted to those offices was sold by the DePieros.

More than 12,000 employees commute to the town's corporate row, and most produce grown on the DePiero farm is sold to people who work in the surrounding corporate offices.

The small borough is home to more than 30 major corporations and several international and national headquarters, including A&P, Butler Service Group, Benjamin Moore Paint, BMW of North America, and IBM. In exchange for the sprawling corporate buildings that grace Chestnut Ridge Road and Grand Avenue, the corporations pay more than $300 million in taxes and make up about 40 percent of the township's tax base.

As a result, borough residents have among the lowest property tax bills in the county.

"Most people around here say Montvale is lucky," said June Handera, the former borough historian.

"Vision had a lot to do with it. The leaders were open to inviting industry in, and you can't say that about every suburb."

To be sure, Montvale was prime for development. Its network of roads is one of the main attractions for corporations. Most of the commercial buildings are near Garden State Parkway exit 172, in the center of the borough.

"The town fathers knew what they were doing," said Ray Woodward, who has lived in Montvale for 29 years. "We have Parkway Exit 172, and we have a nice quiet community. It's a good balance."

Noteworthy historical events

Montvale's famous landmark is the Octagon House, built in 1855 and occupied by many mayors. The builder thought the eight-sided building would be efficient to heat.

Schools

The district serves 777 students from kindergarten through eighth grade. There are two primary schools and one middle school. There are also several special-needs programs, including a gifted and talented program that begins at the elementary level.

High school students go to Pascack Hills High School with students from Woodcliff Lake. Pascack Hills offers more than 100 courses, including 22 honors and 10 advanced placement courses.

About 92 percent of graduates attend two- or four-year colleges. About 85 to 90 percent of high school juniors take the SAT. In 1995, students scored an average of 468 verbal, 562 math.

St. Joseph's High School is located in Montvale.

Houses of worship

International Christian Church; Jerusalem Church; Montvale Evangelical Free Church; and St. Paul's Episcopal Church.

Houses

Single-family houses range in size from three-bedroom Thirties colonials on a quarter-acre, to five-bedroom houses on one acre in the newer developments on the western side of town.

Transportation

New Jersey Transit provides train service to Hoboken, with connecting PATH service to New York City, Jersey City, and Newark.

The Red and Tan bus company offers direct service into Manhattan.

Recreation

The recreation department offers a children's summer camp that includes day trips, arts and crafts, and sports. Other day trips and ski trips are available for a small fee. There are adult fitness classes scheduled throughout the year. The borough has several parks. The Chestnut Ridge Sports Complex consists of two big fields and tennis courts. In the center of town, Huff Park has a pond, tennis courts, basketball courts, and a new play gym. There are fireworks in June and concerts in the park in the summer. The borough is planning a nature walk along the Pascack Brook.

Arts and Culture

The library holds lectures and programs throughout the year.

Child Care Services

Montvale has three private child care facilities.

Senior Services

The town has proposed constructing a senior citizens building.

Recent Developments

The borough is looking at plans to build a new library.

Drawbacks

Residents complain of rush-hour traffic around the parkway, near corporate row.

Prominent Residents

Carl Nelson, former Giants pro-football player, calls the borough home.

Phone Numbers

Township clerk (201) 391-5700
School district (201) 391-1662
Public library (201) 391-5090

— *Barbara Williams*

Demographics

County: Bergen
Size: 4 square miles
Population: 6,946
Density: 1,747/square foot
Median age: 37.8
White: 95 percent
Asian: 3.8 percent
Black: 0.8 percent
Median house value: $291,600
Upper 25 percent: $425,500
Lower 25 percent. $229,800
Median year built: 1964
Median rent: $818
Single-family houses: 1,963
Condominiums: Not available
Median property taxes per household (1994): $6,095
Median household income: $70,272
Industrial property: 6 parcels
Sewers: Public
Library: 35,934 volumes
Media: The Record covers the town, as does the weekly Community Life. TKR provides cable service.
Fire and ambulance: Volunteer
Police: Paid
Crime rate per 1,000 (1994): 23.8
Violent crime rate per 1,000 (1994): 2.4

NEW MILFORD

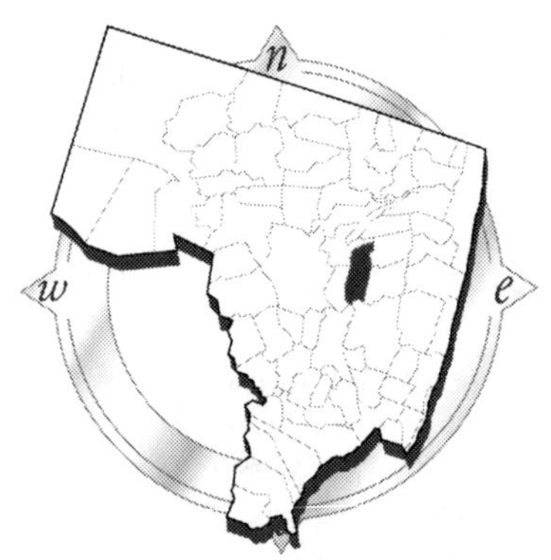

New Milford, which styles itself as "the birthplace of Bergen County," is known today for its small-town atmosphere. The 2.3-square-mile borough is in the heart of the county, convenient to the county seat of Hackensack and a comfortable commute from New York City. But residents are just as likely to look inward, rather than outward, and praise the community's serenity and quality of life. Along its scenic western border, for example, you can open your back door to lush vegetation and the placid Hackensack River.

The borough is next door to Bergenfield, Dumont, Oradell, River Edge, Teaneck, and Hackensack. With its relativity small population of about 16,000, the borough is characterized by friendliness and a spirit of unity.

"Every year, there's a block party on my street," said Councilman Robert Nesoff. "There's a lot of diversity, and people here like to come together for good times."

Equally important, the town's property taxes have remained stable for the last few years, without reductions in essential services. The municipal tax rate is actually below what it was in 1989.

"There's no heavy industry, no pollution, no traffic jams, and we offer terrific services," Nesoff said. "And this town's for everybody. My daughter bought a house in town a few years ago, so that shows that young people can afford to live here."

NOTEWORTHY HISTORICAL EVENTS

David Demarest, a French Huguenot, was the first European to settle in what is now Bergen County, landing at present-day New

Milford on June 8, 1677.

The borough's southern entryway is New Bridge Road, which during the Revolution was a major strategic landing and terminal for both American and British troops.

George Washington crossed through the town several times, pursuing or being pursued by the British. New Milford changed hands four times during the winter of 1776-77, alternating between the British and the patriots.

Schools

Officials of New Milford's school district pride themselves on working closely with parents. And since 82 percent of the district's operating budget comes from local taxes, parents and other residents are often quite vocal in school discussions.

The issue that looms the largest right now is overcrowding: Enrollment is surging at New Milford's four schools. The district is considering a number of options, including expanding the middle school and reconfiguring the grade levels assigned to each school.

Administrators have kept class sizes low by increasing the number of classes in grade levels with the highest enrollment. The average 11th-grade English class has 18 students. The overall student-to-teacher ratio is 14:1.

The high school offers about 20 honors and advanced placement courses and fields 18 interscholastic sports teams. More than 95 percent of high school students graduate, and about 60 percent go on to four-year colleges. Average SAT scores in 1995 were 421 verbal, 487 math; more than 90 percent of the students take the SAT.

Parochial schools in New Milford include Ascension Roman Catholic School, Hovanaian Armenian School of New Jersey Inc., Solomon Schechter Day School, and Workmen's Circle Jewish School.

Houses of worship

Ascension Roman Catholic Church; First Baptist Church of New Milford; Gloria Dei Evangelical Lutheran Church; New Milford Jewish Center; New Milford Presbyterian Church; and St. Matthew's Evangelical Lutheran Church.

Houses

The vast majority of houses in New Milford are Cape Cods, with some older colonial-style homes.

Transportation

New Jersey Transit offers bus transportation to Port Authority in Manhattan — about a 57-minute trip.

Recreation

The recreation department offers year-round activities, including soccer, girls' volleyball, junior football, and cheerleading. Indoor sports for winter include soccer and basketball. New Milford is part of two inter-municipal sports organizations: U-Gals for girls' softball and the Pascack Valley Indoor Soccer League. A summer program offers six weeks of arts and crafts, games, and field trips from 9 a.m. to 12:30 p.m. weekdays.

Arts and culture

The newly established East-West Cultural Arts Center celebrates the borough's diversity, offering classes and shows from Asian and American culture.

The Arts Center of Northern New Jersey regularly showcases the work of local artists.

Child care services

The borough has several private licensed child care facilities.

Senior services

The New Milford Senior Citizen Center offers services including exercise classes, nutrition advice, transportation, needlework, games, and several day trips each year.

Recent developments

The borough just completed an overhaul of the walking trails along the Hackensack River, planting trees, bushes, and berry patches. The borough also is working with businesses at the Brookchester Mall to put up a unified facade for the stores there.

DRAWBACKS

Parts of the borough have historically been subject to severe flooding, although much of the topography has been modified to alleviate that.

Because of shifts in population, the school district is always battling overenrollment. In the late 1980s, with no increase in students projected, the district eliminated two schools to save money on maintenance. In the long run, however, the closings necessitated a reconfiguration of the remaining schools, so that fourth-, fifth-, and sixth-graders attend classes at the middle school, in a separate wing of the building. And, enrollments are on the rise again.

PROMINENT RESIDENTS

Actor Joe Regalbuto, who portrays Frank Fontana on "Murphy Brown," grew up in New Milford.

PHONE NUMBERS

Borough clerk (201) 967-5044
School district (201) 261-2952
Public library (201) 262-1221

— *DeQuendre Neeley*

DEMOGRAPHICS

County: Bergen
Size: 2.31 square miles
Population: 15,990
Density: 6,915/square mile
Median age: 37.8 years
White: 90.6 percent
Asian: 7 percent
Black: 1.9 percent
Median house value: $209,300
Upper 25 percent: $241,900
Lower 25 percent: $183,200
Median year built: 1952
Median rent: $486
Single-family homes: 3,925
Condominiums: 106 units
Median property taxes per household (1994): $5,002
Median household income: $44,600
Industrial property: 4 parcels
Sewers: Public
Library: 66,500 volumes, 1,657 CDs and videos, 125 periodicals
Media: The Record covers the town, as do the weekly Town News and Twin-Boro News. TCI provides cable service.
Fire and ambulance: Volunteer
Police: Paid
Crime rate per 1,000 (1994): 17.2
Violent crime rate per 1,000 (1994): 1.4

NORTHVALE

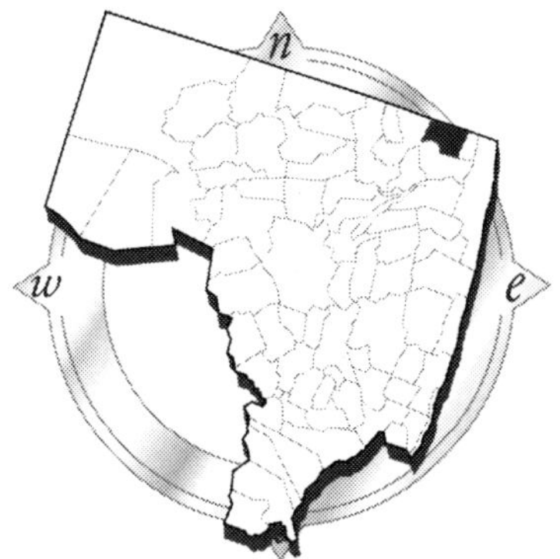

In 1686 the land that is now Northvale was purchased from the Indians by the Tappan Patent Company. At the time, the land was still part of New York state.

That changed around 1800, when a dispute over the land was settled between the states and Northvale became part of Harrington Township, which also included Norwood, Closter, Alpine, and Harrington Park. The town adopted the name Northvale in 1887.

The town's early settlers were German and Dutch. When World War II began, there were 900 people in Northvale, and 180 young men were drafted. Nine did not return.

Anita Rejmaniak, the town's historian, whose brother was one of those killed in the war, said the kindness of the townspeople, especially in times of trouble, is what makes Northvale unique.

Rejmaniak, who has lived in the town all of her 75 years, said another aspect is of particular importance to her. "I think a lot of respect is shown to seniors," she said. "I'm proud of the town that way. They're recognized not as elderly people, but people who have had experience and who are powerful in many ways."

NOTEWORTHY HISTORICAL EVENTS

The Thomas Jefferson Elementary School, dedicated in 1962, was the first circular-shaped school in New Jersey.

SCHOOLS

The borough has two elementary schools, Nathan Hale School and Thomas Jefferson School, with a combined enrollment of about 500. After eighth grade, students attend Northern Valley Regional

High School in Old Tappan. (See the Old Tappan profile for more details on the high school.)

Houses of worship

Community Gospel Church and St. Anthony's Roman Catholic Church.

Houses

Many of the houses are split-levels or ranches. Some of the older homes have extensive additions.

Transportation

There is no train station, but buses make frequent trips to both Port Authority and 178th Street in Manhattan.

Recreation

Northvale has two small parks. Veterans Park has a small swing set, a basketball court, and ball fields. Hogans Park has four ball fields, an ice skating rink, basketball courts, and a play area for children.

Arts and culture

The library has art displays of local artists' work and hosts arts and crafts programs for children.

Child care services

Northvale has a municipally run school-age child care program. There is also one privately run child care facility.

Senior services

There is a senior center at Borough Hall.

Recent developments

A ten-unit affordable rental building for seniors, located on Franklin Street, was completed last year. The Borough Council also is considering rezoning 2.5 acres on Industrial Parkway as affordable housing for senior citizens.

Drawbacks

There is no train station. Northvale has plenty of stores for food shopping, but residents have to go to Closter or the mall in Nanuet, N.Y., to buy clothing. Annual school budget increases have raised taxes, which is hard for seniors on a fixed income who want to continue to live there. There are several vacant industrial buildings; if they became occupied, borough taxes would be reduced. There are no movie theaters.

Phone numbers

Township clerk (201) 767-3330
School district (201) 768-8485
Public library (201) 768-4784

— Hali Helfgott

Demographics

County: Bergen
Size: 1.3 square miles
Population: 4,563
Density: 3,462/square mile
Median age: 37.5 years
White: 88.5 percent
Asian: 10.4 percent
Black: 0.4 percent
Median house value: $227,700
Upper 25 percent: $276,900
Lower 25 percent: $193,300
Median year built: 1961
Median rent: $722
Single-family homes: 1,268
Condominiums: None
Median property taxes per household (1994): $6,193
Median household income: $56,555
Industrial property: 50 parcels
Sewers: Public and septic
Library: 35,000 volumes, 67 periodicals, 600 videos, 200 books on cassette
Media: The Record covers the town, as do the Englewood Press-Journal and the Suburbanite, both weeklies. Cablevision provides cable service.
Fire and ambulance: Volunteer
Police: Paid
Crime rate per 1,000 (1994): 10.5
Violent crime rate per 1,000 (1994): 0.4

Norwood

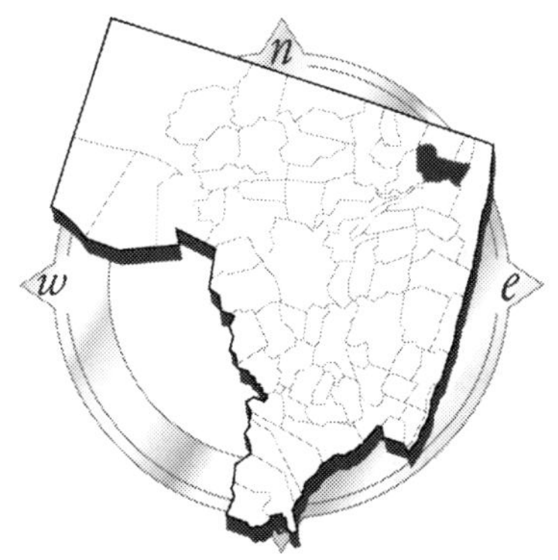

Three centuries ago, Dutch and French Huguenot settlers cultivated the farming community that eventually became Norwood. In the mid-1800s wealthy New York industrialists and their families built summer homes near the railroad stations around Livingston Street and Tappan Road. And over the last 50 years, the town has become one of Bergen County's more affluent bedroom communities.

Norwood today "responds to all the needs of the residents," said Richard Vogler, borough clerk and administrator. It's a rural community, but its location ten miles northwest of the George Washington Bridge gives commuters a convenient route to New York City.

The tight-knit community is what attracts many residents to the borough.

"It's just a lovely place to live," Vogler said. "It has all of the attributes of a small town, with people always extending a helping hand to each other."

The borough is mostly residential, with shops and other commercial buildings located on Livingston Avenue.

Noteworthy historical events

During the Revolution, George Washington and his troops traveled through the town several times.

Schools

Children attend the Norwood Public School from kindergarten through eighth grade.

Enrollment at the elementary school is about 600. After eighth grade, students go to Northern Valley Regional High School at Old Tappan. (See profile of Old Tappan for details on the high school.)

Holy Family Interparochial School is also in Norwood.

Houses of Worship

Church of the Holy Communion (Episcopal); Immaculate Conception Roman Catholic Church; and the Presbyterian Church in Norwood.

Houses

Split-level homes and a mix of contemporary and Victorian styles dominate the architecture. Expensive colonial and contemporary-style homes are available in the recently built Park Place and Rio Vista developments.

Transportation

Rockland Coaches provides daily bus service to New York City. Travel time to Manhattan averages one hour. There is no train service from Norwood.

Recreation

The ten-acre Kennedy Park has baseball, football, and soccer fields. There is a children's park and a duck pond on Broadway.

Arts and Culture

There are no museums or professional performing groups in Norwood.

Child Care Services

The YWCA runs a before- and after-school program at Norwood Public School; there is also a privately run child care facility.

Senior Services

The Heritage Manor of Norwood has 180 units of housing for seniors and a rehabilitation The borough sponsors a senior group at Borough Hall.

RECENT DEVELOPMENTS

A 24-unit rental apartment complex for low- to moderate-income residents was built in 1993, fulfilling the borough's Mount Laurel housing obligation. Construction of 94 units of senior housing is slated to begin July 1997.

About six years ago, Bergen County purchased about 110 acres of the town's East Hill tract for open space. It had been a hot political topic before the sale was finalized.

DRAWBACKS

No movie theaters. Residents have expressed concerns over the fact that the mayor and police chief are brothers, saying that makes it difficult to foster a system of checks and balances.

PROMINENT RESIDENTS

Former Nets player Kenny Anderson. Harry Harrison, who has a WCBS-FM morning radio show. Bruce Harper, former running back with the New York Jets. The late Yankee catcher Thurman Munson lived here. Former third baseman for the Yankees Craig Nettles used to live here.

PHONE NUMBERS

Township clerk (201) 767-7200
School district (201) 768-4321
Public library (201) 768-9555

— *Hali Helfgott*

DEMOGRAPHICS

County: Bergen
Size: 2.8 square miles
Population: 4,858
Density: 1,764/square mile
Median age: 37
White: 83.5 percent
Asian: 14.9 percent
Black: 1.1 percent
Median house value: $276,900
Upper 25 percent: $409,000
Lower 25 percent: $213,000
Median year built: 1962
Median rent: $887
Single-family homes: 1,360
Condominiums: 176 two- and three-bedroom town houses at the 32-acre Northwoods of Norwood, off Broadway
Median property taxes per household (1994): $6,507
Median household income: $63,830
Industrial property: 42 parcels
Sewers: Public and septic
Library: 21,750 volumes, 63 periodicals, 320 videos, 500 music tapes and books on cassette
Media: The Record covers the town, as do the Englewood Press-Journal and the Suburbanite, both weeklies. Cablevision provides cable service.
Fire and ambulance: Volunteer
Police: Paid
Crime rate per 1,000 (1994): 21
Violent crime rate per 1,000 (1994): 0.6

OAKLAND

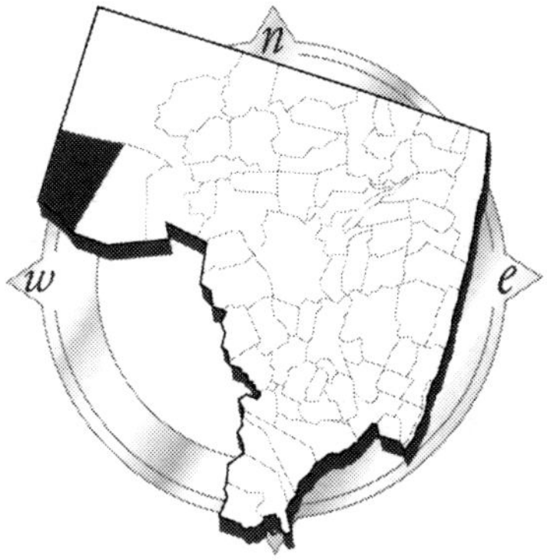

Three hundred years ago — long before state construction crews plowed and paved through the heart of Bergen County — Oakland was a quiet, relatively unknown valley community known for its dirt roads, quaint look, and farming and lumbering trades.

Even with the arrival of the Susquehanna railroad and, in the Sixties, the construction of Routes 208 and 287, Oakland managed to maintain its quiet, secluded atmosphere — despite being located in one of the most well-traveled areas of the county.

In recent days, though, Oakland has shown signs of change. In fact, in an effort to attract home-buyers to the green hills along the Ramapo River, borough officials have approved a project that would turn 303 acres of the Ramapo River Valley into a 400-unit luxury town house development. The plan would increase Oakland's population by ten percent.

The development would not only promote population growth, said Mayor J. Peter Kendall, but would create an economic boom for the town.

NOTEWORTHY HISTORICAL EVENTS

The town was bought from the Minis Indians by Dutch settler Arent Schuyler for 250 pounds of wampum.

After heavy rains washed out the roads through town one stormy night in the mid-summer of 1777, George Washington and his troops were forced to halt their march and stay overnight at the now-historic Van Allen house. While no battles were fought or waged in the municipality, soldiers and families in the valley constantly moved munitions and supplies along the Ramapo Valley Road so that Colonial forces could battle the British farther north. After British troops burned the courthouse in Hackensack on March 22, 1780, Oakland became the county seat for three years. Official records were temporarily stored in the old Ponds Church.

SCHOOLS

The school district has four primary schools, kindergarten through eighth grade, that serve 1,243 students.

Oakland students continue their education at Indian Hills Regional High School, which was listed as No. 52 among the state's top 75 schools by New Jersey Monthly magazine in 1996. There are 15 advanced placement classes offered, including modern European history, economics, and physics. The average scores on the SAT were 523 verbal, 534 math. Seventy-seven percent of its students go on to four-year colleges, with an additional 12 percent continuing at two-year schools.

The school system, however, has been the focus of heated debate in recent years, regarding what has become known as the Franklin Lakes split. The split refers to a 24-year-old arrangement under which Oakland students attend Indian Hills High School in Oakland, Wyckoff students attend Ramapo High School in Franklin Lakes, and students from Franklin Lakes are split between the two.

A proposal to unify Franklin Lakes by sending all its students to Indian Hills recently was rejected by the Board of Education, and debate over the split has raged on.

HOUSES OF WORSHIP

Church of World Messianity; Johrei Fellowship; Korean Presbyterian Church of New Jersey; Messiah Lutheran Church; Our Lady of Perpetual Help Roman Catholic Church; Ponds Reformed Church; Ramapo Valley Baptist Church; and Temple Emanuel of North Jersey.

HOUSES

Houses range from 16th century colonials to small cottages to split-levels to modern luxury homes.

Transportation

Short Line bus has direct routes to New York. New Jersey Transit train service is available in town as well as in nearby Mahwah. Transit lines connect with PATH trains in Hoboken for service to New York City, Newark, and Jersey City.

Recreation

Ramapo Mountain State Forest is a 2,800-acre preserve that includes the Ramapo Lake Natural Area. It is great for hiking and fishing, as well as cross-country skiing and sledding.

The town has an excellent recreation program, with sports such as spring baseball and softball, football, cheerleading, roller hockey, soccer, and wrestling. Summer programs are open to youths from kindergarten through eighth grade. Local Scout troops, mothers' clubs, and veterans' organizations are open to residents.

The Flow Follies is a school district-based drama club that presents annual variety shows to benefit scholarship funds for deserving high school seniors.

Arts and culture

The Van Allen House, at Franklin Avenue and Ramapo Valley Road, is maintained as a museum by the Oakland Historical Society. The museum is open the first and third Sunday of each month. The Native American cultural influence on the town can be seen in the street names, such as Yawpo Avenue, Minsi Place and Lehigh Way — all named for tribes that used to live there.

Oakland is the site of the annual Ramapo Mountain Folk Festival in August and hosts a First Night celebration on New Year's Eve.

Child care services

Oakland has five private child care facilities.

Senior services

Oakland Senior Citizens Center, located at 20 Lawlor Drive, hosts activities including line dancing, card games, dance therapy, and T-shirt painting.

The Oakland Senior Citizens Club, an offshoot of the center, is open to residents age 60 and older.

Recent Developments

In addition to the new housing development, the old Hopper Farm family cemetery — which dates to the 1700s — is being renovated.

Drawbacks

Because of its riverside location, the area is prone to serious flooding during the winter and early spring — often resulting in emergency evacuation and heavy water damage to many homes. A $11.3 million plan to abate flood waters in the borough has been approved by the House of Representatives, but the state has withheld support. At least 330 homeowners in the flood plains are affected.

In addition, controversy has erupted over the burial of illegal trash and refuse by a local Boy Scout organization at Camp Tamarack, an 182-acre site that the county plans to buy and preserve.

Prominent Residents

Sidney Kingsley, playwright.

Phone Numbers

Borough clerk (201) 337-8111
School district (201) 337-615
Public library (201) 337-3742

— *Barbara Williams*

Demographics

County: Bergen
Size: 8.6 square miles
Population: 11,997
Density: 1,394
Median age: 36.6 years
White: 96.2 percent
Asian: 2.3 percent
Black: 1.1 percent
Median house value: $214,300
Upper 25 percent: $260,700
Lower 25 percent: $182,200
Median year built: 1959
Median rent: $855
Single-family homes: 3,831
Condominiums: None
Median property taxes per household (1994): $5,428
Median household income: $63,384
Industrial property: 54 parcels
Sewers: 3,753 septic, 253 public
Library: 4,436 volumes, as well as numerous CDs, audiocassettes, and on-line services via the On-line Public Access Catalog; the library also hosts frequent art displays and guest lecturers.
Media: The Record covers the town, as do the Ridgewood News (a bi-weekly), the Suburban News (a weekly), and Suburban Trends (a bi-weekly). Cable service is provided by TCI, based in Oakland.
Fire and ambulance: Volunteer
Police: Paid
Crime rate per 1,000 (1994): 7.3
Violent crime rate per 1,000 (1994): 0.2

Old Tappan

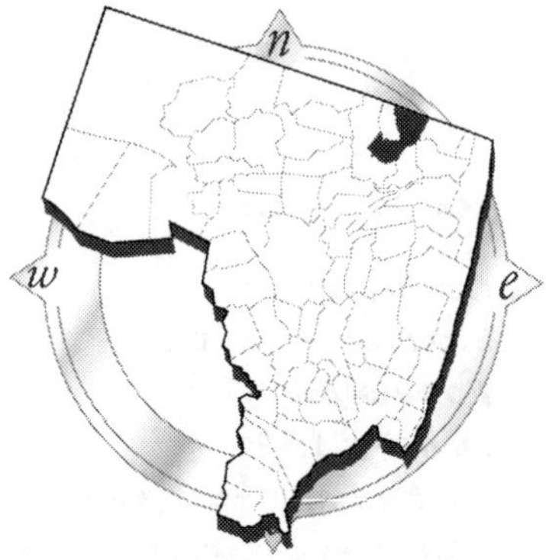

Purchased from the Indians in 1682, Old Tappan is a former farming town with a middle- to upper-class population and a forward-looking attitude. At the end of the 19th century, with the invention of the automobile, Old Tappan became one of the first towns in the county to pave its roads. (Paving consisted of a six-inch layer of stones covered with three inches of dirt.)

The Haring DeWolf house, built in 1704 and considered the oldest home in Bergen County, still stands on its original foundation on DeWolf Road.

Old Tappan was recently in the news because of one of its young residents, 13-year-old Jeffrey Maier. He snagged a fly ball during the first game of the 1996 American League Championship Series before it could land in the mitt of an Orioles outfielder, helping the Yankees to win the game. A media feeding frenzy ensued in Jeffrey's quiet hometown, as well as in New York City, where Jeffrey missed school to appear on talk shows and sign autographs.

Old Tappan Road is the main thoroughfare in town. Borough Hall is located there, as well as the police and fire departments.

The Bi-State Plaza Shopping Center, across the street from Borough Hall, is the town's only shopping plaza. It contains a Blockbuster video store, CVS drug store, several small eateries, and a Starbucks coffeehouse.

The municipality runs a nine-hole golf course.

Noteworthy historical events

John Lachmund was appointed borough clerk in 1897 and served a record 57 years until his death in 1954.

Schools

Students attend the T. Baldwin Demarest School from kindergarten through grade 4 and then the Charles DeWolf School from fifth through eighth grade.

After that, students attend Northern Valley Regional High School at Old Tappan, which receives about 1,027 students from Old Tappan, Harrington Park, Northvale, Norwood, and Rockleigh. (Northern Valley Regional High School at Demarest takes in students from Demarest, Closter, and Haworth.) Northern Valley Regional at Old Tappan was ranked 20th in the state by New Jersey Monthly magazine in 1996.

Both Northern Valley regional high schools were recognized last year by the U.S. Department of Education as "Blue Ribbon" high schools. About 250 schools throughout the country — and only five in New Jersey — received the award.

The Old Tappan high school has placed first in the state's Academic Decathlon for ten of the last 11 years. About 200 courses are offered, including advanced placement and honors classes in English, math, science, foreign languages, and social studies. Students begin foreign language studies in elementary school.

"The Northern Valley regional high schools are probably best described as the jewels of the valley, in conjunction with the seven elementary school districts," said Superintendent of Schools Eugene Westlake. "For 40 years, the regional high schools have been providing a quality education for their students."

Another Department of Education honor was given to the district: Old Tappan is in the top four percent of the nation in technology application and learning. The two high schools own a total of 800 computers.

Ninety percent of the high school graduates attend two- or four-year colleges. Ninety percent of students take the SAT; average scores in 1995 were 540 verbal, 570 math.

Houses of worship

Korean Presbyterian Church of Palisades; Prince of Peace Lutheran Church; St. Pius X Roman Catholic Church; Spanish Eastern District Assemblies; and Trinity Reformed Church.

Houses

Many of the homes built in recent years are quite large and luxurious.

Transportation

Rockland Coaches provides daily bus service to Manhattan. Travel time to Manhattan averages one hour. There is no train service in Old Tappan.

Recreation

Old Tappan has a myriad of sports programs including women's and men's softball, men's basketball, co-ed volleyball, basketball (grades 2 through 8), indoor and outdoor soccer (kindergarten through grade 8), and Little League baseball. The recreation department runs a summer day camp (kindergarten through grade 5). There are two parks in Old Tappan: Stone Point Park and Chestnut Field. Stone Point Park is undergoing a face lift. The renovation should be finished by 1999. There will be three new athletic fields, a walking track, and an area for roller-blading. There is a children's playground at Stone Point Park that was designed and built by a group of volunteer residents.

Arts and culture

The Adelphi Chamber Orchestra, the oldest chamber orchestra in North Jersey, offers free concerts.

Child care services

A new day care center is being built in town.

Senior services

The Golden Age Club is a social group for seniors.

Recent developments

Last year, a $1 million media center was created at the high school, featuring a library, computer center, and classrooms. Under construction are two town house developments: The Village on Orangeburg Road and Le Chateau on Central Avenue.

The town is divided over whether to support a Borough Council proposal for a townwide sanitary sewer system, which could cost about $12,000 per household. Residents recently received petitions that they must sign if they favor the proposal.

Drawbacks

Shopping in town is limited to Bi-State Plaza, so residents must drive to other towns for anything except the drug store, market, or video store. Also, the elementary and middle schools have nearly reached the breaking point with increased enrollments.

Prominent Residents

Former New York WCBS channel 2 news anchor Roseanne Coletti.

Phone Numbers

Township clerk (201) 664-1849
School district (201) 664-7231
Public library (201) 664-3499

— Hali Helfgott

Demographics

County: Bergen
Size: 3.2 square miles
Population: 4,254
Density: 1,317/square mile
Median age: 38.7 years
White: 90.7 percent
Asian: 8.1 percent
Black: 0.9 percent
Median house value: $353,400
Upper 25 percent: $500,001
Lower 25 percent: $257,500
Median year built: 1963
Median rent: $934
Single-family homes: 1,317
Condominiums: None
Median property taxes per household (1994): $6,460
Median household income: $75,372
Industrial property: 1 parcel
Sewers: Public and septic
Library: 25,415 volumes, 51 periodicals, 460 videos, 450 books on cassette
Media: The Record covers the town, as do the Englewood Press-Journal and the Suburbanite, both weeklies. Cablevision provides cable service.
Fire and ambulance: Volunteer
Police: Paid
Crime rate per 1,000 (1994): 9.6
Violent crime rate per 1,000 (1994): 0

ORADELL

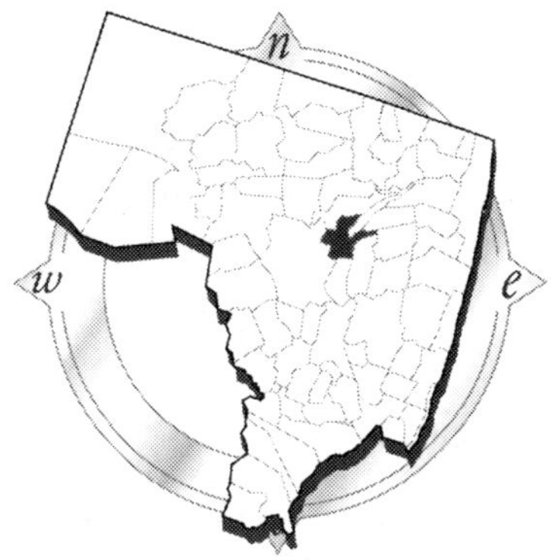

People in Oradell like its small-town atmosphere, closeness to Manhattan, charming downtown, and lovely tree-lined streets. But while other towns share some or all of these, Oradell also boasts of having something unique: the finest community theater group in North Jersey.

In addition to an annual children's holiday show, the Bergen County Players, now in its 65th year, offers a lively season of elaborately produced shows from September through June.

"[The Players] traveled around the county — Teaneck, Bergen Mall — before settling in Oradell," said the group's president, Barbara Warren. Home is an old firehouse that the company has rented from the town for a nominal fee since 1949.

The repertoire includes well-known comedies, dramas, and at least one large-scale musical each year; last season, it was "The Pajama Game." In addition, Warren said, there's "usually something artsy for ourselves."

Oradell's main street, Kinderkamack Road, dates to Colonial times, when the Lenni Lenape Indians had several burial sites in the area. Kinderkamack, whose name means "place of ceremonial dance and worship," is lined with brick- and wood-front stores of all kinds. For grocery shopping, however, residents travel to Emerson, Hillsdale, Paramus, or Westwood.

NOTEWORTHY HISTORICAL EVENTS

The Marquis de Lafayette's division camped on Oradell Heights, at Kinderkamack and Soldier Hill roads, during the Revolution. But Oradell was a Tory stronghold for much of the war.

Parts of Oradell once belonged to three different communities. It was incorporated only after special legislation was passed permitting parts of towns to secede and re-form as boroughs. In 1894, Oradell joined the flurry of Bergen County towns incorporating under this legislation.

Schools

Oradell's school district consists of one school (kindergarten through grade 6) with an enrollment of approximately 650. The district, which is noted for its parental involvement, has won many academic awards. Technology is emphasized as a learning tool.

Students in grades 7 through 12 come under the jurisdiction of the River Dell regional school district, which serves Oradell and River Edge. The district operates two schools: River Dell Middle School in River Edge (grades 7 and 8), and River Dell High School in Oradell (grades 9 through 12).

The high school offers a range of programs, including honors and gifted programs and special education. It was ranked 41st in New Jersey Monthly magazine's 1996 list of the 75 best high schools in the state. River Dell sends 70 percent of its students on to four-year colleges, and an additional 20 percent to two-year schools. SAT scores for 1995 averaged 439 verbal, 523 math.

Oradell's parochial schools include Bergen Catholic High School and St. Joseph's Roman Catholic School.

Houses of worship

Annunciation Episcopal Church; Reformed Church of Oradell; and St. Joseph's Roman Catholic Church.

Houses

A lovely and varied collection of stone and wood-frame, Victorian and modern houses range in price from moderate to expensive. Oradell's typically small-town American streets have become popular with producers of television commercials — so popular, in fact, that for a while they were a disruption. The Borough Council has limited filming to between 8 a.m. and 7 p.m.

Blauvelt Estates and the Greenway section are the borough's

most expensive neighborhoods. Prices there can reach nearly $1 million.

TRANSPORTATION

From the borough's train station, commuters can get to the PATH trains in Hoboken and reach Manhattan, Newark, and Jersey City from there. The Red & Tan bus line runs direct bus service to Manhattan, about a 45-minute trip, and New Jersey Transit buses provide access to most parts of Bergen County and points beyond.

RECREATION

Oradell's recreation department sponsors Little League baseball, softball, senior Little League, men's softball, football, soccer (boys' and girls', grades 1 through 9), wrestling, ice skating, tennis, bridge, and a summer playground program. Some programs require a small fee. There are four major recreational facilities in Oradell; together, they offer athletic fields, basketball courts, lighted tennis courts, handball courts, lighted skating ponds, playgrounds, and picnic areas.

ARTS AND CULTURE

The Bergen County Players, based in Oradell, offers a repertoire of plays and musicals. Bergen County residents are encouraged to audition or join the technical crews, and some well-known actors and actresses have performed on the Players' stage — among them Jonathan Silverman of TV's "The Single Guy."

The town sponsors summer concerts at Memorial Field. The Pascack Art Association offers lectures, demonstrations, and exhibits.

CHILD CARE SERVICES

Oradell has no municipally run child care facilities; however, there are several private facilities.

SENIOR SERVICES

The Oradell Senior Social Club meets once a month to socialize and plan upcoming events.

Recent Developments

The Borough Council recently secured a $3,000 community development block grant for senior citizen activities. The borough also prevailed upon Bergen County to improve Kinderkamack Road, in part through the installation of new traffic signals. The Borough Council recently decided not to develop an island in the Hackensack River on the Oradell/New Milford border. Instead, the Bergen County Freeholders are working on a proposal to turn the island into a 13-acre nature preserve.

Oradell had an unusual experience with historic preservation a few years ago. A group of citizens wanted protection for the town's older homes. There was a backlash, however, when the survey of possible historic sites and districts included a 1950s subdivision on the extreme east side of town. The preservationists believed that the development reflected a significant period in the town's history. The residents of the mostly split-level houses disagreed, and wanted nothing to do with restrictions put on properties deemed historic. The ordinance, which had been passed during the town's centennial in 1994, has since been rescinded.

Drawbacks

Regional development has increased traffic on Kinderkamack Road.

Prominent Residents

Abstract artist Ellsworth Kelly; Mercury astronaut Wally Schirra.

Phone Numbers

Township clerk (201) 261-8200
School district (201) 261-1153
Public library (201) 262-2613

— *Marc Warren Watrel*

Demographics

County: Bergen
Size: 2.4 square miles
Population: 8,024
Density: 3,291/square mile
Median age: 40.6
White: 92.4 percent
Asian: 6.8 percent
Black: 0.4 percent
Median house value: $291,200
Upper 25 percent: $372,400
Lower 25 percent: $231,500
Median year built: 1954
Median rent: $734
Single-family homes: 2,549
Condominiums: 35 units
Median property taxes per household (1994): $6,420
Median household income: $75,324
Industrial property: 1 parcel
Sewer: Public
Library: 70,526 volumes
Media: The Record covers the town, as does the Town News, a weekly. Cablevision provides cable service.
Fire and ambulance: Volunteer
Police: Paid
Crime rate per 1,000 (1994): 16.9
Violent crime rate per 1,000 (1994): 0.5

PALISADES PARK

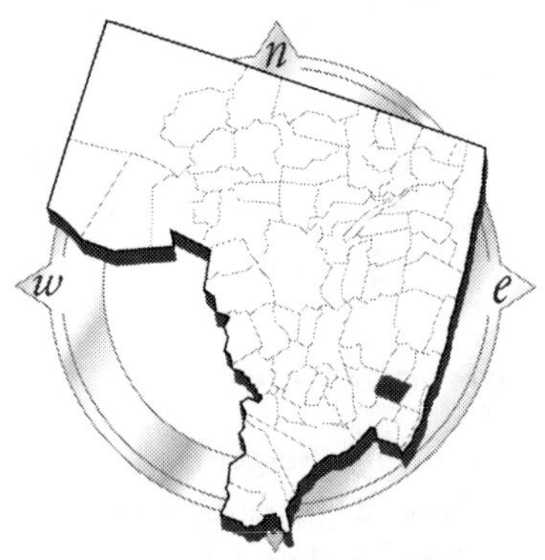

For decades, this working-class town prided itself on its small-town atmosphere and civic-mindedness. Local industry provided numerous jobs, and the town had faith in its school board and its police department.

Yet today, Palisades Park is a town in turmoil.

"Things have deteriorated here," said Mayor Sandy Farber. "It's a different environment."

In 1996, the state Division of Criminal Justice started an investigation into the deficit-plagued school district, while allegations that members of the police force were involved in a burglary ring resulted in the indictment of two officers.

"There were a lot of dishonest, self-serving people running the town," said Farber, whose recent election — along with that of several new council members — is hoped to be a harbinger of better times.

"We're in a state of transition," Farber said. "We've got an FBI man supervising the police department. We've got new school board members and new council members.

"Now we need to attract industry and try to effect a slow turnaround."

There also have been tensions between longtime residents and newly arrived Korean-Americans, who now make up 20 percent of the population and have transformed the large downtown with many new businesses. Korean businessmen charge that recent ordinances limiting business hours and mandating signs in English are racially motivated.

"There wasn't much communication between the two communities. We've established a dialogue. They've been very friendly, cooperative. We're working together to solve these problems," Farber said.

He sees a light at the end of the tunnel for this troubled town. "It's a tough time to write about Palisades Park. Talk to me in a year."

Noteworthy historical events

According to local lore, Chief Oratan of the Achkineshacky Indians had a fort on a hill at the eastern end of Palisades Park. He was reputed to be a man of peace, even when white settlers massacred some of his people in the 17th century.

When the British took control of New Amsterdam from the Dutch (and renamed it New York), they also took control of the area around Palisades Park, which they planned to use as farmland to feed the growing metropolis. Palisades Park remained a quiet farming community until the coming of the railroad after the Civil War.

Schools

Two schools comprise the Palisades Park district: Lindbergh School (kindergarten through grade 6) and the Palisades Park Junior-Senior High School (7 through 12). The elementary school has a traditional curriculum, with special education and bilingual programs for those who need it, as well as classes for gifted children. All students receive computer instruction.

Palisades Park Junior-Senior High School participates in Fairleigh Dickinson University's Middle College program, which grants college credit for certain high school courses. The high school's journalism class designs and writes its own page for local and regional papers. For three consecutive years, the high school literary magazine, Reflections, has won First Place with Special Merit in the American Scholastic Press Association contest. Average SAT scores for 1995 were 400 verbal, 489 math.

Notre Dame Interparochial Roman Catholic School (Elementary Division) is located in Palisades Park.

Houses of worship

Bergen County Choong Hyun Lutheran Church & Korean Christian Center; Central Bible Church; First Presbyterian Church; Fwam Mission Center; GMA US Center; Grace Evangelical Lutheran Church; Korean Presbyterian Church; The Mission 777; St. Michael's Roman Catholic (R.C.) Church; and St. Nicholas's R.C. Church.

Houses

Older houses tend to be wood, while the newer ones are brick and masonry. The styles vary from Victorian and Tudor to Cape Cod. The borough has about a dozen large apartment buildings and many two-family homes.

Transportation

New Jersey Transit runs several bus lines to New York through Palisades Park. The borough's proximity to major highways, including the New Jersey Turnpike and Routes 1, 9, 46, and 80, makes for quick automobile access in or out of the town.

Recreation

Palisades Park offers many youth programs, including Little League, girls' softball, soccer, football, boys' and girls' basketball, cheerleading, and indoor soccer. For adults, there are aerobics, men's softball, and men's basketball. The recreation department sponsors a Halloween party, Christmas tree-lighting ceremony, and Easter egg hunt. It also sponsors a summer indoor program and a summer park program that schedules ten trips per year to such destinations as the Bronx Zoo and the Statue of Liberty. There are four recreational parks in town: Lindbergh Field, Christopher Columbus Park, Charles Tussi Park, and the Little League Field. In 1984, the town's Little League all-star team won the state championship.

Child care services

There is a latchkey program at the elementary school. Palisades Park has a number of privately operated child care centers.

Senior services

The county-sponsored senior citizen activity center offers programs including dance classes and nutritional guidance.

Recent developments

The influx of Koreans has significantly changed the nature and look of the town, and has added tension. That tension, between longtime residents and new immigrants, is being addressed, Mayor Farber said.

Though land is scarce, a ShopRite and a mini-mall are planned for a vacant parcel.

Drawbacks

Houses with more than two families are illegal in Palisades Park; however, several decades ago, people began converting basements or other extra space into apartments, creating what is commonly referred to as illegal three-families. Residents complain that the extra apartments crowd the neighborhood and that the congestion hurts property values.

There is a lack of parking along the main commercial strip. For nearly a decade, the council has been working on one proposal or another to ease the problem.

Phone numbers

Township clerk (201) 585-4100
School district (201) 947-3560
Public library (201) 585-4150

— *Marc Warren Watrel*

DEMOGRAPHICS

County: Bergen
Size: 1.2 square miles
Population: 14,536
Density: 12,032/square mile
Median age: 34.7
White: 75.1 percent
Asian: 20 percent
Black: 1.6 percent
Median house value: $208,500
Upper 25 percent: $249,900
Lower 25 percent: $172,800
Median year built: 1957
Median rent: $649
Single-family homes: 1,297
Condominiums: Not available
Median property taxes per household (1994): $4,414
Median household income: $36,019
Industrial property: 53 parcels
Sewers: Public and private
Library: 38,696 volumes
Media: The Record, a daily, and the Bergen News, a weekly, cover the town. Time Warner provides cable service.
Fire and ambulance: Paid
Police: Paid
Crime rate per 1,000 (1994): 18.8
Violent crime rate per 1,000 (1994): 1.4

PARAMUS

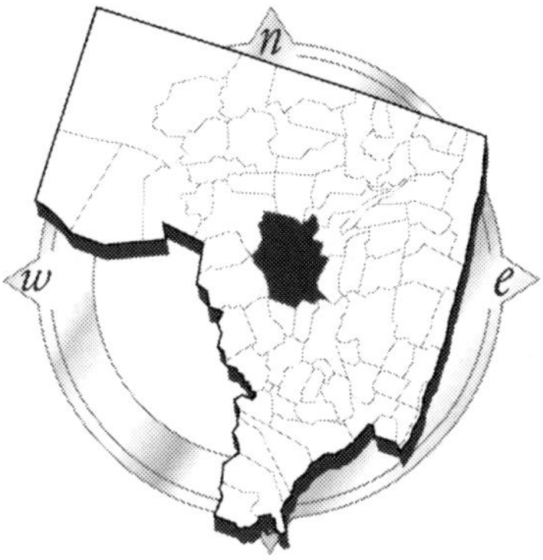

The Paramus of today would be unrecognizable to anyone living here 75 years ago," said Mayor Cliff Gennarelli. "There were maybe two stores back then ... maybe."

The farmers of this 10.2-square-mile town once picked celery by lantern light. Lunch wagons served weary travelers.

Today Paramus is home to no fewer than four malls, numerous retail strips, two multiplex theaters, furniture outlets, two Barnes & Noble superstores, and 22 restaurants.

The transformation began in the Fifties, when officials decided to allow commercial zoning on Routes 4 and 17, reserving the core of the town for residential use. Very soon, the celery and cabbage farmers saw their land being sliced up and used for ramps into the malls and huge parking lots. The Behnke Family farm, which dated to 1886, was broken up to accommodate Paramus Bowling, Huffman-Koos, and Red Lobster.

But the town that's often called the shopping center capital of the Northeast has managed to preserve its homey quality in the midst of all this commercial bustle. Behind the traffic and concrete are block after block of neatly kept homes shaded by tall trees, and even a private riding stable with trails spread over 65 acres.

"This is really a bedroom community and is the best of both worlds," Gennarelli said. "The stores occupy only 15 percent of the space in town."

Many residents say they see the shopping as a major convenience. "I hate to say it, but the shopping was what made me want to move here," said one. "If it were not for the malls I would have picked another town."

The huge tax base that the malls provide — 51 percent of property taxes, or $30 million — has kept taxes relatively low while allowing Paramus to provide top-notch services: good schools, a center for the elderly, a 96,000-volume library, and a 98-member police force.

Paramus is home to Bergen Community College and Bergen Pines County Hospital, as well as many county offices, agencies, and services.

More than 78,000 people come to work in Paramus each day.

Noteworthy Historical Events

According to local history, a farmer and his wife were killed after refusing to feed British troops during the Revolutionary War. Several homes on Dunkerhook Road are said to be the former quarters of slaves who worked for a local family.

Schools

The Paramus school district has one of the best reputations in the county. The district serves 3,823 students, with four primary schools, two middle schools, and Paramus High School. There are also several special-needs programs, including a gifted and talented program that begins at the elementary level.

The high school offers 130 courses, 22 honor programs, and 13 advanced placement programs.

Paramus sends 73 percent of its graduates to four-year colleges and 14 percent to two-year schools. In 1995, the average verbal SAT score was 433; average math was 528.

College credit courses are offered through a cooperative program with Fairleigh Dickinson University and Bergen County Community College.

The high school is nationally known for its advanced music program, which sends students to perform across the country. There is also a television studio where students produce their own news programs.

Parochial schools include Paramus Catholic High School; Frisch Yeshiva High School; Our Lady of the Visitation School; and Yavneh Academy.

Houses of worship

Annunciation Roman Catholic (R.C.) Church; Arcola Korean United Methodist; Arcola United Methodist Church of Paramus; Armenian Presbyterian Church; Central Unitarian Church; Cho Dae Presbyterian Church; Christ Lutheran Church; Church of Jesus; Church of the Nazarene; Community Church of Paramus; Congregation Beth Tefillah; Congregation K'hal Adath Jeshurun; Jewish Community Center of Paramus; Lutheran Church of the Savior; The Mission Church; Orthodox Christian Church of Christ the Savior; Our Lady of the Visitation R.C. Church; Paramus Baptist Church; Paramus Congregational Church; Presbytery of the Palisades; St. Athanasios Greek Orthodox Church; St. Matthew's Episcopal Church; St. Therese Carmelite Chapel; Sung Rock Baptist Church of New Jersey; and Trinity United Presbyterian Church.

Houses

Houses in Paramus range from starter homes on small lots for $175,000, to $650,000 mansions.

Transportation

Paramus is about 14 miles from midtown Manhattan. Short Line runs buses to and from Port Authority — about a 45-minute trip.

Recreation

During the summer, the recreation department runs an all-day six-week children's program that includes trips, games, and crafts.

The recreation department offers adult volleyball, indoor soccer, basketball, and softball. Youth programs include basketball, soccer, softball, roller hockey, wrestling, and arts and crafts.

The recreation department also offers special community events during holidays, including an Easter egg hunt and a winter holiday party for preschoolers.

The town has about 300 acres of parkland, including a municipal golf course, a community pool, two hockey rinks that are also used for ice skating, and loads of baseball and football fields. There are several walking paths. Paramus is home to the 140-acre county-run Van Saun Park, which offers fishing, ice skating, and a zoo.

Arts and Culture

Paramus is home to the Bergen Museum of Art and Science, which occupies a wing of the county office building and displays the work of local artists. It also has Indian artifacts and a collection of tools from the Stone Age, Bronze Age, and Iron Age. Paramus is also home to the Laboratory Theatre, which produces student plays and occasionally presents touring arts groups.

Child Care Services

The school district offers free preschool services, including a half-day program for 4-year-olds. There are 15 private child care facilities in Paramus.

Senior Services

Township officials pride themselves on the borough's senior services. There is a very active senior center and a bus that enables seniors to get around town. Other programs include an adult day care center; Hope House Inc.; Institute for the Aging; a senior citizen center; and a senior citizen nutrition program.

Recent Developments

Garden State Plaza just went through a major expansion, adding a new wing and two department stores. During the last five years, about 125 units of affordable senior housing have been built.

Drawbacks

The malls contribute to the borough's crime rate, particularly car thefts. Speeding is common on the highways, but the residential neighborhoods are safe. Traffic that spills onto local streets from the highways can be a nuisance, however, and can be especially maddening between 5 and 7 p.m. on weekdays.

Phone Numbers

Township clerk (201) 265-2100
School district (201) 261-7800
Public library (201) 599-1302

— *Emily Wax*

Demographics

County: Bergen
Size: 10.5 square miles
Population: 25,067
Density: 2,391/square mile
Median age: 41.0
White: 88.2 percent
Asian: 10.5 percent
Black: 0.8 percent
Median house value: $246,200
Upper 25 percent: $305,200
Lower 25 percent: $206,000
Median year built: 1957
Median rent: $958
Single-family homes: 7,340
Condominiums: None
Median property taxes per household (1994): $4,707
Median household income: $62,513
Industrial property: 39 parcels
Sewers: Public
Library: 96,509 volumes
Media: The Record covers the town, as does the weekly Post Review. Cable service is provided by Cablevision and TCI.
Fire and ambulance: Volunteer
Police: Paid
Crime rate per 1,000 (1994): 11
Violent crime rate per 1,000 (1994): 0.5

PARK RIDGE

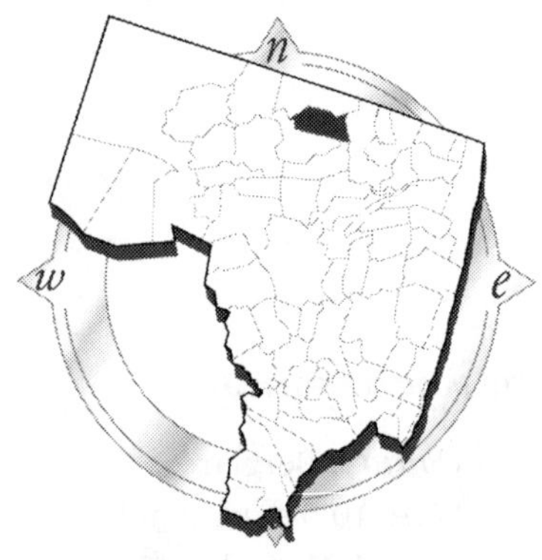

The cowpaths surrounded by mountain ridges, and the large parklike areas, gave birth in the 1800s to the name Park Ridge, an affluent community nestled in the northern section of the Pascack Valley.

Fondly referred to as "our little Camelot," Park Ridge, said Councilman Donald Ruschman, has everything residents could ask for. "The people are very friendly, the school system is good — which is basically the fabric that holds the community together — and our services are excellent," he said.

The 2.6-square-mile community is the only town in Bergen County with its own electric company and water distribution system. A direct result has been seen: Electric bills are 40 percent less than in neighboring boroughs and water rates are 20 to 25 percent lower.

"I think having our own school system, without regionalizing, helps set our town apart from others and makes us a more close-knit community," said Mayor Richard Mancinelli. "It's a great place to raise children; many of our residents who are empty-nesters are selling their homes to their children, who remain in the community."

"Living in Park Ridge affords you the luxury of being able to commute almost anywhere," said Muriel Speer, a local real estate agent. "In less than an hour, you can get to White Plains, New York City, or Rockland County, so you can work in a variety of areas."

Park Ridge is home to several corporate headquarters, reinforcing the borough's motto, "By industry we flourish." Sony electronics, Hertz rental cars, National Utility Services, and the Park Ridge Marriott contribute heavily to the community's tax base.

NOTEWORTHY HISTORICAL EVENTS

Park Ridge was one of the pioneer boom towns, with the Hackensack and New York Extension Railroad Company stopping at the stationhouse built in 1871 (it was restored in October 1986). The town prospered as the real estate market took off, and the population grew from 1,200 to 8,000 in this century.

The borough's first electric system was created in 1904 on Mill Road, and by 1907, the system had 18 customers. The company still serves as a substation, resulting in lower electric rates for Park Ridge residents.

SCHOOLS

The Park Ridge school system is self-contained, with two elementary schools and a junior/senior high school, serving about 1,050 students. Most live within walking distance of all three schools.

In 1996, Park Ridge High School was ranked 35th in the state by New Jersey Monthly magazine, and one of the top eight in Bergen County. Eighty-seven percent of the graduating students attend two- or four-year colleges. Average SAT scores for 1995 were 458 verbal, 518 math.

A National Science Foundation grant has enabled the district to establish a polar satellite link with Ramapo College so elementary school students can learn weather imaging brought in on a scanner.

The borough has one parochial school, Our Lady of Mercy Interparochial School (Catholic), for students in kindergarten through grade 8.

HOUSES OF WORSHIP

First Congregational Church; Our Lady of Mercy Roman Catholic Church; Park Ridge United Methodist Church; Pascack Reformed Church; and Temple Beth Sholom of Pascack Valley (Conservative).

HOUSES

Homes are of the typical suburban variety: center-hall colonials, split and bi-levels, Cape Cods, and some small ranches that are sold mainly as starter homes. Condominiums and town houses are also plentiful, though most of the town houses start at half a million dollars or more.

TRANSPORTATION

There is direct bus service to New York City. Trains depart from Park Ridge for Hoboken and the PATH system, with connections to New York City, Newark, and Jersey City.

RECREATION

In addition to the recreation department's standard fare of football, baseball, soccer, and basketball, many activities are offered throughout the year for children and adults. The annual town picnic, Halloween parade, Easter candy hunt, summer day camp, and summer fitness program are well attended.

The Park Ridge Golf Classic, in its second year in 1996, promises to be an annual event. In 1996 it raised $1,000 for D.A.R.E., a student drug-awareness program.

There's always a large turnout for the Garden State Bicycle Classic, held in partnership with Park Ridge officials and now in its 12th year.

ARTS AND CULTURE

Outdoor concerts are held in town parks throughout the year. There are theater workshops for children, and several bus trips to Broadway shows are offered to Park Ridge residents.

CHILD CARE SERVICES

Park Ridge has eight private child care facilities.

SENIOR SERVICES

The town contributes to the Park Ridge Golden Age Social Club, a private group that offers activities and trips for seniors.

RECENT DEVELOPMENTS

Final approval was granted recently for 100 town houses to be built in the Bear's Nest Development. Prices for these exclusive homes range from $500,000 to $600,000. This will mean a $60 million tax ratable for the town.

Continuum Care of New Jersey was granted approval to build an assisted living facility at the corner of Grand Avenue and Mill Road. The building will contain 100 condominium units with 200 beds.

Drawbacks

No major highway intersects the small community, so residents must travel on local roads before reaching highways for commuting and shopping.

The teachers in the school district were working without a contract in the fall of 1996.

Prominent residents

Former President Richard Nixon lived in Park Ridge for several years until his death in April 1994.

Phone numbers

Borough clerk (201) 573-1800
School district (201) 573-6000
Library (201) 391-5151

— *Barbara Williams*

DEMOGRAPHICS

County: Bergen
Size: 2.6 square miles
Population: 8,102
Density: 3,118/square mile
Median age: 36.7 years
White: 94.7 percent
Asian: 4 percent
Black: 0.7 percent
Median house value: $254,800
Upper 25 percent: $308,900
Lower 25 percent: $212,800
Median year built: 1959
Median rent: $811
Single-family homes: 2,226
Condominiums: 350 units
Median property taxes per household (1994): $5,048
Median household income: $59,780
Industrial property: 4 parcels
Sewers: 3,052 public, 11 septic
Library: 56,000 volumes, 150 periodicals
Media: The Record covers the town, as do the weeklies Pascack Valley News and Community Life. Cable service is provided by TCI.
Fire and ambulance: Volunteer
Police: Paid
Crime rate per 1,000 (1994): 11
Violent crime rate per 1,000 (1994): 0.5

PASSAIC

An urban center with a small-town mindset, the City of Passaic has a diverse population, a bustling downtown, and easy access to three major highways.

Nestled in the southeast corner of Passaic County, this 3.1-square-mile city is bordered on three sides by Clifton, with the Passaic River serving as the border with Bergen County.

The most recent census figures estimate that more than half the city's population is of Hispanic origin. There are also large Jewish, Polish, and Indian sections of the community, with businesses catering to each segment. The school district spends about 14 percent of its budget on bilingual education in more than 24 languages.

A bright spot in Passaic has been the revitalization of its downtown, which once had many empty stores. Now the downtown is crowded with shoppers every weekend and some nights. The small, Everything Under $10 stores seem to be taking over where large department stores once ruled. The main downtown shopping area has many of those discount stores as well as clothing and jewelry shops, and ample parking. Several smaller business areas cater to the various ethnic communities. Nearly all these businesses charge 3 percent sales tax under urban enterprise zoning.

"This city has so much to offer," said Glenn Carter, community development director. "There is such a rich ethnic diversity that our shopping areas, all of which can be walked to from almost anywhere in town, are filled with a variety of products and food.

"There is also a wide selection of private schools, numerous community organizations for people to get involved in, and a new community policing effort."

Noteworthy Historical Events

American Revolutionary forces under the command of George Washington rested and restocked in Passaic after crossing the Acquanock River in their retreat from Fort Lee. Passaic rose to industrial prominence because of its location at the headwaters of the Passaic River. Raw materials from New Jersey's interior would make their way to Passaic, where they would be loaded onto barges and ships and taken down-river to Manhattan and other ports.

Schools

The school district is rebounding from years of neglect and indifference. Schools Superintendent Robert Holster has implemented districtwide changes that have put the district on course for recertification and prominence. There are approximately 10,000 students in the district.

Passaic has 11 public elementary schools, one junior high school, one senior high school, and a learning center (for adult and overage special education). There are also ten private and parochial schools in Passaic. With so many students speaking Spanish as a first or second language, emphasis is placed on English studies throughout the district.

Some elementary schools boast such extras as a greenhouse, a photography darkroom, language labs, computers, and a home economics room. Scores on the Early Warning Test, a state requirement for eighth-graders, have been steadily rising.

The district recently spent $10 million for additions to the high school and one elementary school. Passaic High School has a new science and math wing, featuring a greenhouse and 27 state-of-the-art classrooms.

The library has been updated to include a fully computerized research lab. The World Language Department also has a new language laboratory. Courses include several advanced placement and honors classes, speech, drama, creative writing, and multicultural literature, as well as standard academic subjects.

Sixty-two percent of Passaic High School students go on to four- or two-year colleges. Average SAT scores for 1995 were 304 in verbal, 365 in math.

Houses of Worship

Bethel African Methodist Episcopal Church; Church of God La Hermosa; The Church of God of Passaic; Church of Prophecy; Church of the Nazarene; Congregation Bais Medrash L'Torah Inc.; Congregation Bais Torah Vtfilah; Dayspring Outreach Ministries; First Baptist Church; First Presbyterian Church; First Spanish Baptist Church; First Spanish Free Methodist Church; First United Methodist Church; Holy Rosary Roman Catholic (R.C.) Church; Hopewell Holiness Church; Hungarian Reformed Church; Iglesia Bautista de Passaic; Iglesia Cristiana Principe de Paz; Iglesia de Cristo; Iglesia Pentacostal Smiran Inc.; Iglesia Reformada Bethel; Jehovah Witness of Passaic; Living Water Pentecostal Church; Most Holy Name of Jesus; Mt. Zion Baptist Church; Mt. Moriah Baptist Church; Mt. Pilgrim Missionary Church; New Jerusalem Pentecostal Church; New Testament Church of God; Nuevas de Salvacion; N.Y. Conference Free Methodist Church; Our Lady of Fatima R.C. Church; Our Lady of Mt. Carmel R.C. Church; Passaic Church of God; St. Anthony of Padua R.C. Church; St. John Lutheran Church; St. John the Baptist Russian Orthodox Church; St. Kosma & Damian Russian Orthodox Church; St. Mary's Assumption R.C. Slovak Church; St. Michael the Archangel Byzantine Catholic Cathedral; St. Nicholas Ukrainian Catholic Church; St. Paul's Baptist Church; St. Peter's & Paul's Russian Orthodox Cathedral; Salvation Army; Spanish 7th Day Adventist Church; Spanish Evangelical Pentecostal Church; Spirit & Life Word Ministries; Talmudic Research Center; Temple Emanuel; Trinity Assembly of God; and Young Israel of Passaic-Clifton.

Houses

Passaic presents a variety of housing choices — everything from Victorian-era homes, small cottages, and condominiums to large apartment buildings and three public housing complexes. Although homes are not expensive, many neighborhoods are nicely maintained. Some neighborhoods, however, are less desirable than others.

The distinctive Passaic Park section is filled with majestic, Victorian-style homes. The centerpiece of Passaic Park is Third Ward Memorial Park, a sprawling, nearly mile-long park that zigzags through neighborhoods as it stretches from the Clifton border to Main Street.

Transportation

Several major highways run through or near Passaic, providing easy access to the entire metropolitan area. Community Coach Lines and New Jersey Transit provide bus service to Port Authority in Manhattan. NJ Transit also provides train service to New York via the PATH system in Hoboken. Amtrak provides passenger service to Newark.

Recreation

The city's eight parks feature three major athletic fields, three sets of tennis courts, a cross-country track, and eight children's playgrounds. Municipally run programs include boys' and girls' gymnastics, night gym basketball, co-ed adult volleyball, soccer, junior league football, baseball (all ages), tennis, and bowling. There is a program for handicapped youth and young adults. There is also a six-week summer day camp and an evening activities program.

Arts and Culture

The Hungarian Folklore Museum is located on Third Street. The Passaic Museum Board is working to create a museum showcasing the city's past in the historic Aycrigg Mansion.

Child Care Services

Passaic has no community-sponsored child care programs; however, there is Passaic City Head Start, a federal program that uses matching funds from the city. There are about a dozen private child-care facilities.

Senior Services

Passaic offers an extensive program for its senior citizens. The Annabelle Shimkowitz Senior Center has a large cafeteria, fully equipped kitchen, lounge area, and sewing room. It runs activities five days a week, including bingo, arts and crafts, and film screenings. Programs include Meals on Wheels, homebound telephone reassurance, and transportation, escort, shopping, and information referral services. An annual health fair offers free eye and ear screenings and flu shots to Passaic seniors. There is also a privately run nursing home in Passaic. The city has three major hospitals.

RECENT DEVELOPMENTS

The city has spent millions of dollars in recent years to rebuild its ailing infrastructure. Several retail stores have opened, including a ShopRite supermarket.

DRAWBACKS

Passaic is struggling to deal with a fleeing middle class and an influx of immigrants. Though parts are still well maintained, Passaic has been a city in decline for several decades. The city is making repairs, but many roads still need reconstruction. Crime continues to be a problem in some neighborhoods.

PROMINENT RESIDENTS

Passaic was the home of the 1960s rock group the Shirelles. It is the former home of Sol Zantz, Academy Award-winning producer of "One Flew Over the Cuckoo's Nest" and "Amadeus."

PHONE NUMBERS

Township clerk (201) 365-5500
School district (201) 471-5201
Public library (201) 779-0474

— Steve Marlowe, Marc Warren Watrel

Demographics

County: Passaic
Size: 3.1 square miles
Population: 58,041
Density: 18,711/square mile
Median age: 30.3
White: 45.3 percent
Black: 20.1 percent
Asian: 7 percent
Median house value: $165,100
Upper 25 percent: $198,500
Lower 25 percent: $126,800
Median year built: 1944
Median rent: $443
Single-family homes: 2,708
Condominiums: 738 units
Median property taxes per household: $6,709
Median household income: $26,669
Industrial property: 141 parcels
Sewers: Public and private
Library: 138,282 volumes, periodicals, videos, audiobooks, and compact discs
Media: The Record and the North Jersey Herald & News cover the town, as do the Dateline Journal of Clifton, the Daily Challenge, and the Passaic Citizen, all weeklies. TCI of North Jersey provides cable service.
Fire and ambulance: Paid and volunteer
Police: Paid
Crime rate per 1,000 (1994): 63.8
Violent crime rate per 1,000 (1994): 11.2

PATERSON

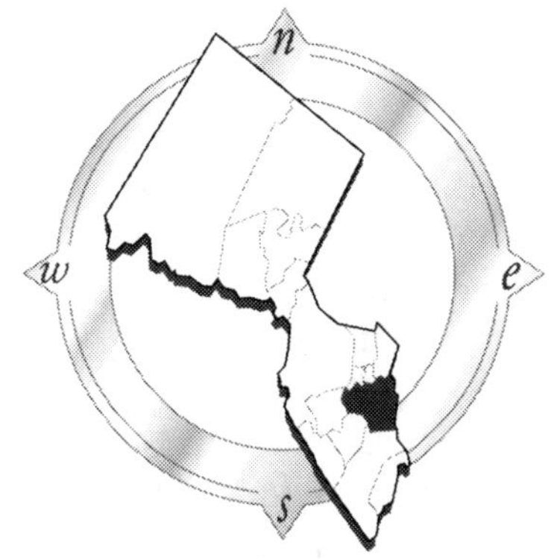

Paterson's reputation as a poverty-stricken city, a prime example of urban decay, is misleading. New Jersey's third-largest city (after Newark and Jersey City) is actually rather suburban, with plenty of single-family homes with well-tended lawns.

Certain parts of the city remain pocked by abandoned buildings or broken-down houses, but many neighborhoods are vital, sometimes breathtaking reminders of a bygone, more glamorous era.

Paterson's bad press can be a bonus for home buyers: It's one of the few places in North Jersey where it's possible to find big, lovely houses for bargain prices.

Many neighborhoods have hardly changed since the mid-19th century, when Paterson was known as the "Silk City" for its dominance in that industry.

One example is the Eastside section, where the wealthy silk magnates once lived. This charming neighborhood, nestled between Route 20 and one of Paterson's urban communities, boasts stunning columned mansions accentuated by leaded and stained-glass windows, ornate cornice moldings, and spectacular porticos. Many once-sprawling estates have been subdivided over the years, and the quaint carriage houses are now single-family dwellings. Also zoned for single-family housing are the Hillcrest and Lakeview sections.

In the industrial part of town, it's still possible to visit the historic silk mills and factories of downtown Paterson, some of which have been transformed into artists' housing.

From the beginning, industry was Paterson's core, driven by the water power of the Passaic River's Great Falls — at 77 feet, second in size only to Niagara in the Eastern United States. In the 19th century, Paterson was the birthplace of the Colt revolver and the submarine, as well as being a major producer of locomotives, airplane engines, cotton, and silk.

Today, the ever-evolving city is known for its diverse neighborhoods. City Councilman Marty Barnes, who has lived in Paterson for 48 years, likes the city for its "wide variety of people and culture, with all lifestyles within walking distance of one another." Dominicans, African-Americans, Arabs, Italians, Puerto Ricans, and people from numerous other backgrounds have found a niche in Paterson, resulting in a highly integrated city offering eclectic cultural events and some of the finest ethnic cuisine in New Jersey.

Because of Paterson's grand civic buildings, widely varied churches, and historic factories, Hollywood has often used it for location shooting; exterior shots of Paterson have been seen in "Angel Heart," "Billy Bathgate," "The Preacher's Wife," and, of course, "Lean on Me," which is based on the true story of principal Joe Clark and his crusade to keep drug pushers out of his high school.

In a city as large as Paterson — the county seat of Passaic — crime is a major concern, and Paterson's crime rate remains high compared with that of other cities of similar size. But City Councilman Barnes said the crime rate has plummeted in recent years (dropping to 70.4 crimes per 1,000 population in 1994, compared with 106.6 per 1,000 in 1981). Still, he admitted, "there are a few neighborhoods no one should venture into alone."

NOTEWORTHY HISTORICAL EVENTS

Paterson, the first designed industrial city, was the brainchild of Alexander Hamilton. The first factory strike in American history took place here in 1828. In 1835, Samuel Colt began mass production of firearms in Paterson. The city was a major stop on the Underground Railroad, which carried escaping slaves to freedom in the North. John Hotland had his first successful submarine run in the Passaic River in 1878. In 1902, the so-called Great Fire destroyed a large portion of the downtown area. When the city was rebuilt, large amounts of capital were invested in design and construction — giving Paterson what city historian Flavia Alaya called "a continuity of architecture and an identifiable city center." In 1913, members of the Industrial Workers of the World (IWW) manned the picket lines for months in a strike that ultimately failed.

Paterson eventually began an economic slide that started with the loss of the textile industry and locomotive manufacturing businesses. Like many urban centers, Paterson later suffered from the civil unrest of the late 1960s and successive, lingering recessions. A wave of bank failures in the early 1990s emptied several downtown branches.

Schools

Paterson's public schools, which have been state-run since 1991, have had steadily declining test scores. Average SAT scores in 1995 were 307 verbal, 369 math. Fortunately, the city has some excellent private and parochial schools.

Paterson also has two vocational schools — Don Bosco Technical High School and Passaic County Learning Center.

Religious schools include: Dawn Treader Christian School; Gilmore Memorial Christian Academy; Most Blessed Sacrament Roman Catholic (R.C.) School; Our Lady of Lourdes R.C. School; Paterson Catholic Regional High School; Paterson Community Christian School; St. Anthony of Padua R.C. School; St. George R.C. School; St. Gerard's R.C. School; St. Mary's R.C. School; and St. Therese R.C. School.

Houses of worship

Agape Christian Center-Word of Faith; All-Nation United Church of God; Assembly Holy House of Prayer; Beth Hamedrosh; Bethel African Methodist Episcopal Church; Bethel Church of Christ; Blessed Sacrament Roman Catholic (R.C.) Church; Calvary Baptist Church; Canaan Baptist Church; Central Baptist Church; Cheeck Temple UHC Inc.; Christ United Methodist Church; Christ Temple Baptist Church; Christian Fellowship Center & OM, Inc.; Church of God; Church of God of Prophecy; The Church of God Pentecostal; Church of Jesus Christ Apostolic; Church of Jesus Christ of Latter-Day Saints; Church of Jesus Christ the Lord Inc.; Church of the Brothers United in Christ; Church of the Holy Communion;

Community Baptist Church of Love; Community Holiness Church; Congregation of Yahweh; Conzillo Presbiteriano Hispano Presbiterio de Palisades; C-U-M-A-C-E-C-H-O; East Side Seventh-Day Adventist Church; Faith Chapel; Faith Soul Saving Station; Faith With Love Fellowship Church; Family Circle Baptist Church; First AME Zion Church; First Baptist Church of Paterson; First Hispanic Baptist Church; First Presbyterian Church of Paterson; Friendship Baptist Church; Gilmore Memorial Tabernacle; Glory Gospel Assembly; Good Shepherd Baptist Church; Good Shepherd Pentecostal Church; Grace Chapel Baptist Church; Grace Gospel Church; Greater Bible Way Church of Christ; Greater Mount Calvary Church of God Love in Christ; Highway Church of Christ Association; Highway to Heaven Tabernacle; Holy House of Prayer Interdenominational Church; Hope of Deliverance Holiness Church; Hope of Glory Church of Christ; House of Faith Church of Christ; Iglesia Cristiana Ebenezer Inc.; Iglesia de Cristo Misionera Beter Inc.; Iglesia de Dios Pentecostal; Iglesia Pentecostal Puerta de Refugio; Islamic Center of Passaic & Paterson; Italian Christian Church; Jehovah's Witness Paterson Congregation — West Unit; Latin American Pentecostal Church of God; Love of Jesus Church; Madison Avenue Baptist Church; Madison Avenue Christian Reformed Church; Madison Park Epworth; Masjid Al-Nur Islamic Center; Mission Church of God; Missionary Church of God; Mohanmadia Islamic Assoc. of Afghan Inc.; Moslem Mosque Inc.; Mt. Zion Full Gospel Church; Mt. Zion Missionary Baptist Church; Neighborhood Baptist Church; New AME Zion Church; New Birth Baptist Church; New Christian Fellowship of Deliverance; New Christian Missionary Baptist Church; New Christian Tabernacle; New Shiloh Missionary Full Gospel Church; New York Free Methodist Conference; Non-Sectarian Church of God; Northside Community Chapel Christian Reformed Church; Olivet Good Shepherd Church of Christ; Omar Mosque; Our Lady of Lourdes R.C. Church; Our Lady of Pompei R.C. Church; Our Lady of Victories R.C. Church; Paterson Assemblies of God; Paterson Avenue United Methodist Church; Paterson Community Church; Paterson Deliverance Center; Paterson Seventh-Day Adventist Church; Pentecostal Church of God the Great Commission Inc.; Pentecostal Lighthouse Church; Philadelphia Church; Prayer of Faith Pentecostal

Church; Prophetic Church of God; Reborn Evangelist Church Inc.; Reformed Church of God; St. Agnes R.C. Church; St. Anthony of Padua R.C. Church; St. Augustine Presbyterian Church; St. Bonaventure R.C. Church; St. Casimir Church; St. George R.C. Church; St. Gerald Majella R.C. Church; St. John the Baptist Cathedral; St. John Serbian Orthodox Church; St. Joseph R.C. Church; St. Luke Baptist Church; St. Luke Evangelical Lutheran Church; St. Mary, Help of Christians, R.C. Church; St. Michael Orthodox Church; St. Michael R.C. Church; St. Paul Episcopal Church; St. Paul Lutheran Church; St. Peter FBH Church; St. Stephen Apostolic Faith Church; St. Stephen R.C. Church; St.Therese Church; Salvation Army; Second Baptist Church; Seminary Baptist Church; Serenity Baptist Church; Solid Rock Baptist Church; Solomon's Temple; Spanish Pentecostal Church; Spanish Seventh-Day Adventist Church; Temple Emanuel of North Jersey; Thankful Baptist Church; Tri-County Scholarship Fund; Trinity Episcopal Church; Trinity Pentecostal Church; True Witness Circle of Jesus Christ; Union Avenue Baptist Church; United American Muslim Assoc.; United Church of Jesus Christ Inc.; United Islamic Center; United Missionary Church; United Presbyterian Church; Unity Missionary Church; Upper Room Church of Christ; Victory Temple; and Westside United Methodist Church.

Houses

Paterson offers spacious Victorian homes at affordable prices; modest one-, two- and three-family houses; project housing, garden apartments, condos, and co-ops.

Besides Victorians, there are also a number of Cape Cods, Tudors, and colonials.

Transportation

New Jersey Transit provides bus service to Port Authority in Manhattan, about a one-hour trip, and there is a station in town for the Main Line train, which brings passengers to the PATH station in Hoboken. From there, connections can be made to New York City, Newark, and Jersey City.

About 15 bus routes pass through Paterson.

Recreation

Paterson runs many sports programs, including softball, baseball, and basketball. The city runs a summer camp program for ages 5 to 12 (registration required) and a summer playground for ages 5 to 12 (registration not required). The city also offers support to several non-municipal sports leagues, including flag football. There is a program for handicapped adults and an after-school gym program at ten schools. There are athletic fields and playgrounds scattered throughout Paterson, which non-resident groups can apply for city permission to use. The Garret Mountain Reservation consists of 570 acres of peaceful woodlands overlooking the city.

Arts and culture

The Paterson Museum showcases the city's industrial, technological, and geological history.

Numerous arts and cultural groups are based in Paterson, including the Ballet Folklorico "De Columbia Con Sabor," a folkloric dance group; the Association of Hispanic Artists and Writers, which preserves and presents Hispanic writing and art; Colombianos en Accion de N.J., which offers art exhibits and performances of dance, music, and poetry representing Colombian folklore; the Congress of Russian Americans, which presents music and dance programs celebrating Russian culture, and the Learning Theater, which presents original theatrical productions for children.

Tours of the Great Falls are offered. Westside Park exhibits John Holland's first successful submarine. Broadway and LRC Galleries of Passaic County Community College provides a series of rotating art exhibits. The Paterson Public Library has ongoing art and lecture series. Passaic County Community College offers theater and music events. There are also numerous cultural events, such as the annual Dominican Day Parade.

Child care services

The city has 37 child care centers, including a Head Start program, and 23 school-age programs. Most of the centers are multicultural, but some are unicultural. Some school-age programs offer a hot dinner.

Senior services

There are numerous senior programs, including Gordon Canfield Senior Center; Medical Day Care Center; Mi Casa es su Casa; Paterson Senior Citizens Adult Day Care; Senior Citizen Outreach Program; and Seniors and Community Service Program.

Recent developments

An elegant housing development off Route 80, set in the mountains and with a view of Manhattan, was completed recently. The city is planning a subsidized housing project, with restaurants and stores, in the Great Falls Historic District, a 119-acre tract close to the river and the downtown area. Two old stone bank buildings on Market Street are being converted into restaurants, with upstairs office space or possibly a hotel. Also in the advanced planning stages is a trolley system to shuttle passengers from the Market Street train station to the historic district.

Drawbacks

The Paterson school district has been in trouble for decades; a state takeover in 1991 has yet to result in substantial improvement. Paterson's numerous tax-exempt businesses, churches, and schools constitute about one-third of the city's property, resulting in higher taxes for homeowners.

Prominent residents

Comedian Lou Costello; poet Allen Ginsberg; Albert Sabin, developer of the oral polio vaccine; and Larry Doby, first African-American to play in the American League, all hailed from Paterson. Also associated with Paterson, but never a resident, is William Carlos Williams, who wrote a series of poems about the city.

Phone numbers

Township clerk (201) 881-3400
School district (201) 881-6213
Public library, (201) 345-8120

— *David Schaublin*

Demographics

County: Passaic
Size: 8.4 square miles
Population: 140,891
Density: 16,691/square mile
Median age: 29.5
White: 41.2 percent
Black: 36 percent
Asian: 1.4 percent
Median house value: $138,700
Upper 25 percent: $170,300
Lower 25 percent: $100,100
Median year built: 1948
Median rent: $444
Single-family homes: 7,242
Condominiums: Not available
Median property taxes per household (1994): $4,971
Median household income: $26,960
Industrial property: 453 parcels
Sewers: Public and private
Library: 359,159 volumes
Media: The Record and the North Jersey Herald & News cover the city. Cable services is provided by U.S. Cable.
Fire and ambulance: Paid
Police: Paid
Crime rate per 1,000 (1994): 70.4
Violent crime rate per 1,000 (1994): 14.0

Pompton Lakes

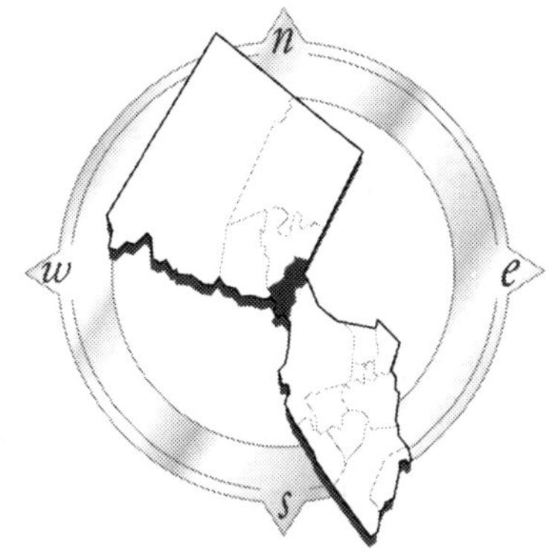

Pompton Lakes is a classic small town, often compared by residents to Bedford Falls, the fictional locale of the 1946 Jimmy Stewart film "It's a Wonderful Life."

In real life, Pompton Lakes High School was chosen as the set of a new Hollywood film, "In and Out," about the life of a popular teacher in a Midwestern town.

With the 1994 closing of the DuPont explosives plant that was the borough's major employer, as well as competitive pressure on the downtown business district by regional shopping malls, residents have banded together to preserve the community's charm.

"We bail each other out when it rains and we shovel each other out when it snows," said longtime residents Ted and Bonnie Ott, who helped form a civic group for busy parents. "In Pompton Lakes, we can't walk from our house to town without visiting with an old friend and making a new one."

Built on a plain between two rivers, Pompton Lakes' compact network of tree-lined streets lures people young and old to go walking, jogging, or biking. The town borders Wayne, and its natural features invite fishing, boating, and watching families of swans glide over the water.

Snugly nestled into the waist of Passaic County, on the edge of the Highlands, the borough also borders Wanaque, Riverdale in Morris County, and Oakland in Bergen County.

Noteworthy historical events

Pompton Ironworks provided shot for the French and Indian War and filled military orders for George Washington during the

Revolution. An explosives plant built in 1886 was later purchased by DuPont, which produced munitions for two world wars and built DuPont Village, a housing development. In the Thirties, heavyweight boxing champion Joe Louis trained in town.

Schools

The district has two elementary schools, a middle school, and a high school. There's also a parochial school, St. Mary's, and a private academy for special education students, the Windsor School.

Pompton Lakes High School received an Excellence in Education award from the U.S. Department of Education in 1987. Since 1991, students from neighboring Riverdale have attended the high school, making a combined population of 583 in fall 1996. Seventy-eight percent of the class of 1996 continued on to four- or two-year colleges. In 1995, the average SAT score for the class was 397 verbal, 465 math.

Houses of worship

Christ Episcopal Church; Congregation Beth Shalom; First Church of Christ, Scientist; Lutheran Church of the Incarnation; Pompton Lakes Congregation of Jehovah's Witnesses; Pompton Reformed Church; and St. Mary's Roman Catholic Church.

Houses

An attractive mix of Victorian and 20th century housing styles.

Transportation

New Jersey Transit provides all-day bus service to Port Authority in Manhattan, a trip of less than 60 minutes.

Recreation

There's hiking in Ramapo Mountain State Forest in the north end of town. Canoeing and boating are available on lake and rivers. Soccer, football, and Little League baseball teams play on borough ball fields. The borough recreation commission offers a summer day camp, swimming programs, gymnastics, men's basketball, women's softball, and a ski club.

Arts and culture

The borough has an active Historic Commission. Residents rebelled against a school board cost-cutting proposal to eliminate the music program. In addition to its local concerts, the Pompton Lakes High School Marching Band played at Walt Disney World in spring 1996.

Child care services

The public school district provides child care at two elementary schools, called Pompton Lakes Day Care Center, for preschool through fifth grade. Six private child care facilities are available.

Senior services

The borough has a 100-unit non-profit senior citizen housing complex; a county para-transit program for shopping and doctor appointments; and county nutrition and Meals on Wheels programs. Catholic Family & Community Services Project also provides services for the elderly.

Recent developments

The downtown business district has been undergoing a revival, with more than a dozen new stores joining older establishments on Wanaque Avenue, the main drag. Plans are in the works for commuter railroad service to New York.

Drawbacks

DuPont is completing a cleanup of lead, mercury, and chlorinated solvents that contaminated stream banks, backyards, and groundwater in parts of the borough. In 1994, the state issued a health advisory on fish taken from Pompton Lake. Flooding occurs in low-lying areas of town.

Phone numbers

Borough clerk (201) 835-0143
School district (201) 835-4334
Public library (201) 835-0482

— *Jan Barry*

Demographics

County: Passaic
Size: 3.16 square miles
Population: 10,539
Density: 3,522/square mile
Median age: 35.7 years
White: 97.2 percent
Asian: 1.5 percent
Black: 0.5 percent
Median house value: $178,600
Upper 25 percent: $201,100
Lower 25 percent: $156,800
Median year built: 1957
Median rent: $701
Single-family homes: 2,666
Condominiums: 250 units
Median property taxes per household (1994): $5,320
Median household income: $48,864
Industrial property: 5 parcels
Sewers: Public and septic
Library: 34,738 volumes
Media: The Record covers the town, as do the bi-weekly Suburban Trends and WKER radio. TCI provides cable service.
Fire and ambulance: Volunteer
Police: Paid
Crime rate per 1,000 (1994): 17.1
Violent crime rate per 1,000 (1994): 0.7

RAMSEY

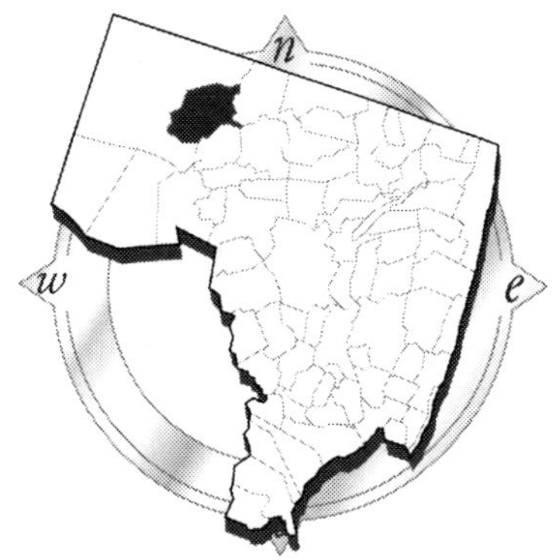

It started as an outgrowth from a railroad station before the turn of the century. Today, the borough of Ramsey offers everything from spacious, elaborate homes with sprawling lawns to easy commuting to great schools.

"We are a family-oriented community, with a lot of recreation programs geared toward children," said Councilman John Pajanowski. "Although our taxes may be a little higher than in some other towns, our municipal services are better than most."

Ramsey boasts a busy Main Street, a large municipal pool complex, thorough snow removal, and an effective library with an updated computer system — along with those excellent schools.

"Ramsey has everything, from a downtown area to a recreation department that offers everything from Ping-Pong to football," said Mayor John Scerbo. "Our small-town community has such a high degree of volunteerism, it's a great place to live and raise children."

This suburban municipality is likely to remain basically unchanged, since 98 percent of the borough is developed and no major projects are on the drawing board. Restaurants, retail shops, groceries, a movie theater, and fast-food chains contribute to the community's ratables, and there are few vacant stores.

NOTEWORTHY HISTORICAL EVENTS

Ramsey came into being with the opening of the Paterson and Ramapo Railroad in the 1800s. Built to transport the huge crop of strawberries grown in the area, the train eventually became what it is today — a passenger service moving people from northwest Bergen County to New York City and the surrounding areas.

SCHOOLS

Ramsey's school district offers outstanding programs and updated facilities. In 1995, voters approved a $9.5 million referendum for the school district, which serves about 2,400 students. The funding will go toward improvements in facilities and technology.

New Jersey Monthly magazine listed Ramsey High School 42nd on its list of the 75 best high schools in the state in 1996. Average SAT scores for 1995 were 459 verbal, 538 math. About 78 percent of the graduates go on to four-year colleges, while 12 percent attend two-year schools. Interactive television allows students to monitor classes being held in other locations, and a formal student exchange with schools in Japan continues to be very successful. A leadership camp, available to all high school students, helps recognize inherent qualitities of good leadership and assists the participants with problem-solving.

Parochial schools in Ramsey include Don Bosco High School and St. Paul's Interparochial Roman Catholic School.

HOUSES OF WORSHIP

Covenant Community Church; First Presbyterian Church; Grace Baptist Church of Ramsey; Lutheran Church of the Redeemer; St. John's Memorial Episcopal Church, and St. Paul's Roman Catholic Church.

HOUSES

Residents can find a one-bedroom condominium for $85,000, or a three-bedroom ranch or small split-level for less than $250,000. Some larger homes sell for just over a half-million dollars.

TRANSPORTATION

Commuting from Ramsey is easier than from other area towns, because a park-and-ride facility provides 525 parking spaces for commuters. There is direct bus service from town into Manhattan. Train service is provided to Hoboken and the PATH system, where connections can be made to New York City, Newark, and Jersey City.

RECREATION

The recreation department offers sports from Ping-Pong to football. A dozen playing fields are available, and more than 800 participate in the soccer program alone.

ARTS AND CULTURE

There are no museums or professional performing groups.

CHILD CARE SERVICES

The Ramsey School-Age Child Care Program (Ram-Sacc, for short) is available at each of the elementary schools. There are several private preschools.

SENIOR SERVICES

A van is available to transport residents to shopping centers, doctors' offices, etc. The Woodlands, a 100-unit apartment complex, provides affordable housing for those over 55 years of age. The recreation department organizes bus trips into Manhattan.

RECENT DEVELOPMENTS

When New Jersey Transit proposed an additional 200 parking spaces in downtown Ramsey, municipal officials fought the plan all the way to the governor's office. Ramsey won; NJ Transit is looking at alternative sites.

DRAWBACKS

Occasionally, congestion from Route 17 makes entering and exiting Ramsey a little frustrating, and the traffic down Main Street can be a slow go. Because of Ramsey's location in the heart of northwest Bergen County, residents of many other towns travel through it to get to their homes, adding to the congestion.

PROMINENT RESIDENTS

Actor Danny Aiello.

PHONE NUMBERS

Township clerk (201) 825-3400
School district (201) 327-6800
Public library (201) 327-1445

— *Barbara Williams*

Demographics

County: Bergen
Size: 5.5 square miles
Population: 13,228
Density: 2,387/square mile
Median age: 35.6
White: 94.1 percent
Asian: 4.4 percent
Black: 0.7 percent
Median house value: $263,300
Upper 25 percent: $341,800
Lower 25 percent: $215,500
Median year built: 1960
Median rent: $900
Single-family homes: 3,648
Condominiums: 1,100 units
Median property taxes per household (1994): $5,547
Median household income: $65,590
Industrial property: 26 parcels
Sewers: Public and private
Library: 90,086
Media: The Record covers the town, as do the Reporter, the Ridgewood News, Suburban News, and Home and Store News, all weeklies. TCI provides cable service.
Fire and ambulance: Volunteer
Police: Paid
Crime rate per 1,000 (1994): 25.2
Violent crime rate per 1,000 (1994): 0.8

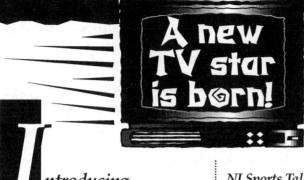

RIDGEFIELD

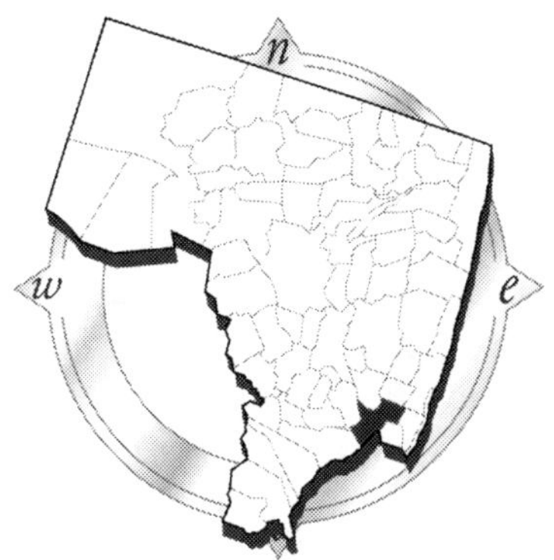

If New Jersey could be telescoped into a single, representative town, that town might look like Ridgefield. Once an untamed expanse of woodland and marsh, the area that is now Ridgefield — bordered by Ridgefield Park and Palisades Park to the north, Cliffside Park to the east, Fairview to the south, and the Meadowlands to the west — has gradually been transformed by the forces of immigration, transportation, and commerce into a compact mix of industry and suburban living.

"We're close to New York City, and we have very nice people," said Stewart V. Veale, who has served as mayor for 19 of his 37 years as a borough resident.

Veale said low, stable taxes and good municipal services, such as parks, a swimming pool, and police, fire, and ambulance service, are among the biggest advantages the borough offers its residents.

Ridgefield was incorporated in 1892, and its population has ranged from 600 at the turn of the century to a peak of 11,000 in the 1970s.

Though it sounds like a contradiction, Ridgefield is aptly named: Near Broad Avenue, the borough's main north-south thoroughfare, the steep, eastern hills of the Palisades flatten into the western lowlands of the Hackensack River.

"It's mostly a blue-collar town," said real estate salesman Leslie Noonan, who handles residential property in Ridgefield. Italian-Americans make up the largest portion of the borough's population — 3,359, according to the 1990 U.S. census. Other ethnic groups include 1,912 German-Americans, 1,683 Irish-Americans, 680 Hispanics, and 570 Asians.

The Asians, particularly Korean-Americans, have been one of the borough's fastest-growing ethnic groups, representing less than 1 percent of the population in 1980 and nearly 6 percent in 1990. Hispanics have doubled their presence in the borough, growing from 3.5 percent in 1980 to nearly 7 percent in 1990.

Ridgefield has a large and active senior population. The average resident is just over 40 years old — three years older than the county's median age. One reason Ridgefield residents stick around longer than their neighbors in surrounding communities is that they have enjoyed lower tax bills over the years.

The borough experienced a tax windfall in 1961, when the Public Service Electric and Gas Company built a coal-burning power plant in the Meadowlands. For a decade, the utility paid nearly all the borough's taxes, supporting municipal services and schools. The only drawback was the pollution the plant created before it switched to oil.

Industry in general has found Ridgefield a friendly host. Routes 80 and 46, as well as the Conrail railroad lines, cut through the borough, making commuting and freight hauling relatively easy.

The Great Bear Spring Water Co. was located in Ridgefield from 1920 to the late 1980s. The water's source was a natural spring located in the Morsemere section of town near Palisades Park. The neighborhood was named for Samuel F. B. Morse, inventor of the Morse code, who owned a large estate there in the 1860s.

Another neighborhood in the eastern section of town, called Ridgefield Heights, was known as an artists' community in the 1920s. Surrealist photographer Man Ray and several lesser-known artists lived there. Reminders of that era remain in the street signs: Art Lane, Studio Road, and Sketch Place.

Noteworthy Historical Events

Ridgefield, which sits on the Ramapo fault line, experienced an earthquake in 1976 that registered 3.0 on the Richter scale. There were no serious injuries.

Schools

Ridgefield's school system, with an enrollment of close to

1,500, has two elementary schools, one middle school, and one high school. Two other schools — the Shaler Academy and the Bergen Boulevard School — are facilities specifically suited to special-education students. The district has received state recognition for its exemplary leadership in special-education programs and serves as a magnet school for students with disabilities from 55 other districts in five counties.

The district received the Redbook magazine award for most improved high school in 1991.

Because so much of the enrollment consists of tuition-paying special-needs students, only 53 percent of the Ridgefield taxpayer's dollar goes to the school district. This is considerably less than in other county districts, which generally spend between 60 and 70 percent of their local tax dollars on their schools.

The district's median teacher salary of $41,053 represents 63 percent of the district's budget, which is on a par with that of most of Bergen County. But the median salary of $89,530 for school administrators is the lowest in the county.

The high school has a 100 percent graduation rate and offers four advanced placement courses: English, calculus, European history, and biology. Seventy-three percent of juniors took the SAT in 1996; the scores averaged 467 verbal, 520 math. In 1996, 70 percent of graduates planned to continue their education at a four-year college, and 21 percent were opting for a two-year school.

Ridgefield also has a parochial school, the Notre Dame Interparochial Roman Catholic School (Primary Division).

Houses of worship

Assembly of God New Jersey Central Church; Emmanuel Mission Church Subsidiary of the Korean Evangelical Church; English Neighborhood Reformed Church; Igreja Evangelica O Bom Pastor Inc.; Jehovah's Witness Congregation; St. James Episcopal Church; St. Matthew's Roman Catholic Church; St. Vartanantz Armenian Apostolic Church; and Zion Evangelical Lutheran Church.

Houses

Ridgefield's social divisions tend to coincide with its geography.

Garden apartments at the lower altitudes give way to one-story, single-family homes as you climb any of the east-west streets. Toward the higher elevations sit larger, two-story, brick and stone homes in Tudor, Victorian, and Dutch colonial styles.

The borough's residential lot sizes tend to be small — 50 feet by 100 feet or less. But the houses and lawns, while diminutive, are well tended.

Transportation

New Jersey Transit schedules bus service from several locations in Ridgefield to Port Authority in Manhattan, about a 45-minute trip.

A light-rail commuter train is planned from Ridgefield to Hoboken, with PATH connections to New York, Newark, and Jersey City.

Recreation

Veterans Memorial Park is the hub of recreation in Ridgefield. It is also the site of band concerts and the annual Fourth of July fireworks display.

The borough also has a four-acre wooded preserve with a nature trail. The swimming pool at Veterans Park offers lessons for all age groups. The town sponsors a basketball league for adults. For teens, there's a recreation center with evening hours, also at Veterans Park.

Arts and Culture

The New Jersey Chorale, a choral music group, performs two concerts each year.

Child Care Services

The borough's health department runs a Baby Keep-Well program, and there are several private day care services in the borough.

Senior Services

Borough seniors have a shuttle bus to transport them to shopping and recreational stops such as the community center, where they can take part in card games and meetings.

Recent developments

In June, the Ridgefield Board of Education promoted Marcella Gleie from vice principal to principal of the high school, making her the first female high school principal in district history.

Also this year, the library opened its own Web page on the Internet. The address is http://www.rfld@buccls.org.

Drawbacks

There is a downside to Ridgefield's proximity to major transportation routes. As one resident said, "We get transients from New York because we are so close to the George Washington Bridge." Also, the Park-n-Ride stop on the N.J. Turnpike has been the scene of car thefts and robberies, which has distorted the borough's crime statistics.

Phone numbers

Borough clerk (201) 943-5215
School district (201) 945-4455
Public library (201) 941-0192

— *Scott Moritz*

DEMOGRAPHICS

County: Bergen
Size: 2.7 square miles
Population: 9,996
Density: 3,665/square mile
Median age: 40.1 years
White: 92.7 percent
Asian: 5.7 percent
Black: 0.8 percent
Median house value: $204,400
Upper 25 percent: $286,300
Lower 25 percent: $188,800
Median year built: 1949
Median rent: $618
Single-family homes: 1,690
Condominiums: 87 units
Median property taxes per household: $4,178
Median household income: $36,879
Industrial property: 87 parcels
Sewers: Public
Library: 67,971 volumes
Media: The Record covers the town, as does the weekly Sun Bulletin. Cable service is provided by Time Warner Cable.
Fire and ambulance: Volunteer
Police: Paid
Crime rate per 1,000 (1994): 21.9
Violent crime rate per 1,000 (1994): 1.3

RIDGEFIELD PARK

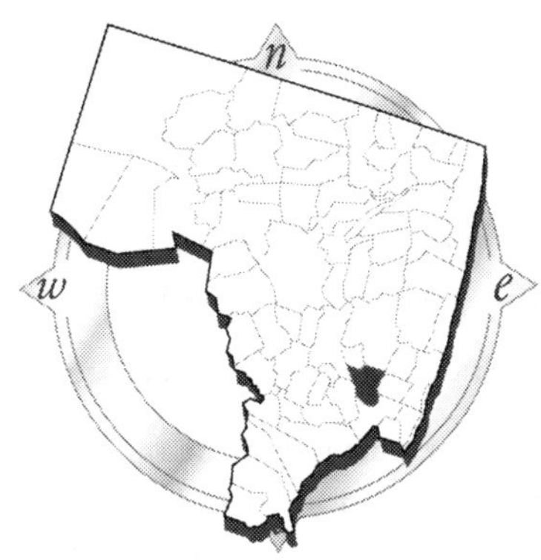

Ridgefield Park, founded more than 300 years ago, still clings to its small-town roots in the mid-1990s. The tiny village comprises one square mile in southeastern Bergen County, and many of its families have been in the town for generations.

In fact, direct descendants of Ridgefield Park's first settlers in 1685 still call the town home.

"The town has changed some in the 31 years I've lived here, but it remains a small town with small-town sensibilities," said one resident who declined to be identified. "It's corny in a way, but it's refreshing."

"Everybody knows everybody and everything that's going on," said 48-year resident Catherine Houston. "That small-town flavor is very enjoyable."

Local politics have a decidedly non-partisan air; the Board of Commissioners has never had Republicans or Democrats — just citizens. "It gives us the ability to get things done without taking shots at each other for party reasons," said Mayor George Fosdick.

The town is located right in the middle of everything — Routes 46, 80, and 95 all run through it — and it's just as easy a trip to New York City to the east as to Passaic and Morris counties in the west.

A significant number of Ridgefield Park's homes were built more than 100 years ago. Most are charming and very well maintained.

The village is also home to a handful of apartment complexes and condominiums. The eastern edge of the community is filled with recreation areas — a town pool, numerous fields, and baseball diamonds. Smaller parks with tennis and basketball courts are scattered throughout the village. It even has its own roller hockey rink.

"This town is alive. Civic spirit is very strong, and there are always things going on — parades, meetings, dances, car washes, live concerts, etc.," Fosdick said.

Noteworthy Historical Events

The village has the oldest continuous Fourth of July celebration in the nation. For 103 years, neither war, economic turmoil, nor social upheaval have interrupted the annual day-long event.

Schools

The district serves approximately 1,500 students, including students grades 9 through 12 from Little Ferry, who attend Ridgefield Park Junior-Senior High School.

There are two grammar schools for kindergarten through grade 6, and one high school (7 through 12). The high school offers honors programs, advanced placement courses, and three foreign languages — Spanish, French, and Italian.

There are several special-needs programs, including a gifted and talented program for elementary-level students.

The district has just set up a technology committee that will draw up proposals for the purchase of new equipment. The eventual goal is to hook up with the Interactive Television Network, which broadcasts more than 30 televised classes to and from other Bergen County schools.

Average SAT scores for the high school in 1995 were 461 verbal, 466 math. About 85 percent of the students go on to two- or four-year colleges.

The high school is also a model for extracurricular and athletic involvement. More than 70 percent of its student body is involved in some sort of after-school activity.

"Our athletic and extracurricular programs are excellent, and academic improvement is under way," said Schools Superintendent David Rightmyer.

"We have good kids, and we are concentrating on putting a lot of money toward the kids and the things that directly affect them, rather than spending a great deal on administration."

Houses of worship

Christ Lutheran Church; Church of the Good Shepherd; First Baptist Church; First Presbyterian Church; First United Methodist Church; Han Moory Church; Reformed Presbyterian Church; St. Francis Roman Catholic Church; St. Mary the Virgin Episcopal Church; and Temple Emanuel of Ridgefield Park.

Houses

Most are quaint, well-maintained colonial-type homes built around World War I. There are some older and some newer homes, as well as some apartments and condos. The average lot is about 50 by 100, and the average price for a home is around $155,000.

There is some light industry — Crystal Clear Industries is the major industrial presence. It is located near the Hackensack River in the southwest corner of the village. On the other side of I-95 is an upscale office park development and the Sony Twelveplex movie theater. The village and the theater have an agreement in which the theater pays for the use of the land and donates a percentage of its gross receipts to the village.

Transportation

New Jersey Transit bus service provides all-day service from Ridgefield Park to Port Authority in Manhattan — a 25-minute trip.

Recreation

There are scores of fields, parks, and tennis courts. McGowan Park on Bergen Turnpike hosts summer band concerts every year from May through August. There's a municipal pool, which offers lifeguard certification programs.

Each Independence Day, the town sponsors breakfasts, a baby parade, civic parade, backyard barbeques, concerts, fireworks displays, and more. "On the Fourth of July, Ridgefield Park does more as a community than most towns ever do," Mayor Fosdick said.

Arts and culture

There are no museums or professional performing groups in the village.

Child care services

There are two private child care facilities in Ridgefield Park.

Senior services

The Ridgefield Park Senior Citizens Activity Center is a non-profit organization offering a range of activities, from daily pinochle games to the making of stuffed toy animals that are donated to hospitalized children.

Recent developments

In 1995, the Ridgefield Park High School football team won a state championship.

Drawbacks

Traffic can be a problem, especially since train service stopped in the mid-1980s.

Also, many of the older homes were built without automobiles in mind. This makes for a lot of parking on the streets in some areas of town, making it feel crowded and congested.

Prominent residents

Early television actor Ozzie Nelson graduated from Ridgefield Park High School in 1923. The street in front of the school was renamed Ozzie Nelson Drive six years ago. Bud Lewis, the co-pilot of the Enola Gay, the plane that dropped the atomic bomb on Hiroshima, graduated from the high school in 1938.

Phone numbers

Township clerk (201) 641-4950
School district (201) 641-0806
Public library (201) 641-0689

— *Steven C. Johnson*

Demographics

County: Bergen
Size: 1.7 square miles
Population: 12,454
Density: 7,194/square mile
Median age: 34.9
White: 91.2 percent
Asian: 4.2 percent
Black: 2 percent
Median house value: $172,800
Upper 25 percent: $197,100
Lower 25 percent: $150,100
Median year built: 1939
Median rent: $641
Single-family homes: 1,948
Condominiums: 400 units
Median property taxes per household (1994): $4,405
Median household income: $42,464
Industrial property: 23 parcels
Sewers: Public and private
Library: 77,032 volumes
Media: The Record covers the town, as does the weekly Sun-Bulletin. Cable service is provided by Time Warner.
Fire and ambulance: Volunteer
Police: Paid
Crime rate per 1,000 (1994): 18.5
Violent rate per 1,000 (1994): 1

RIDGEWOOD

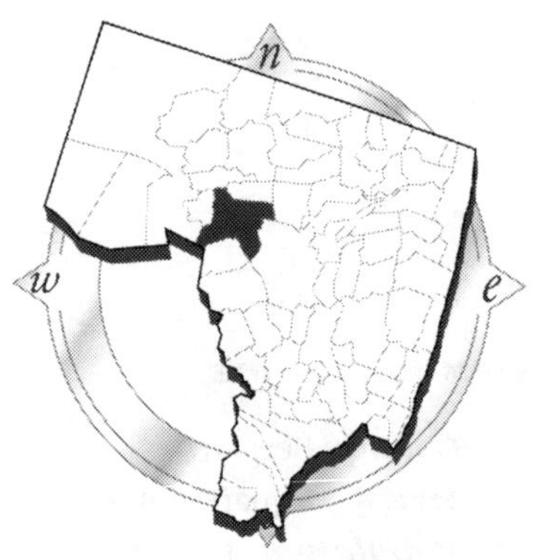

Ridgewood is one of those suburban towns that seems just perfect, a leafy village with a self-sufficient downtown, neighborhoods of wonderful old houses, a low crime rate, no industry, one of North Jersey's best school systems, and a great recreation program.

Its reputation was confirmed in 1975 by a poll in Ladies Home Journal, which ranked the village as one of the ten best suburbs in the country.

Traditional in appearance and conveniently located within an hour of New York City, Ridgewood — like most towns in North Jersey — was founded in the 1660s by Dutch settlers, who bought the deeds to property in the area from royalists and local Indian tribes in the hopes of achieving a safe haven in the New World.

The village today is considered a prime refuge for New Yorkers seeking a change from the hustle, bustle, crime, and cramped conditions of big-city life. Many prominent Ridgewood officials say they chose the small village over an apartment in midtown Manhattan.

"I came from New York City, and the funny thing is, I didn't want to live in New Jersey," said Mayor Patrick Mancuso. "But when we took Route 17 to Linwood Avenue and we came down the hill and saw Veterans Field on the left and Graydon pool on the right, it was just wonderful. We just fell in love with it and never looked back."

Others, like Marge Downs, a Ridgewood resident for 38 years, has fond memories of some traditional village events, such as her high school graduation ceremony, a dinner dance instead of the usual setup of folding chairs in the football field. Instead of caps and gowns, the women wore long white evening dresses and carried bouquets of red roses, while the men wore white dinner jackets and red rose boutonnieres.

"That tradition, still in practice, has gone on since the 1920s," Downs said. "And people from other communities come to see those things, if just to visit, to dine, or stroll along the avenue or watch the parades pass by."

NOTEWORTHY HISTORICAL EVENTS

Parts of Ridgewood served as a sort of military crossroads during the American Revolution, specifically the Dutch Reformed Church (now the Old Paramus Reformed Church at 660 East Glen Ave.), which served as George Washington's headquarters, the site of Aaron Burr's wedding, and the location of Charles Lee's court-martial.

SCHOOLS

Ridgewood schools were ranked 17th in the state in a 1996 survey by New Jersey Monthly magazine. (The schools were ranked sixth in the same survey in 1994.)

There are six primary schools, two middle schools, and one high school serving some 4,790 students. Ridgewood High School, the largest in Bergen County, offers 257 courses, with a strong emphasis on writing and computer literacy. It has 22 advanced placement classes, including Pascal, English 12, and A History of the Arts, in addition to courses in the sciences; music; fine arts; English; mathematics; TV production; Chinese; myth, legend, and the Bible; occupational graphics; and advertising.

Ridgewood High School has been recognized by the Middle States Association of Colleges and Secondary Schools for an outstanding advanced placement program. In 1995, eight students were finalists in the National Merit Scholarship program. Ridgewood students annually score in the top four percent nationally on the California Achievement Tests, while the average SAT scores in 1995 were 489 verbal and 566 math. About 80 percent of high school graduates attend four-year colleges; 9 percent go on to two-year schools.

Houses of Worship

The Baha'i Faith of Ridgewood; Bethlehem Evangelical Lutheran; Christ Church; Emmanuel Baptist Church ABC; First Church of Christ Scientist; First Presbyterian Church; First Reformed Church; Grace Evangelical Church; Megumi Evangelical Lutheran Church; Metropolitan AME Zion Church; Mount Bethel Baptist Church; Mount Carmel Church; New Hope Community Church; Old Paramus Reformed Church; Our Lady of Mount Carmel Roman Catholic Church; Reorganized Church of Jesus Christ of Latter Day Saints; Ridgewood Christian Reformed Church; Ridgewood United Methodist Church; St. Elizabeth's Episcopal Church; Temple Israel and Jewish Community Center of Ridgewood; Unitarian Society of Ridgewood; Upper Ridgewood Community Church; West Side Presbyterian Church; and Zion Wesleyan Church.

Houses

Ridgewood is known for houses of individual character. The town has only one housing development and there has been no significant growth since immediately after World War II. On block after block one finds great old Victorian houses — Queen Annes with wraparound porches and Second Empires with mansard roofs — and early 20th century houses in colonial, Tudor, or eclectic styles.

Ridgewood is one of the few North Jersey towns to have resisted condo development, opting instead to maintain its traditional small-town appearance and an atmosphere remarkably unchanged from decades past.

Transportation

There's direct bus service to Port Authority in Manhattan. New Jersey Transit trains are linked to the PATH system in Hoboken, with connections to New York City, Newark, and Jersey City. By car, it is an estimated 60-minute commute to Manhattan.

Recreation

During the summer, families often gather on Tuesday and Thursday nights outside the village square to hear live bands perform in concert, buy ice cream from the local vendors, or take a leisurely stroll around the nearby duck pond.

The Graydon pool - actually a filtered, man-made lake - is one of the biggest attractions for children and adults. Surrounded by tall trees and lush green lawns, the 2 1/2-acre pool is excellent for swimming.

The village also hosts one of the largest and most popular Fourth of July celebrations in the county. Since 1993, Ridgewood also has sponsored a First Night New Year's Eve celebration, a family-oriented alternative to traditional New Year's Eve parties.

The department of recreation sponsors an array of programs for Ridgewood citizens including a summer day camp for children grades 1 to 6 and H.I.L.T. (Highlights in Leisure Time) activities for residents over 60. There is also an open gym, arts and crafts, roller hockey, soccer camp, and women's volleyball. There are basketball, baseball, football, lacrosse, wrestling, and softball programs. Annual events include the fishing derby, art exhibits, and children's shows.

In addition to Graydon pool, municipal facilities include Citizens Park, Kings Pond Park, Grove Park, Van Neste Square, Maple Park, Leuning Park, Twinney Pond Park, Pleasant Park, and Veterans Field.

Arts and Culture

The Kasschau Memorial Shell Committee holds an annual performing arts series during the summer. The Irine Fokine Ballet Company is a professional performing dance company.

"People laugh and call us the restaurant capital of New Jersey," Mayor Mancuso joked. "But we were the ones who introduced sidewalk cafes a few years ago, and that took off quite well."

In addition to its restaurants, the downtown Ridgewood shopping district has a variety of specialty shops, including a number of national stores.

Child Care Services

Ridgewood has some 14 private child care facilities.

Senior Services

The recreation department offers H.I.L.T. activities for seniors. The municipality is also home to Valley Hospital.

Recent developments

There is ongoing restoration of the downtown region, as well as a revamping of the local library, much of which is being accomplished through resident volunteer efforts and funding.

Drawbacks

High tax rates seem to be the downside of the comfort and solitude of living in a village without industry or high-rises. The average rate is almost $4 per $100 of assessed valuation, with the median tax bill running nearly $7,000 a year.

Prominent residents

CBS humorist and commentator Bill Geist, author of "Little League Confidential," about his experiences coaching his son's baseball team in Ridgewood. Former baseball commissioner Bowie Kuhn lived in Ridgewood until 1989. Former Yankee Jim Bouton, author of "Ball Four," spent his teenage years in Ridgewood.

Phone numbers

Village clerk (201) 670-5510
School district (201) 670-2700
Public library (201) 670-5600

— *Kevin Byrne*

Demographics

County: Bergen
Size: 5.8 square miles
Population: 24,152
Density: 4,180/square mile
Median age: 37.9 years
White: 90.3 percent
Asian: 7.2 percent
Black: 2 percent
Median house value: $299,800
Upper 25 percent: $421,400
Lower 25 percent: $233,600
Median year built: 1945
Median rent: $867
Single-family homes: 6,972
Condominiums: None
Median property taxes per household (1994): $6,984
Median household income: $75,221
Industrial property: None
Sewers: Mostly public, some private
Library: 147,974 volumes
Media: The Record covers the town, as does the Ridgewood News. Cable service is provided by TCI.
Fire and ambulance: Paid and volunteer
Police: Paid
Crime rate per 1,000 (1994): 12.2
Violent crime rate per 1,000 (1994): 0.6

RINGWOOD

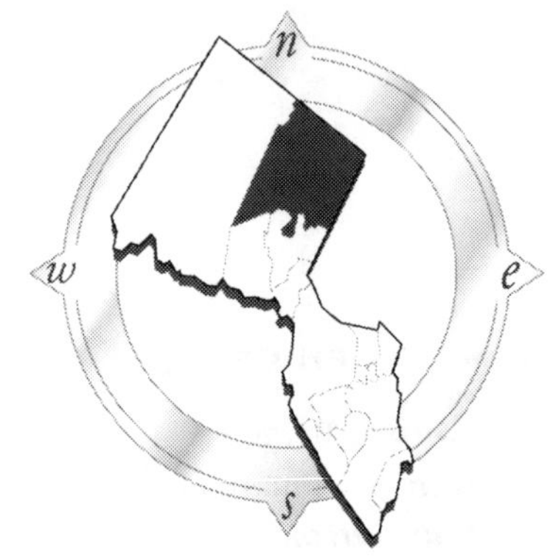

With mountain views of the New York skyline, state forests, and reservoirs that attract eagles and black bears, Ringwood is a favorite haunt of urban commuters who like to commune with nature. Founded in 1740 as an iron manufacturing works high in the Ramapo Mountains, the Passaic County community of 13,000 people is bordered by Bergen County on the east and Sterling Forest in New York State on the north. Neighboring towns include West Milford, Bloomingdale, and Wanaque.

Sixty percent of the Highlands borough, located 30 miles from Manhattan, is protected open space, including the Wanaque and Monksville reservoirs, Ringwood State Park, and the New Jersey Botanical Gardens at Skylands Manor.

The borough has five lake communities — Cupsaw, Erskine, Harrison Mountain, Riconda, and Skyline — several leafy subdivisions, a sprawling rural area called Stonetown, and the former mining hamlet of Upper Ringwood. The borough, which is spread across 28 square miles, also has a small industrial park and three small shopping areas.

To preserve their historic bucolic views, residents have formed active civic organizations, including volunteer fire and ambulance services and support groups for Ringwood Manor and Skylands Manor. After battles over plans for high-density housing developments, a consensus was reached to promote tourism and light industry to help stabilize property taxes.

People move to Ringwood from urban areas mainly for two reasons: "Wildlife and elbow room," said William Brunkhardt, a local Realtor and borough Planning Board chairman. "That's why we came here 25 years ago" from New Milford in Bergen County, he said.

Noteworthy historical events

Ringwood's mines and forges played a major role in the American Industrial Revolution, producing cannonballs for George Washington's Continental Army, shot for the Civil War, and iron for the Brooklyn Bridge.

In the 19th century, Ringwood Manor was the summer home of the prominent Cooper and Hewitt families of New York.

In the 1920s, one of the largest reservoirs in the state was formed by flooding a farm valley in Ringwood and neighboring Wanaque.

Schools

The district has three elementary schools and a middle school. Because of the rugged terrain and lack of sidewalks, nearly all students are bused.

Ninth- through 12-graders attend Lakeland Regional High School in Wanaque. The school was designated a Star School in 1995 by the state Department of Education for innovative uses of computers in the classroom.

In 1994, Lakeland garnered two state Best Practices Awards for vocational education and citizenship. Its ERASE (End Racism and Sexism Everywhere) program also won a $10,000 Noxzema Extraordinary Teens Award.

Lakeland has 1,050 students from its two districts. Eighty-one percent of Lakeland graduates attend two- or four-year colleges. The average combined SAT score for the Class of 1995 was 929. (Separate verbal and math scores were not available.)

The borough also has two private schools, the Ringwood Christian School and St. Catherine of Bologna School.

Houses of worship

Christ the King Lutheran Church; (Episcopal) Church of the Good Shepherd; Community Presbyterian Church; Ringwood Baptist Church; and St. Catherine of Bologna Roman Catholic Church.

Houses

An eclectic mix of winterized summer cabins, modern colonials and ranches, and posh hideaways.

Transportation

New Jersey Transit buses provide all-day service to Port Authority in Manhattan, about a 60-minute trip. There's a municipal park-and-ride lot at Ringwood Commons off Skyline Drive.

Recreation

Two state forests, two state parks, and Sterling Forest offer recreational possibilities including hiking, mountain biking, cross-country skiing, fishing, boating, swimming, hunting, bird-watching. Nature courses, summer camp, and swimming are offered at New Jersey Audubon Society's Weis Ecology Center. Camping, swimming, and outdoor recreation are available at Spring Lake Day Camp. There is a riding academy at Triangle Acres. Little League baseball, softball, football, and soccer fields, tennis and boccie courts, and horseshoe pits are located at Hoffman municipal recreation complex. There is a roller hockey rink at E.G. Hewitt School. Pioneer Park has a children's playground with special-needs equipment. There are five membership lake associations.

Arts and Culture

Ringwood Manor Association of the Arts sponsors art shows in a historic barn and outdoor painting classes in Ringwood State Park. Iron Mountain Stage Company performs classics and new plays. Ringwood Friends of Music sponsors musical events.

Child Care Services

Ringwood has six private child care facilities.

Senior Services

There is a county para-transit program for shopping and doctors' appointments. Ringwood seniors are served by a county nutrition program in Pompton Lakes and at Camp Hope in West Milford. Ringwood senior citizens groups sponsor day and overnight trips.

Recent developments

Plans are in the works for a 100-unit senior citizens complex to be built by the Franciscan Sisters of Ringwood near the order's religious retreat off Morris Road. The Borough Council adopted a zoning change to encourage development of golf courses. Passaic County purchased 2,000 acres of Sterling Forest in Ringwood and West Milford.

Drawbacks

Snowy weather often closes Skyline Drive, which links Ringwood with major commuter routes. When that happens, traffic is funneled through Wanaque, where there is a new interchange of Route 287. (Commuters can also take nearby Route 17 in New York State to Route 287.)

An active stone quarry off West Brook Road has upset many nearby residents. Wooded high points soon may host towers for cellular telephone companies and a radio station.

Prominent residents

Former Giant football player George Martin.

Phone numbers

Borough clerk (201) 962-7002
School district (201) 962-7029
Public library (201) 962-6256

— *Jan Barry*

Demographics

County: Passaic
Size: 28 square miles
Population: 12,623
Density: 505/square mile
Median age: 33.8 years
White: 95.4 percent
Black: 1.8 percent
Asian: 1.4 percent
Median house value: $189,000
Upper 25 percent: $231,700
Lower 25 percent: $160,100
Median year built: 1963
Median rent: $844
Single-family homes: 4,063
Condominiums: None
Median property taxes per household (1994): $5,649
Median household income: $60,026
Industrial property: 15 parcels
Sewers: One package treatment plant and septic tanks
Library: 32,230 volumes
Media: The Record covers the town, as does the bi-weekly Suburban Trends. TCI of Oakland provides cable service.
Fire and ambulance: Volunteer
Police: Paid
Crime rate per 1,000 (1994): 9
V***iolent crime rate per 1,000 (1994):*** 0.2

River Edge

River Edge is a small borough full of vitality and rich in history. It's ideally located for commuters to New York City and major hubs of the county, including Hackensack, the county seat, and the shopper's haven, Paramus — both of which it borders. Its name comes from its long eastern border with the Hackensack River. Just south of the borough is Route 4.

New Bridge Landing, a major strategic point during the Revolutionary War, is in River Edge. A nine-member commission has been appointed by the state to oversee the landing, now a county park. The only historical park in the county, it is also the site of the Van Steuben house, a command center and sleeping quarters of sorts for George Washington.

Though population has declined from a high of 13,260 in 1960 to more than 10,000 in the last decade or so, River Edge continues to be a magnet for young families and new immigrants, many of them Asian. The borough also is working to make it easier for the elderly to remain here.

Although it is dominated by single-family homes, about 25 percent of the dwelling units in the borough are garden apartments.

Within its 1.9 square miles, the borough maintains 29 acres of open space, parks, athletic fields, playgrounds, and vegetation. A portion of the county's Van Saun Park also lies in River Edge.

Noteworthy historical events

Washington crossed New Bridge retreating from the British on Nov. 20, 1776, inspiring Thomas Paine to write his pamphlet "American Crisis." ("These are the times that try men's souls ..."), according to Steuben House curator Kevin Wright. Several battles were fought in and around River Edge, giving Steuben House — a historical landmark — the honor of being the structure that survived the most Revolutionary War battles. Historic New Bridge Landing is now the site of the Ackerman-Zabriskie-Steuben House, the Campbell-Christie House, and the Demarest House.

Schools

The River Edge elementary school district consists of two schools, Cherry Hill and Roosevelt, each with an enrollment of about 350 students in kindergarten through grade 6. Each school has newly equipped computer labs. A recently installed satellite receiving unit allows students to capture live weather images as well as images broadcast by satellites around the world.

"Through the Classroom Window," an award-winning illustrated literary publication written and edited by River Edge's elementary schoolchildren, is published annually by the district. Teachers cull the poetry and short pieces of fiction from schoolwork submitted throughout the year, and a committee of teachers and students selects the works to be published. Illustrations are submitted, and volunteers from the fourth, fifth, and sixth grades edit and lay out the book.

The Columbia (University) Scholastic Press Association has awarded Medalist Ranking to four volumes and nominated two volumes for a Crown Award.

"The project has been embraced by the entire community," said superintendent of schools Dr. Roger Bayersdorfer. "It celebrates and memorializes our students' work. And it defines our commitment to providing our students with the best education possible."

Other programs include a Shakespeare drama performance, choral and instrumental performances, and a Festival of the Fine Arts. There is also a program for gifted children and an array of remedial programs.

River Edge students continue on to River Dell Regional Schools, which include River Dell Junior High School in River Edge and River Dell High School in Oradell. (See Oradell for details about the high school.)

Houses of worship

Cherry Hill Reformed Church; First Congregational Church; Grace Lutheran Church; New Jersey Ark Church; St. Peter the Apostle Roman Catholic Church; and Temple Sholom.

Houses

Housing stock includes turn-of-the-century Victorians, quaint stone and brick Tudors, ranches, and Cape Cods. The average home is assessed at $215,000, and residents have praised the borough for keeping the tax rates manageable, spending frugal, and services ample.

Transportation

New Jersey Transit provides direct bus service into Manhattan and train service to New York via PATH connections in Hoboken.

Recreation

River Edge has three municipal parks — Memorial Park, Brookside Park, and Kenneth B. George Park. The River Edge recreation commission sponsors baseball, football, boys' and girls' basketball, soccer, girls' bowling, girls' softball, and wrestling for eligible school-age participants. Adult programs include aerobics, basketball, softball, and volleyball. The commission also sponsors bus trips; past excursions have visited the Culinary Institute of America, Radio City Music Hall, and Atlantic City.

Arts and culture

The recreation commission organizes holiday events including the annual Easter egg hunt, the Halloween Ragamuffin Parade, a holiday ceremony for all faiths in December, and the River Edge 5K Run-Healthwalk-Fun Run. At the River Edge Cultural Center, events include the West Point Concert, Fine Crafters Fair, and a performance by the Rutgers Chorus.

Child care services

The River Edge Extended Day-Care Program is a non-profit organization providing morning and afternoon day care service to River

Edge residents. Day care is offered at both elementary schools for a modest fee. Enrollment is limited to 30 children at each location, from 7:30 to 8:30 a.m. and from 3 to 6 p.m., Mondays through Fridays. In addition, there are several private preschools in town.

Senior services

Senior Citizens of River Edge (SCORE), partially funded by the municipality, meets every Monday and Tuesday at Temple Sholom. Programs include card games, exercise classes, line dancing, a glee club, day trips, and discussion groups. There is one annual five-day trip. Housing is provided at the Senior Residence of River Edge.

Recent developments

The River Edge Board of Education is considering ways to deal with increased enrollments. A $6 million bond issue, which would pay for additional classrooms, is being debated.

Drawbacks

River Edge has easy access to all major thoroughfares, but rush-hour traffic on Route 4 and Kinderkamack Road backs up on the side streets, upsetting the quiet community atmosphere. A rising number of complaints have centered around Van Saun Park, where residents say non-county residents take up valuable parking spaces.

Prominent residents

The late Mickey Mantle lived in River Edge for several summers while playing baseball for the New York Yankees. Big Band saxophonist and flutist Walt Levinsky lives here. Singer Tony Bennett and his family lived here in the Forties and Fifties. Artist Joseph Domjan, famous for his wood carvings, lived here.

Phone numbers

Township clerk (201) 599-6300
School district (201) 261-3408
Public library (201) 261-1663

— *Marc Warren Watrel, DeQuendre Neeley*

Demographics

County: Bergen
Size: 1.9 square miles
Population: 10,603
Density: 5,624/square mile
Median age: 39.6 years
White: 90.3 percent
Asian: 8.4 percent
Black: 0.6 percent
Median house value: $224,000
Upper 25 percent: $252,700
Lower 25 percent: $196,300
Median year built: 1948
Median rent: $716
Single-family homes: 3,041
Condominiums: 16 units
Median property taxes per household (1994): $5,231
Median household income: $52,126
Industrial property: 6 parcels
Sewers: Public and private
Library: 84,152 volumes
Media: The Record covers the town, as does the weekly newspaper Town News, Zone 9. TCI provides cable service.
Fire and ambulance: Volunteer
Police: Paid
Crime rate per 1,000 (1994): 19.0
Violent crime rate per 1,000 (1994): 0.4

River Vale

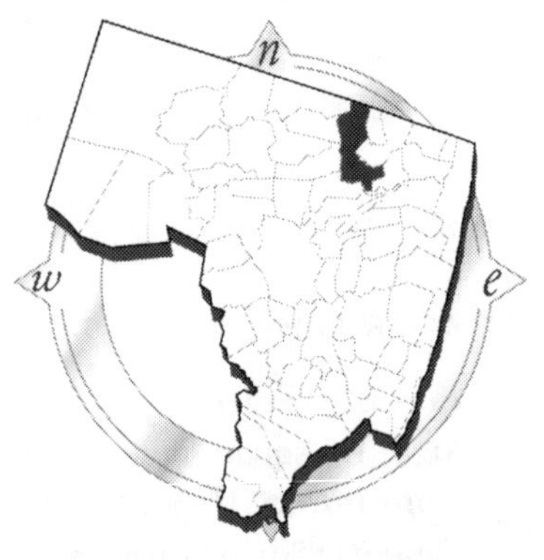

This affluent township's motto is "Garden Spot of the Pascack Valley." In addition to its close-knit community atmosphere, its rural character is what draws residents to River Vale.

"I think a lot of people buy homes in River Vale because of the beautiful trees," said township administrator Roy Blumenthal, who has served for 25 years.

River Vale is located in the Pascack Valley (shortened from the original Indian name, "Pack-a-Gee-Achen," which meant "where the paths divide"). During the 19th and early 20th centuries, River Vale was mainly a farming community, although its industrial phase began in 1857, when the water power of the Hudson and Saddle rivers was harnessed. The town was incorporated in 1906. A baseball diamond and horse track were built in the years around World War I, and River Vale became a resort town, evolving into a bedroom community after World War II.

Noteworthy historical events

The Baylor Massacre, one of the Revolutionary War's most horrific events, took place in River Vale on Sept. 28, 1778. About 90 Colonial soldiers were killed or wounded in a surprise attack by the British on the Third Continental Light Dragoons. Six soldiers were buried in tanning vats, which were discovered in the 1960s. A commemorative site was created a few years ago on Rivervale Road, where the bones of some of the soldiers were discovered. In the Thirties, an ice skating rink larger than the one at Madison Square Garden was built and became the home of the Jersey Skeeters, a semi-professional hockey team affiliated with the New York

Rangers. The games were popular until World War II, when a lack of public transportation and gasoline rationing reduced attendance. The site today is occupied by a manufacturing company.

Schools

There are two elementary schools: the Roberge School and the Woodside School, both for kindergarten through grade 5; students attend the Holdrum School from grades 6 through 8. The three schools have a combined enrollment of about 2,000. After eighth grade, students go to Pascack Valley Regional High School in Hillsdale. (See Hillsdale for more details about the high school.)

Houses of worship

Community Evangelical Free Church and Valley Baptist Church.

Houses

River Vale contains mostly single-family homes with styles ranging from ranch to Tudor to colonial. The tallest building in the township is a 150-unit five-story condominium complex.

Transportation

The Red and Tan bus line travels into New York City, leaving from Rivervale Road and Prospect Avenue Mondays through Fridays. River Vale does not have a train station. Residents can buy parking permits for the Hillsdale station for an annual fee of $240.

Recreation

Ranges Field has playing areas for soccer and baseball. Alexander Field has areas for soccer, football, baseball, basketball, tennis, and a new children's playground called the Frank Giordano Memorial Playground, named for the late councilman. Once a popular resort town, River Vale still has one country club, which is private, and two public 18-hole golf courses.

Arts and culture

The River Vale library has lectures and photo exhibits throughout the year. From noon to 2 p.m. on Fridays, there is a program called "Lunch and Learn," where different speakers come in to discuss various topics. In the spring, the library holds a classical concert series.

Child care services

A group of young mothers organized a preschool morning and afternoon program called River Vale Friends, which has activities for toddlers age 4 and under.

Senior services

The very active Senior Friendship Club is primarily a social club. It has an arrangement with a school bus company to transport members to the meetings, which are held Wednesday nights.

Recent developments

The Planning Board is reviewing construction plans for multifamily homes.

The sternplate from the Enterprise, the most decorated ship in World War II, is the subject of a lawsuit in town. The plate is hanging at Hoffman Field, where Little League batters use it as an outfield target. The town's war veterans want it moved to the site near Borough Hall, where a veterans memorial is going up. The town's baseball association is suing.

Drawbacks

During the morning and afternoon rush hours there is often extra traffic on the back roads.

Phone numbers

Township clerk (201) 664-2346
School district (201) 358-4020
Public library (201) 391-2323

— *Hali Helfgott*

Demographics

County: Bergen
Size: 4.1 square miles
Population: 9,410
Density: 2,308/square mile
Median age: 38
White: 93 percent
Asian: 5.8 percent
Black: 0.7 percent
Median house value: $287,900
Upper 25 percent: $376,500
Lower 25 percent: $227,700
Median year built: 1964
Median rent: $920
Single-family homes: 2,716
Condominiums: 150 units
Median property taxes per household (1994): $6,342
Median household income: $73,125
Industrial property: 1 parcel
Sewers: Public and septic
Library: 45,000 volumes, 215 periodicals, 500 videos, 1,700 audio, including audiobooks and compact discs
Media: The Record covers the town, as does the weekly Community Life. Cablevision provides cable service.
Fire and ambulance: Volunteer
Police: Paid
Crime rate per 1,000 (1994): 3.9
Violent crime rate per 1,000 (1994): 0.2

ROCKLEIGH

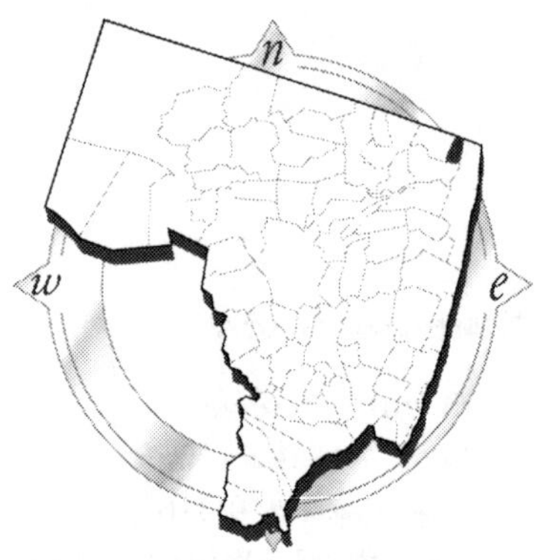

Located in the northeast corner of Bergen County, Rockleigh is a lush, rural community on the New York State line. A sleepy town of about 300 residents, it is divided into three sections: the industrial park, a Bergen County golf course, and a historic residential area with some homes dating to the 18th century. Houses are set on one-acre lots.

Despite the age of its houses, Rockleigh is one of the youngest towns in the county; it broke away from Northvale in 1923.

Rockleigh has no retail stores. There is one gas and service station and a horse farm. There is no police station; Bergen County police patrol the area. There is also no school system; Rockleigh's children attend school in neighboring towns.

The industrial park, which was built in the Sixties and Seventies, houses Volvo Corp. of America and United Airlines. Besides the golf course, the town is home to a county-operated nursing home, an alcohol and drug rehabilitation center for teenagers, and a day school for special-education children.

Unburdened by a school system or police department, and with a strong corporate tax base, Rockleigh's taxes are exceptionally low: The median tax bill is only $4,000 in a town where the median house is valued at a half-million dollars.

NOTEWORTHY HISTORICAL EVENTS

About half the borough was designated the Rockleigh Historic District in 1976 and was listed in the New Jersey and National register of historic places. Eleven of the borough's single-family homes have been named state and national historic sites.

Schools

The borough has no schools. Students attend elementary school in Northvale and high school at Northern Valley Regional High School at Old Tappan. (See Old Tappan for details about the high school.)

Houses of worship

None.

Houses

Rockleigh is lined with large single-family homes that range in price from $599,000 to more than $1 million, according to John Falcone, a real estate agent at RE/MAX in Oradell. "People ask for it because of the charm of the town," Falcone said. "It's very tiny and very quaint."

Transportation

Buses into New York City leave frequently from the Rockleigh Corporate Center on King Road.

Recreation

There is the privately owned Rockleigh Country Club, which has seven tennis courts, a pool, and picnic areas. The club, which has been in Rockleigh since 1941, is currently being refurbished. There is also the Rockleigh Equestrian Center, which has riding lessons and trains horses. The county-owned Rockleigh Golf Course is in town.

Arts and culture

There are no museums or professional performing groups located in Rockleigh.

Child care services

There are no municipally run child care facilities.

Senior services

The borough contributes funds to a senior center in Northvale.

Recent developments

The borough plans to build ten units of moderate and low-income housing.

Drawbacks

Because it doesn't have its own schools or police and must rely on other towns or agencies for these services, citizens have less input into education and policing than in other communities.

Phone numbers

Township clerk: (201) 768-4217

— *Hali Helfgott*

Demographics

County: Bergen
Size: 1 square mile
Population: 270
Density: 278/square mile
Median age: 53
White: 95.2 percent
Asian: 3 percent
Black: 1.5 percent
Median house value: $500,000
Upper 25 percent: Not available
Lower 25 percent: Not available
Median year built: 1965
Median rent: $1,001
Single-family homes: 62
Condominiums: None
Median property taxes per household (1994): $4,001
Median household income: $73,221
Industrial property: 14 parcels
Sewers: Public and septic
Library: None
Media: The Record covers the town, as do the Englewood Press-Journal and the Suburbanite, both weeklies. Cablevision provides cable service.
Fire and ambulance: Volunteer
Police: None; covered by Bergen County police
Crime rate per 1,000 (1994): Not available
Violent crime rate per 1,000 (1994): Not available

RUTHERFORD

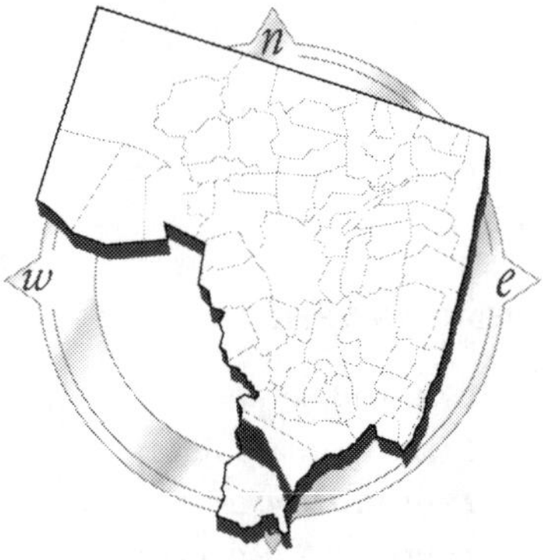

Having endured years of political backbiting, the expansion of Fairleigh Dickinson University (and its subsequent departure to Teaneck), and the rising crime rate just beyond its borders, Rutherford has somehow maintained its multicultural, middle-class identity with style and grace.

Located eight miles from Manhattan, Rutherford is primarily a residential community whose tree-lined streets and charming homes lend the borough an air of 1950s Americana. Rutherford's thriving downtown, located along Park Avenue, serves as home to an array of shops and professional services.

For Mayor Andrew Bertone, the reason Rutherford has held up so well for so long against outside elements is simple. "Our citizens take pride in the community," Bertone said. "Volunteers recently built the children's playground at Memorial Park. [They] are ready to tackle any problem."

Once a settlement known as Boiling Springs, Rutherford was developed in 1862 on land owned by John Rutherford, a patriot and close friend of George Washington's. It was incorporated as a borough of Bergen County in 1881.

The population boomed during the early 1940s with the opening of Fairleigh Dickinson, and it has since grown to approximately 18,000. "Our population is not very transient," Bertone said. "Once people move here, they stay."

Noteworthy historical events

George Washington used the now-historic Nathaniel Kingsland house on Union Avenue as a rest stop along his journey from

Newburgh to Princeton; some sections of the structure date to 1670, making it one of the state's oldest homes.

SCHOOLS

There are three elementary schools (Lincoln, Sylvan, and Washington Schools) for kindergarten through grade 5, two elementary schools (Pierrepont and Union Schools) for K-8, and one high school. There is also one alternative education program for grades 7 and 8.

The curriculum, while traditional, includes some unusual programs: third-graders receive violin instruction; fourth- and fifth-graders receive swimming instruction; and elementary French is taught to fifth- and sixth-graders. About 90 percent of the high school students take the SATs. The average math score for 1995 was 424 verbal, 482 math. Eighty-seven percent of graduates attend two- or four-year colleges. Rutherford High School offers seven advanced placement classes and many honors courses, along with standard academic fare.

St. Mary's is the only parochial school.

Rutherford Adult School offers a variety of courses.

HOUSES OF WORSHIP

Community of God's Love; First Church of Christ Scientist; First Presbyterian Church of Rutherford; Grace Episcopal Church; Grace Korean Presbyterian Church of N.J.; Living Gospel Baptist Church; Mt. Ararat Baptist Church; New Jersey Ephesus Church; Rutherford Bible Chapel; Rutherford Congregational Church; Rutherford United Methodist Church; St. John's Lutheran Church; St. Mary's Roman Catholic Church; and Temple Beth-El.

HOUSES

Housing prices range from $175,000 to $450,000. Rutherford has more than 900 rental apartments, averaging around $800 per month for a two-bedroom. There are also condominiums.

TRANSPORTATION

Rutherford boasts easy access to areas both north and south. A commuter may take the train or bus directly into Manhattan (its turn-of-the-century train depot has just been restored), or hop in the car and reach the New York State Thruway, the New Jersey Turnpike, or the Garden State Parkway in minutes. A borough-operated shuttle bus travels within the borough.

Recreation

The borough has three recreational parks, ten baseball fields, eight tennis courts, and several leisure parks. The 30-acre Memorial Park is known for its large football and soccer fields, as well as boccie and workout tracks. The Fourth of July fireworks attract people from all over North Jersey. The Nereid Boat Club recently renovated the site of the former Rutherford Yacht Club on Riverside Ave.

Arts and culture

The old Dutch Yereance-Berry House contains the Meadowlands Museum, which displays fine and decorative arts and crafts, as well as area history.

Rutherford is the home of the William Carlos Williams Center for the Performing Arts, which offers lectures, musical events, poetry readings, drama, workshops, seminars, and children's theater. The center, built as a vaudeville theater in 1922, also houses two movie theaters.

Summer concerts are held at the William Hutzel Band Shell in Lincoln Park, across from Borough Hall.

The borough is close to the Continental Airlines Arena (formerly the Brendan Byrne Arena) and Giants Stadium, where indoor and outdoor sporting events range from Giants and NBA playoff games to rock concerts and festivals.

Child care services

Rutherford has several private child care facilities, as well as a program run by the Sylvan School PTA.

Senior services

Seniors — who make up more than 30 percent of the population — have access to 55 Kipp Center, an active senior citizen center and residence. Seniors also have easy access to a number of hospitals, including Hackensack Medical Center, just beyond the borough border. Hospice care services can be found outside the borough in Teaneck and Paramus.

Recent developments

In 1995, Sony Corp. expressed interest in developing a theme park on land in Rutherford and in adjacent East Rutherford and Lyndhurst.

In an attempt to boost its shopping district, the borough invested $2.8 million in a new parking garage a few years back, and also lifted its overnight parking ban. However, some residents say that parking is still a hassle.

Borough officials are still trying to decide what should become of the site formerly occupied by Fairleigh Dickinson University.

Drawbacks

Rutherford's limited industrial base has forced yearly tax increases. Borough officials plan to develop a plot of land for commercial use but are hampered by the Meadowlands Development Commission, which has zoned the property for residential use.

Rutherford is also among the South Bergen towns opposed to a proposed $1.2 billion tunnel project to ease flooding in the Passaic River basin. Residents fear that the 19.5-mile project, which would divert rising Passaic and Pequannock river water and stretch from Wayne to Newark Bay, would require dikes and levees and eventually result in land condemnation.

Prominent residents

Poet-physician William Carlos Williams, who wrote about Rutherford, giving it national prominence.

Phone numbers

Borough clerk (201) 939-0020
School district (201) 939-1717
Public library (201) 939-8600

— *Marc Warren Watrel*

Demographics

County: Bergen
Size: 2.8 square miles
Population: 17,790
Density: 7,390/square mile
Median age: 36.6 years
White: 89.4 percent
Asian: 6.5 percent
Black: 3 percent
Median house value: $206,200
Upper 25 percent: $241,300
Lower 25 percent: $181,000 (affordable units)
Median year built: 1939
Median rent: $618
Single-family homes: 3,875
Condominiums: 1,630 units
Median property taxes per household (1994): $4,906
Median household income: $46,499
Industrial property: 26 parcels
Sewers: Public and private
Library: 120,000 volumes
Media: The Record covers the town, as do two weeklies: the News Leader and the South Bergenite. Comcast provides cable service.
Fire and ambulance: Volunteer
Police: Paid
Crime rate per 1,000 (1994): 19.1
Violent crime rate per 1,000 (1994): 1.2

Saddle Brook

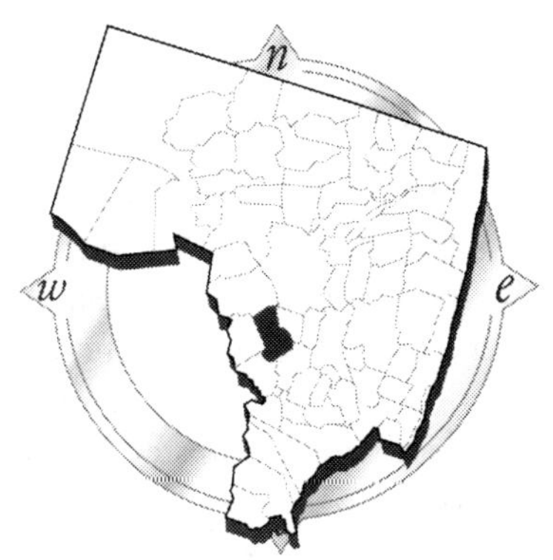

If there is a tradition that best defines the sense of community in Saddle Brook, it is the township's annual picnic. Almost 4,000 people attend the event, to which 75 local organizations donate time and materials. Women's organizations prepare much of the food, and residents join with volunteers from the public works department to set up the tables and barbecues. It's an afternoon of children's rides, jugglers, and face-painters, capped off by a softball game between the fire and police departments. No municipal funds go toward the event.

This densely populated, middle-class Bergen County enclave works hard to maintain its sense of community, especially for its youth.

In 1995, Mayor Raymond SantaLucia created the Mayor's Catch of the Day, an annual fishing contest for Saddle Brook's youngest citizens. The same year, the mayor established the Youth Advisory Board to encourage high school students to be more active in community affairs; the board helps organize the township picnic, the holiday tree lighting, and many sporting events. Saddle Brook has active Boy and Girl Scout troops. There are also myriad sports teams.

Noteworthy Historical Events

Saddle Brook was once part of a larger entity, Saddle River Township, one of the oldest in Bergen County. The area that comprises Saddle Brook was the hub of several Indian trails that led to Hackensack and Newark. Inns and hotels sprang up followed by homes and several grist and saw mills. In the 19th and 20th centuries, other industries moved in along the Saddle River.

SCHOOLS

Saddle Brook has 1,395 students enrolled in several elementary schools, a middle school, and a high school. Computer and Spanish instruction begin in kindergarten.

Saddle Brook High School offers the standard academic and honors courses, along with advanced placement classes in English, U.S. history, and chemistry. The math and science labs were recently renovated.

Forty-nine percent of the high school students go on to four-year colleges, and 29 percent to two-year colleges. Seventy-eight percent of high school juniors took the Scholastic Assessment Test in 1995; average scores were 399 verbal, 460 math.

St. Philip the Apostle Roman Catholic School is located in town.

HOUSES OF WORSHIP

Abundant Life Worship Center; Holy Apostles Eastern Orthodox Church; First Reformed Church of Saddle Brook; and St. Philip the Apostle Roman Catholic Church.

HOUSES

Homes are mostly small, single-family dwellings in brick or Cape Cod style.

TRANSPORTATION

New Jersey Transit offers direct bus service into Manhattan. NJ Transit trains stop in Saddle Brook en route to Hoboken, where connections to the PATH system can be made. Saddle Brook is located near Routes 4, 17, 20, 46, and 80, and the Garden State Parkway.

RECREATION

The town offers boys' and girls' basketball, cheerleading, football, Little League, soccer, softball, summer playground, track, and wrestling. The Saddle Brook Community Project and Activity Committee offers the following programs, among others: the Saddle Brook Community Theater, the annual township picnic, parks and playground committee, the holiday tree lighting and children's holiday party. Saddle Brook is renovating its five parks and playgrounds.

Arts and Culture

There are no museums or professional performing groups in town.

Child Care Services

The township provides a child health care conference, in cooperation with the County of Bergen Health Department and the Lodi Board of Health. Residents may obtain free inoculations for children ages 6 months to prekindergarten.

Senior Services

A senior citizen municipal complex provides social services and an active social calendar.

Recent Developments

A freight train line running through Saddle Brook is being considered for possible commuter use. New Jersey Transit hopes to ease congestion on already-crowded Bergen County roads and provide easier access to New York City and other points in the area.

Drawbacks

Saddle Brook teenagers have been clashing with those in neighboring Elmwood Park.

Phone Numbers

Township clerk (201) 587-2900
School district (201) 843-2133
Public library (201) 843-5512

— *Marc Warren Watrel*

DEMOGRAPHICS

County: Bergen
Size: 2.7 square miles
Population: 13,296
Density: 4,882/square mile
Median age: 37.6
White: 95.6 percent
Asian: 2.7 percent
Black: 1.1 percent
Median house value: $193,300
Upper 25 percent: $227,200
Lower 25 percent: $172,600
Median year built: 1954
Median rent: $687
Single-family homes: 3,373
Condominiums: 21 units
Median property taxes per household (1994): $4,053
Median household income: $46,082
Industrial property: 86 parcels
Sewers: Public and private
Library: 59,339 volumes
Media: The Record covers the town, as does the Shopper News, a weekly. TCI provides cable service.
Fire and ambulance: Volunteer
Police: Paid
Crime rate per 1,000 (1994): 31.7
Violent crime rate per 1,000 (1994): 1.3

SADDLE RIVER

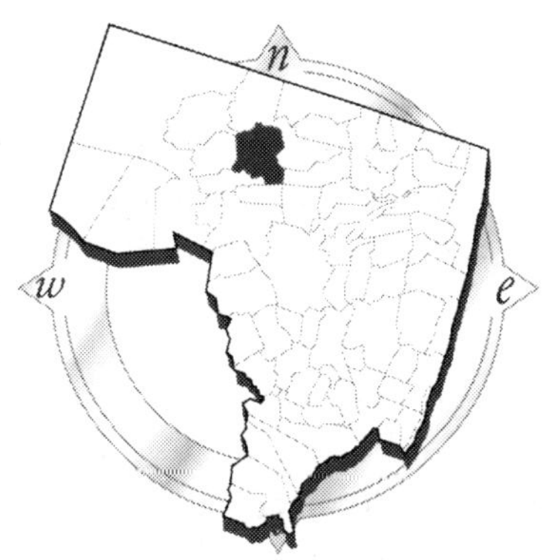

Its proximity to Manhattan, its majestic houses, and the prestige of living close to best-selling authors and, until recently, a former U.S. president, have made Saddle River one of Bergen County's most upscale boroughs.

Located off Route 17, where superstores and shopping centers draw thousands of bargain seekers, Saddle River is close to the conveniences of mass urbanization but far enough away to retain a genteel, small-town charm. Those who live in the borough say they moved there to escape city pressures without isolating themselves in the middle of nowhere. The borough's low taxes — among the lowest in Bergen County — are another incentive.

"We privatize most of our services," Mayor Theodore "Ted" Anthony explained. "We have a very small town center. There's a barber shop, a nail salon, a hardware store. Saddle River is probably more of a bedroom community than many other towns."

Saddle River was home to the Lenni Lenape Indians, who in 1702 deeded the land to Albert Zaborowsky, a Polish immigrant who was the first white settler in Ho-Ho-Kus. The deed is displayed in the municipal building on Allendale Road. Zaborowsky later deeded half the land to Thomas Van Buskirk, whose son, Andries Thomas, built Saddle River's first home in 1724.

By the late 1750s, the formidable power of the nearby Saddle River had turned the borough into an established commercial center, where river water powered up to 13 cotton, grain, and corn mills. Others farmed the land, and Saddle River remained a quiet country community for many years. But the farms and mills eventually died out. By the mid-1800s, families seeking refuge from New

York City had begun to build spacious summer houses. Those seasonal houses evolved into permanent homes, and many are listed in the National Register of Historic Places.

But many homes are new. And massive. "We have several that are over 30,000 square feet," Anthony said.

Construction has been constant, but with the expected addition of a 27-acre office park and a 56-unit affordable-housing complex to help meet Saddle River's Mount Laurel requirements, there is little space left to develop.

"We're about to tap out soon," Anthony said.

Homes can cost as much as $4 million; "cheap" ones go for $300,000.

Although it is still known as a safe, quiet, and upscale borough, Saddle River has been unable to avoid encroaching development completely. To get to new offices in nearby Montvale, commuters now cut though town.

And the traffic is "horrendous" at times, said resident Sandy Van Benschoten.

"The commuter traffic is terrible. But if you get off East Allendale and East Saddle River roads, it's very quiet," added Van Benschoten, who recently wrote a book on the borough's history. "I think residents like the quiet, peaceful, bucolic atmosphere. It's 20 miles from the city. That's a convenience."

Noteworthy Historical Events

In July 1938, Babe Ruth, who had friends in Saddle River, umpired part of a borough Blue Jays semi-pro game.

Schools

Saddle River schools enjoy widespread support from residents, who routinely pass budgets, raise hundreds of thousands of dollars for school programs, and donate their time and skills.

Because the district is small — just 300 students — it is difficult for anyone to slip through the cracks. There are 16 students in an average class. "Every student is known. Every family is known," said Superintendent Mark Mangon.

Students begin their education at Wandell Elementary, which

has classes from prekindergarten through grade 8. High school students attend Ramsey High School (see Ramsey profile for details) or private or parochial schools.

Wandell is housed in two buildings: a stone-and-mason schoolhouse dating to 1917, and a brick schoolhouse built in 1954. (Daylong prekindergarten classes are held across the street in a building rented from a local church.) Wandell boasts state-of-the-art science and computer labs, funded by the Wandell School Education Foundation. This private group, formed by parents in 1991, has donated $750,000 to the district, Mangon said. The money has paid for computers and printers in all classrooms, the lab, and the library. The district is working on getting e-mail and expanding its links to the Internet, which can be accessed through the library and computer lab.

"In-kind gifts have taken care of us," Mangon said. "When we had to do major asbestos removal, it was donated by a person who does that for a business."

French — the only foreign language offered — begins in kindergarten and continues through eighth grade.

Perhaps not surprisingly, students do extremely well on national achievement tests, scoring an average of 92 in 1996.

They tend to do well at Ramsey High, Mangon said. The Board of Education, after studying Ramsey and Northern Highlands High School recently, decided to extend its sending agreement with Ramsey.

Saddle River Day School, a co-ed college-preparatory campus, is located in Saddle River.

Houses of Worship

St. Gabriel the Archangel Roman Catholic Church and Zion Evangelical Lutheran Church.

Houses

Homes range from 10,000-square-foot "cottages" to sprawling, 30,000-square-foot mansions. Some are listed on the state Register of Historic Places, but many families moved to the borough in the 1980s, when Saddle River's larger homes were constructed. Lot sizes are a minimum of two acres, which helps protect the borough's private wells and septic systems. There are no public sewerage or water systems.

Transportation

There is no direct bus or train service from Saddle River. Commuters can take Short Line buses from Ramsey or Allendale to Port Authority in Manhattan and destinations in North Jersey. New Jersey Transit trains to the Hoboken PATH station, with connections to New York and elsewhere, leave from nearby Ridgewood and Ramsey.

Recreation

Saddle River teams up with the Ho-Ho-Kus Recreation Commission to organize youth sports ranging from football and soccer to softball. Working together ensures there will be enough players on the team. The recreation association organizes holiday events, such as the Halloween parade and visits from Santa Claus to private homes on Christmas Eve. There are two parks, Rindlaub and Ice Pond, and walking trails. The Saddle River is stocked with trout for fishermen.

Arts and culture

There are no community arts programs, said Mayor Anthony. Most people travel to Manhattan for cultural events and performances.

Child care services

The public school system includes all-day prekindergarten and kindergarten classes. Parents also organize after-school activities at the Wandell School during January and February. But "a lot of people have housekeepers, and child care is taken care of at home," Mangon said.

Senior services

Bergen County Special Transportation, based in Hackensack, can transport elderly and handicapped residents to medical appointments or food shopping. Patrons are asked to pay a suggested $1 round-trip fee.

RECENT DEVELOPMENTS

Saddle River Properties, a private development, is turning 27 acres near Route 17 into offices. There also will be a retirement home, geared toward assisted living.

DRAWBACKS

Saddle River's blessings might also be considered drawbacks. The borough keeps taxes low by providing few amenities, such as sewers, streetlights, sidewalks, or a library, and contracting out for services such as snow plowing. Because there is no direct bus or rail line from Saddle River, commuting is complicated and tedious for those without a car. And Saddle River teens must go to other towns to find even such mundane entertainment as a movie theater.

PROMINENT RESIDENTS

Mystery writer Mary Higgins Clark lives in Saddle River, and former President Richard M. Nixon was a resident for a time in his later years.

PHONE NUMBERS

Township clerk (201) 327-2609
School district (201) 327-0727

— Leslie Haggin

Demographics

County: Bergen
Size: 5 square miles
Population: 2,950
Density: 592/square mile
Median age: 44.9
White: 94.8 percent
Asian: 4.6 percent
Black: 0.4 percent
Median house value: $500,001
Upper 25 percent: $3 million
Lower 25 percent: $300,000
Median year built: 1966
Median rent: $1,001
Single-family homes: 1,052
Condominiums: 56 units, currently under construction
Median property taxes per household (1994): $4,133
Median household income: $135,662
Industrial property: None
Sewers: Private
Library: Saddle River does not have its own library. Patrons use the Ridgewood and Upper Saddle River libraries.
Media: The Record covers the town, as do the Villadom Times, the Suburban News, and the Town Journal, all weeklies. Cablevision provides cable service.
Fire and ambulance: Volunteer
Police: Paid
Crime rate per 1,000 (1994): 15.6
Violent crime rate per 1,000 (1994): 1

TEANECK

People who move to Teaneck choose diversity; it's who we are," said 23-year resident Marie Warnke. Proud of its multi-ethnic character and its progressive history of racial tolerance — in 1964 it became the first American town with a white majority to voluntarily desegregate its schools — Teaneck today is a suburban melting pot with a vibrant downtown, an active cultural life, well-maintained parks, an excellent library, and a sense of connection to New York City that is stronger than that in most other bedroom communities.

Adding to Teaneck's diversity in recent years has been an influx of Orthodox Jews who have opened businesses along Cedar Lane, the town's main shopping street. The variety of restaurants now includes Israeli, Chinese (including vegetarian and *glatt* kosher), Indian, Spanish, and Italian.

However, the Orthodox Jewish businesses are closed Friday nights and Saturdays — typical eating-out and shopping times — creating a sense of two parallel downtowns.

But Teaneck works hard to make its melting pot work, striving to help its youngest citizens overcome ignorance and prejudice. A recent two-day program in the Thomas Jefferson Middle School replaced regular school work with a program to help black and white students better understand each other.

"Both of my children graduated from Teaneck's school system," Warnke said. "They always said that [Teaneck's diverse population] prepared them to face life after high school, not just academically, but socially and emotionally."

Teaneck has a major medical facility in Holy Name Hospital,

where services include 41 dialysis stations, a center for treating multiple sclerosis, the area's only all-Korean outpatient clinic, and a cardiac rehabilitation program.

NOTEWORTHY HISTORICAL EVENTS

Teaneck witnessed George Washington's withdrawal from Fort Lee to New Bridge Landing (today's Brett Park). There are seven stone houses built by Dutch settlers and their descendants during the 17th and 18th centuries: the Adam Vandelinda House, 586 Teaneck Road; the James Vandelinda House, 566 Teaneck Road; the Brinkerhoff-Demarest House, 493 Teaneck Road; the Caspar Westervelt House, 20 Sherwood Road; the John Ackerman House, 1286 River Road; the Banta-Coe House, 884 Lone Pine Lane; and the Kipp-Cadmus House, 664 River Road.

SCHOOLS

Teaneck prides itself on its school system. In 1996, Teaneck High was ranked 75th best high school in the state by New Jersey Monthly magazine. One all-day kindergarten school, four elementary schools for kindergarten through grade 4, two middle schools (5 through 8), and one high school serve more than 4,300 students. Teaneck strives for racial balance, so students in elementary and junior high may be bused to schools outside their neighborhood. Parents are encouraged to participate in their children's education, and many become actively involved.

Teaneck High School offers more than 125 courses (including "Television Production" and "The Young Executive"), a broad range of electives, an in-school alternative program for students who perform better with closer student-teacher contact, an off-site program for students with special needs, vocational and industrial arts classes, and special-education programs.

Honors and advanced placement courses are offered, although admission to honors classes is not merit-based. They are open to all students on a first-come, first-served basis, but the larger proportion of white students in these classes has led to charges from the black community that black students are steered away.

Ninety percent of high school graduates attend two- or four-year colleges; on average, two to four percent attend Ivy League schools. Average SAT scores for 1995 were 448 verbal, 511 math.

Parochial schools include Grace Lutheran Church School; St. Anastasia's; and Yeshiva High School for Girls of Bergen County.

The Board of Education also runs the Teaneck Community Education Center, an independent, self-supporting continuing education program for adults and children that offers courses in arts and crafts, computers, culinary arts, investment and finance, among others. There are also several popular school vacation programs.

Fairleigh Dickinson University has its main campus in Teaneck.

Houses of worship

Abundant Grace & Truth Ministries Church; Christ Episcopal Church; Christian Science Reading Room; Church of Scientology Mission of N.J.; Congregation Beth Aaron; Congregation Beth Am; Congregation Beth Sholom; Congregation B'nai Yeshurun; Congregation Rinat Yisrael; Elim Missionary Church; Ethical Cultural Society of Bergen County; First Baptist Church of Teaneck; Grace Lutheran Church; Jehovah's Witness Congregation of Teaneck; Jewish Center of Teaneck; Jewish Conversion Center; Masjid-Al-Islah; New Life Covenant Church; Northern Teaneck Synagogue; Our Savior's Lutheran Church; Presbyterian Church of Teaneck; St. Anastasia's Roman Catholic Church; St. Andrew Kim Korean Catholic Mission; St. Mark's Episcopal Church; St. Mark's Syrian Orthodox Cathedral; St. Michael's Ethiopian Orthodox Tewahedo; St. Paul's Lutheran Church; Seventh Day Adventist Church; Teaneck Assembly of God; Teaneck Bahai Center; Teaneck United Methodist Church; Temple Emeth Reformed Congregation; Trinity Evangelical Free Church; and Victory Tabernacle FBH Church.

Houses

Teaneck has many distinct neighborhoods, ranging from those with elegant Tudors and stone mansions to those with modest Cape Cods and starter homes — and just about everything in between. The influx of Orthodox Jews has sent home prices soaring in neighborhoods near Orthodox synagogues, while prices elsewhere have declined or remained flat. Apartments are rent-controlled.

Transportation

New Jersey Transit runs buses through Teaneck. Route 4, which becomes a shopping strip farther west, maintains a green belt where it passes through Teaneck and provides quick access to the George Washington Bridge. Express buses to the bridge can be picked up at stops on Route 4. Others go through downtown and ultimately to Port Authority in Manhattan via the Lincoln Tunnel.

Recreation

Teaneck has excellent recreation facilities, with many well-maintained fields for baseball, football, and soccer; basketball and tennis courts; and picnic areas. Many of the parks have above-ground and in-ground swimming pools. The Teaneck recreation department offers a range of programs for every age group, including swimming lessons, roller skating, skiing, softball, Little League, and bingo.

Arts and culture

The American Stage Company, northern New Jersey's newest and Bergen County's only professional Actors Equity theater, is in residence at Fairleigh Dickenson University. It presents classics and premieres new American works. The Art Center Chamber Music Concerts, a series of four annual concerts by professional chamber music artists, is presented at Benjamin Franklin Middle School Auditorium. The Teaneck Public Library has a Sunday afternoon concert series, often featuring local musicians. In addition, many musicians, artists, and writers live in Teaneck. At various times, as many as nine members of the New York Philharmonic have lived in town.

Child care services

Teaneck administers the Child Health Conference and Immunization Center in conjunction with Holy Name Hospital, providing medical care for preschoolers. Child care programs include ten private facilities.

Senior services

The Senior Citizen Service Center is open daily. A hot lunch is served for a small suggested donation; a homebound lunch program is available for those who qualify. There are scheduled activities. A county van transports participants to and from the center daily. Other senior programs include: Bergen County Nutrition Center; Generations; and Senior Medical Outreach Program. Classic Residence by Hyatt is a senior citizens residential facility.

Recent developments

A dispute has arisen over the Teaneck Swim Club, a three-pool complex that is privately owned but occupies ten acres of town land. The club has come under attack from a citizens' group that says the facility is subsidized by tax dollars. It wants the town to take over the facility. The group charges that membership is too expensive, that waiting lists are too long, and that the membership is almost exclusively white.

Drawbacks

Racial tensions surface in the town periodically. The shooting of a black teenager by a white policeman in 1990 sparked youth riots, demonstrations, and two trials. Tensions in the high school are evident in the black students' preference for using a separate door to enter and exit the building.

Prominent residents

Leonard Jeffries, former head of the Black Studies Department at City College of New York, controversial for his claim that Jews financed the slave trade as well as other anti-Semitic and racist remarks; rap star Biggie Smalls (Christopher Wallace); talk show host Rolanda Watts; minister and black activist the Rev. Herbert Daughtry; former Yankee Jim Bouton, author of "Ball Four."

Phone numbers

Township clerk (201) 837-1600
School district (201) 833-5510
Public library (201) 837-0410

— *Marc Warren Watrel*

Demographics

County: Bergen
Size: 6.1 square miles
Population: 37,825
Density: 6,249/square mile
Median age: 37.2
White: 66.6 percent
Black: 26.6 percent
Asian: 5.6 percent
Median house value: $210,800
Upper 25 percent: $259,000
Lower 25 percent: $178,800
Median year built: 1944
Median rent: $565
Single-family homes: 10,118
Condominiums: 520 units
Median property taxes per household (1994): $5,765
Median household income: $56,598
Industrial property: 19 parcels
Sewers: Public and private
Library: 120,553 volumes
Media: The Record covers the town, as do the Teaneck Suburbanite and the Connection, both weeklies. Cable service is provided by TCI.
Fire and ambulance: Paid
Police: Paid
Crime rate per 1,000 (1994): 30.8
Violent crime rate per 1,000 (1994): 3.1

TENAFLY

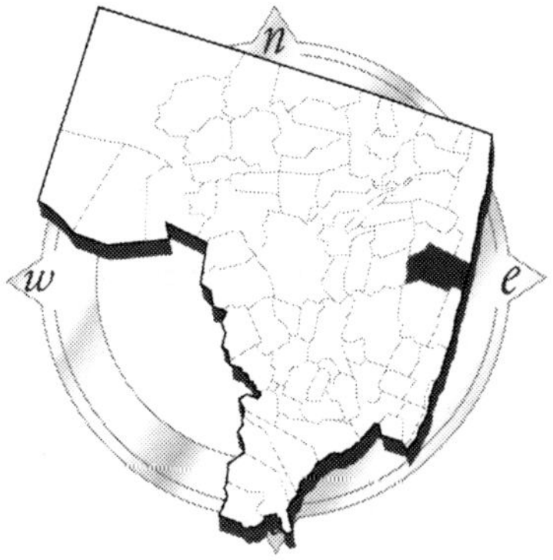

Curled up in a green valley just north of Englewood, Tenafly has the friendly, good-natured, American-as-apple-pie appearance of any Frank Capra-esque small town. And it doesn't only look that way, said Mayor Ann A. Moscovitz. Tenafly is still a place where residents can meet with the mayor and council formally or informally to talk out matters of local concern, and take an active part in how their tax dollars are spent.

Like many of North Jersey's towns, Tenafly's name was derived from the Dutch colonists who settled it in the 1800s. Historians translate the original Dutch name, "tiene vly," as "garden valley."

The railroad, which now divides the town, was the impetus for its development in the 1870s. Rail service shut down in the 1960s, and the old station was converted into a shop. Today, the town is mostly residential, with a compact business area in the center and a small industrial area in the north-central section along the tracks. Old-timers may recall that a trolley line once paralleled the railroad; but it is the old railroad tracks that literally split the town down the middle from north to south, separating the million-dollar houses and trimmed lawns of the many lawyers, accountants, doctors (an oft-heard remark is that Tenafly has more physicians per square foot than the Mayo Clinic), and well-to-do in the east from the older, more modest homes inhabited by bus drivers, mechanics, and hospice workers in the west.

Despite this split, there are no high-rises, no industrial encroachments, nothing to suggest a class struggle. Real estate broker Joseph Marevich attributed the town's success in marrying working-class values with a high standard of living to "good management," something that ultimately gives residents a reason to take pride in Tenafly as one of North Jersey's better towns.

Noteworthy Historical Events

Elizabeth Cady Stanton, the rebel suffragette, moved into 135 Highwood Ave. in 1869; fellow feminist activist Susan B. Anthony joined her there a few years later.

In the 1970s, residents successfully fought development of 700 acres of wooded property — the last open area in town — as high-rise housing. The tract, which remains woodland today, is responsible for much of Tenafly's rural atmosphere.

Schools

Tenafly's school system is the icing on the cake. The district serves 3,680 students, with four primary schools, a middle school, and a high school, which was named by New Jersey Monthly in 1996 as the sixth best in the state.

Tenafly boasts a broad range of advanced placement and honors courses including an interdepartmental humanities honors class which focuses on the historical and cultural development of Western Civilization. For its special education students, the school offers in-class support, a resource room, and supplemental instruction. With average SAT scores in 1995 of 551 in verbal and 602 in math, more than 87 percent of Tenafly's students go on to attend four-year colleges. An additional five percent continue on to attend two-year schools.

Another noteworthy aspect of the school system is its music program, which runs from kindergarten through graduation. Students are selected annually to perform in all-county and regional orchestra and band competitions.

There is also a gifted and talented program called the Talent Bank, which provides volunteers to boost classroom programs with their practical experience. Parents frequently visit the lower grades, where they tell stories about their life experiences and careers and answer questions.

The borough's parochial school is Our Lady of Mount Carmel, located in the center of town.

HOUSES OF WORSHIP

Chavurah Bethshalom; Church of the Atonement (Episcopal); Grace Chapel; Greek Orthodox Cathedral of St. John the Theologian; Jewish Community Center on the Palisades Inc.; Lubavitch on the Palisades; Our Lady of Mount Carmel Roman Catholic Church; The Presbyterian Church at Tenafly; St. Thomas Armenian Apostolic Church; The Society of African Missions; Temple Sinai of Bergen County; Tenafly United Methodist Church; and Trinity Lutheran Church.

HOUSES

Housing ranges from old Victorians to ranches, with prices running from $180,000 to $2 million mansions on the East Hill. Condominiums and co-ops begin at $80,000 and $100,000, but vacancies are very rare. According to local real estate broker Joseph Marovich, most residents are so satisfied with the quality of life that if they actually decide to sell their houses, they often simply move to larger homes in town.

TRANSPORTATION

There is direct bus service to New York, as well as points in South Jersey. From Route 9W, which puts the community within minutes of the George Washington Bridge, the approach to town along East Clinton Avenue winds through woodlands and luxury homes. There is no train station.

RECREATION

Open space is abundant throughout the town, though some of it is not officially designated for park purposes. The 165-acre Greenbrook Sanctuary on Route 9W, atop East Hill, has a five-acre pond, seven guided nature trails, 150-year-old hemlock trees (a number of which are endangered), and a large study hall for research into the annual cycle of native flowers and other botany. Hiking is permissible, but the sanctuary is open by appointment only.

The schools are located near Roosevelt Common (named after famed outdoorsman and President Theodore Roosevelt), a huge park and recreation area with playing fields and a new track.

The borough's recreation commission sponsors "Mother's Morning Out," tennis programs for all ages, and occasional trips to New York City. A teen center is popular with local youths looking to play table tennis, shoot pool, or just hang out.

There is also the Knickerbocker Country Club, which has a reputation as a rather exclusive, cliquey establishment. The club features golf, tennis, and a swimming pool. There is also an indoor tennis club in town, and two popular neighboring private swimming clubs just north of the high school.

Arts and Culture

Tenafly has a Jewish Community Center, which has amassed a library with a huge selection of classic music tapes and CDs. There is also the S.M.A. Fathers of African Art Museum. The museum features a diverse collection of wood, ivory, bronze, and brass exhibits and sponsors outreach programs and crafts programs.

Child Care Services

There are four private child care facilities in Tenafly. Neighboring towns such as Englewood also provide child care and au pair services. The Board of Education offers before- (7 to 8:40 a.m.) and after-school (3 to 6 p.m.) care for kindergarten through fifth grade.

Senior Services

The town has a senior citizens center with 35 residential units. Unfortunately, the rooms are usually filled.

Recent Developments

The downtown center, which has several small book and clothing outlets and a few convenience stores, has been targeted for a commercial redevelopment project, although no concrete plans have been put into effect.

In 1995, the council adopted an ordinance designating the Tenafly railroad station, the Theodore Roosevelt Monument, the Elizabeth Cady Stanton Station House, Christie-Parsels House, Sickels-Melbourne House, Demarest-Lyle House, and Roelof-Westervelt House as historic sites.

Drawbacks

The major controversy in recent years has been a lawsuit that started when the school board voted to allow Englewood Cliffs high school students to attend Tenafly High School. Englewood Cliffs has been trying to sever its ties with Dwight Morrow High School in Englewood. Residents fear that the dispute, which has dragged on for years, could lead to regionalization with Englewood, resulting in one high school for students in two or three towns.

Prominent Residents

Glenn Miller, Big Band leader of the late 1930s and early 1940s.

Phone Numbers

Township clerk (201) 568-6100
School district (201) 816-4500
Public library (201) 568-8680

— *Kevin Byrne*

Demographics

County: Bergen
Size: 4.6 square miles
Population: 13,326
Density: 2,890/square mile
Median age: 40.5
White: 84.7 percent
Asian: 14 percent
Black: 0.9 percent
Median house value: $353,200
Upper 25 percent: $500,000
Lower 25 percent: $247,650
Median year built: 1947
Median rent: $899
Single-family homes: 4,898
Condominiums: 100 units
Median property taxes per household (1994): $8,194
Median household income: $68,742
Industrial property: 15 parcels
Sewers: Mostly public, some private
Library: 67,891 volumes
Media: The Record covers the town, in addition to weekly publications including the Twin Borough News, the Press Journal, and the Suburbanite. Cable service is provided by Cablevision.
Fire and ambulance: Paid and volunteer
Police: Paid
Crime rate per 1,000 (1994): 15.2
Violent crime rate per 1,000 (1994): 0.8

TOTOWA

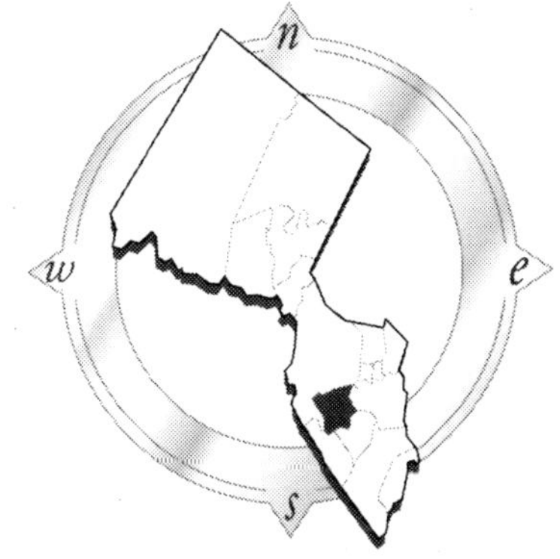

Rock-bottom taxes — the lowest in Passaic County — and exceptional schools are what draw people to this small, working-class borough of neatly trimmed homes.

"It's a suburban community with an excellent school system that attracts a lot of volunteers and has a very appealing tax rate," said Borough Councilman John Coiro.

A concentration of light industry on the east end of town allows officials to keep the tax rate low while providing excellent services.

But while low taxes attract newcomers, they stay because of the volunteerism and community spirit that animates this close-knit community of 10,000 people.

In an effort to spruce up the downtown area, for instance, local businesses have funded the planting of trees and the installation of cement-block sidewalks along Union Boulevard. So far, the beautification project hasn't cost residents a single penny in taxes.

And, through the award-winning Totowa Education Foundation, businesses and other local groups have raised more than $100,000 for after-school and Saturday enrichment programs, as well as activities for adults and seniors.

"The foundation has found a way to provide programs that don't cost the taxpayers," said Coiro. "They have really expanded the role of the school system in the community by making our schools community learning centers, not just for children but for adults and seniors."

Pam Cherba, a Totowa native and councilwoman, said all three characteristics — low taxes, good schools, and a strong sense of community — have made Totowa a great community.

"I walk around town and see a lot of people I went to school with," she said. "People tend to stay here. It's home."

Noteworthy historical events

Totowa was a crucial link in the defense of George Washington's army, with troops positioned along the eastern slope of the Totowa Ridges and artillery stationed near Totowa Road. In a little-known skirmish known as the Battle of Totowa, the Continental Army defeated the British, thwarting a plan to capture Washington masterminded by the traitor Benedict Arnold.

Schools

The Totowa school system serves 825 students, with one elementary and one middle school. Known for its exceptional after-school and Saturday enrichment programs, the district offers extra-curricular courses ranging from computer applications to journalism. The free courses are made possible by business and civic-group donations to the non-profit Totowa Educational Foundation.

Students in grades 5 through 8 attend Memorial School, where programs include after-school study groups, math and reading competitions, French, and peer tutoring.

Students in kindergarten through grade 4 attend Washington Park School. A $2 million, voter-approved addition to the school was completed in 1996, adding 12,500 square feet of classroom space devoted primarily to a computer lab, music and art rooms, an expanded media center, and a full-day kindergarten program. The school also started a preschool program in 1996.

Programs include a school newspaper; lunchtime enrichment classes in the performing, literary, and visual arts; an award-winning, student-run, in-school postal service called Wee Deliver, and The Little People Depot, a student-run school supply store whose proceeds fund special activities.

Older students attend Passaic Valley Regional High School in Little Falls, which serves 980 students from Totowa, Little Falls, and West Paterson. It offers more than 100 courses, with advanced placement programs in computer science, biology, chemistry, physics, calculus, American history, and English literature.

About 80 percent of the junior class of 1996 took the SAT; average scores were 497 verbal, 495 math. Sixty percent of the class went on to four-year colleges, while 21 percent enrolled in community college programs. Four seniors were recognized as Garden State Scholars, and seven were recognized by Rutgers University as Edward J. Bloustein Distinguished Scholars.

There is one parochial school, St. James Roman Catholic School.

Houses of Worship

Christ Episcopal Church; Han Wool Church; St. James Roman Catholic Church; St. Nikola Macedonian Orthodox Church; and Totowa United Methodist Church.

Houses

Totowa neighborhoods are composed mostly of single-family homes built in the 1940s and 1950s, with a few hundred two-family homes and one 84-unit town house complex.

Transportation

New Jersey Transit provides regular bus service to surrounding towns, with connections to New York City in Paterson and at Willowbrook Mall. A bus to Port Authority in Manhattan leaves from Riverview Drive and Route 46. Newark Airport is ten minutes away, as is the Meadowlands Sports Complex.

Recreation

The borough prides itself on its athletic programs and other activities, which are run cooperatively through its board of recreation and the Police Athletic League. Programs include organized team sports for kids, aerobics classes, adult men's and women's basketball teams, a six-week summer camp program, outdoor summer concerts, field trips, and holiday celebrations. Facilities include six playgrounds with jungle gyms and well-maintained ball fields, tennis courts (slated for renovations), and a municipal pool.

The borough cooperates with West Paterson and Little Falls to provide activities for disabled children.

ARTS AND CULTURE

The borough's board of recreation sponsors occasional trips into Manhattan for plays and performances.

CHILD CARE SERVICES

There are five private child care facilities.

SENIOR SERVICES

Totowa operates a free door-to-door bus service to area doctors' offices and shopping locations. The Triborough Seniors provides free lunches on weekdays for residents of West Paterson, Totowa, and Little Falls at the neighboring West Paterson Boys and Girls Club. They also run the Meals on Wheels program.

The Deerfield Senior Day Center, a privately run organization, provides medical assistance and daytime activity programs for seniors. Transportation and three meals are provided.

RECENT DEVELOPMENTS

A $650,000 expansion and renovation of Municipal Hall is under way. A downtown beautification project, paid for with donations from local businesses, is ongoing. Arlington Estates, 80 units of upscale single-family housing, is under construction.

DRAWBACKS

No senior or low-income housing.

PROMINENT RESIDENTS

Uncle Floyd Vivino, the comedian/actor whose television show became a cult hit in the 1980s.

PHONE NUMBERS

Township clerk (201) 956-1009
School district (201) 956-2125
Public library (201) 790-3265

— *Kelly David*

DEMOGRAPHICS

County: Passaic
Size: 4 square miles
Population: 10,177
Density: 2,547/square mile
Median age: 40.4
White: 96.8 percent
Asian: 1.3 percent
Black: 1.2 percent
Median house value: $190,700
Upper 25 percent: $240,100
Lower 25 percent: $161,300
Median year built: 1954
Median rent: $618
Single-family homes: 2,587
Condominiums: 80 units
Median property taxes per household (1994): $3,439
Median household income: $46,309
Industrial property: 67 parcels
Sewers: Public and private
Library: 37,373 volumes
Media: The Record and the North Jersey Herald & News cover the town. TCI provides cable service.
Fire and ambulance: Paid
Police: Paid
Crime rate per 1,000 (1994): 43.1
Violent crime rate per 1,000 (1994): 2.6

UPPER SADDLE RIVER

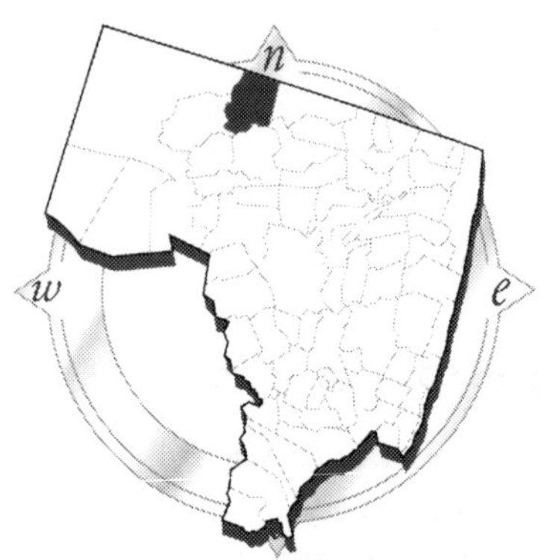

Incorporated in 1894, Upper Saddle River was once a farming community of apple orchards, strawberry fields, and dairy farms. Today, it is one of the most affluent towns in Bergen County.

The borough borders New York State and adjoins some of the county's other wealthy towns, including Allendale, Saddle River, Montvale, and Ramsey.

Upper Saddle River is a bucolic community with many luxurious homes. Many houses in the borough are new; a number of long-time residents have enlarged their older homes or demolished them to build new ones on the land.

The borough has one-acre zoning. It recently completed construction of 24 units of affordable housing. Residents have been vocal about new development, with many charging it is a threat to the borough's small-town charm and rural beauty.

A group of local residents has been trying to raise funds to save the town's last working farm — Mettowee Farm — from development. The Martin family, which has owned the farm since the 1950s, recently put the 17-acre tract up for sale.

Upper Saddle River lacks a downtown center, but Elmer's Country Store is a common meeting place for residents. Located on the corner of Lake Street and East Saddle River Road for more than 50 years, Elmer's was at one time a cow barn.

Nearby Route 17 has many businesses, but residents do most of their shopping in neighboring towns. Some borough council members and many residents are fighting a proposed multiplex movie theater that has been proposed for a lot on Route 17. Many teenagers in Upper Saddle River and surrounding towns are in favor of the theater, which they say would give them something to do besides hang out at the Route 17 diners.

One well-known historic landmark is the Old Stone Church, which is still in use today.

Noteworthy Historical Events

George Washington and his troops passed through the town in 1778. He stopped at the sandstone house at 199 East Saddle River Road to thank residents for baking bread for his soldiers. Several Revolutionary War soldiers are buried in the cemetery at the Old Stone Church.

A huge flood on July 23, 1945, destroyed many homes and a lot of property in the area.

Schools

Until the late Forties, the school system employed one teacher. Today, of course, the educational standards in the K-8 district are somewhat higher: Superintendent of Schools Nathan Parker boasted of "the highest-quality staff around, an innovative curriculum, forward thinking, and a lot of community and parent involvement."

The district serves about 1,060 students. Students in kindergarten through grade 2 attend Robert Reynolds School. Emil Bogert School is for grades 3 and 4; Cavallini Middle School is for grades 5 through 8. Upper Saddle River is the only district in the county that has a fourth-grade newspaper, as well as a middle-school newspaper, desktop-published by the students. Five students in the district recently qualified for the Center for the Advancement of Science and Technology at Bergen County Technical College. The schools are working to get their students on the Internet.

Upper Saddle River and Allendale elementary and middle schools feed into Northern Highlands Regional High School in Allendale, which enrolls about 750 students. Northern Highlands was ranked No. 4 among the state's high schools by New Jersey Monthly magazine in September 1996. The district sends 98 percent of its students to two- or four-year colleges. Average SAT scores in 1995 were 501 verbal and 574 math. (See Allendale for more details on the high school.)

Houses of Worship

Bergen Highlands United Methodist Church; Church of the Presentation (Roman Catholic); and the Saddle River Reformed Church (the historic Old Stone Church).

Houses

Houses run the gamut from small to large; many are ranch-style or two-story. There are also numerous mansions.

Transportation

A Short Line bus into New York City leaves from and returns to Elmer's Country Store. There is also a bus into New York City from Route 17. It's easy to get around the borough by car, bike, or foot. Upper Saddle River is a few miles from the Garden State Parkway and the New York State Thruway.

Recreation

The 12-acre Lions Park on Lake Street, bordered by streams and woods, has playing fields for soccer, baseball, and softball, and a children's playground.

In addition, there's the seven-acre Hess Court Park off West Saddle River Road; and five tennis courts on West Saddle River Road in front of the Reynolds/Bogert school complex.

Arts and Culture

The Hopper-Goetschius House Museum and the Saddle River Valley Cultural Center are located in town. The library schedules monthly art exhibits.

Child Care Services

The school district sponsors the Upper Saddle River after-school program. There are also several privately run child care facilities in town.

Senior Services

The borough appropriates funds for a local senior citizens group.

Recent developments

In the summer of 1996, 24 units of affordable housing were built on East Crescent Avenue.

Prominent residents

Former New York Giants linebacker Lawrence Taylor used to live here.

Phone numbers

Township clerk (201) 327-2196
School district (201) 327-4401
Public library (201) 327-2583

— *Hali Helfgott*

Demographics

County: Bergen
Size: 5.3 square miles
Population: 7,198
Density: 1,360/square mile
Median age: 40
White: 94.1 percent
Asian: 4.5 percent
Black: 0.9 percent
Median house value: $479,200
Upper 25 percent: $500,001
Lower 25 percent: $383,900
Median year built: 1964
Median rent: $1,001
Single-family homes: 2,396
Condominiums: None
Median property taxes per household (1994): $8,192
Median household income: $94,200
Industrial property: 4 parcels
Sewers: Public and septic
Library: 44,656 volumes, 225 periodicals, 1,500 videos, 1,500 audiobooks, 700 compact discs
Media: The Record covers the town, as do the Town Journal, the Suburban News, the Villadom Times, and the Ridgewood News, all weeklies. Cable service is provided by TCI.
Fire and ambulance: Volunteer
Police: Paid
Crime rate per 1,000 (1994): 18.9
Violent crime rate per 1,000 (1994): 0.4

WALDWICK

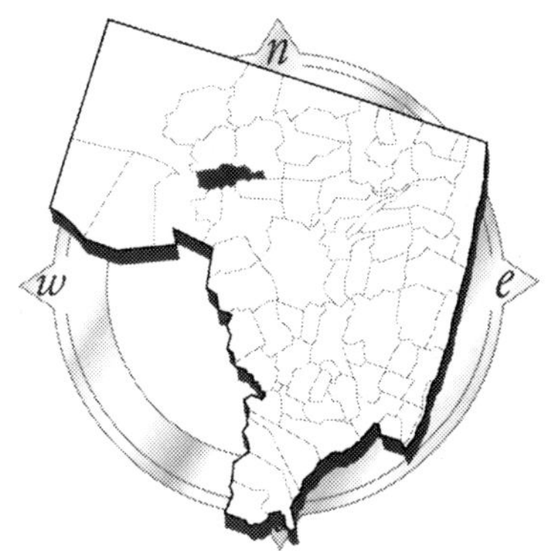

Incorporated in 1919, Waldwick was once home to railroad workers and farmers. Today, it's a middle-class bedroom community for commuters who work in the region. The original settlers were Dutch and English; now, it's a mini-melting pot.

The town derived its name from an old German word that means "a light in the woods": In its early history, the train's light was the area's only illumination. The phrase became the town motto.

Waldwick is a tight-knit community, where many residents get involved in local affairs. For example, parents here volunteer on a graduation ball committee, which helps plan a big party for graduating seniors every year. The town also has many sports programs.

"In my 40 years as a resident I have found that Waldwick is a friendly, caring town of people willing to volunteer their time and energy for their neighbors," said George Fredricks, the town historian.

There are several commercial districts. The main district occupies a six-block area on both sides of Prospect Street, Franklin Turnpike, and Wyckoff Avenue and comprises more than 50 stores. An industrial area lies near the Allendale border.

A trolley once ran through Waldwick, and the town has one of the last remaining railroad towers in the county.

One of the more amusing events in Waldwick history happened in 1962. About 400 pigs from a Wyckoff farm escaped and lumbered down Wyckoff Avenue into Waldwick. Farmers retrieved only about half of them; the remaining pigs probably became pork dinners.

NOTEWORTHY HISTORICAL EVENTS

In 1971, Nathaniel T. Bogdanove ran for mayor against the

incumbent. Just before the election, he died of natural causes while taking the train home from work, but it was too late to remove his name from the ballot. The dead man beat his opponent by about 200 votes. The incumbent ended up staying in office.

George Washington stayed here during the American Revolution. Poet Joyce Kilmer immortalized the town by mentioning it in a poem, "The Twelve-forty-five," which is when the train got into Waldwick.

Schools

The district serves about 1,300 students in the Crescent School, Traphagen School, and Waldwick High School. In 1996, New Jersey Monthly magazine ranked Waldwick High School 71st in the state.

The high school offers 127 courses, including six advanced placement programs. Honors classes are offered in 17 academic subjects, including foreign languages, in grades 9 through 12. Students learn Russian via a satellite cable hookup.

Of last year's graduates, 72 percent went on to attend four-year colleges; 12 percent, to two-year schools. Almost all students take the Scholastic Assessment Test; the district's average SAT scores were 509 verbal and 523 math.

The Seventh Day Adventist School is located in Waldwick.

Houses of worship

Christ Community Church and Waldwick United Methodist Church.

Houses

Many of the homes in town are single-story, some in the ranch style popular during the Sixties.

Residents have expanded many of the smaller homes, and the new homes in town tend to be larger. There are still some houses from the Twenties.

Transportation

There is direct bus service from Route 17 into Manhattan. New Jersey Transit trains run from the borough to Hoboken, with connections to PATH trains for New York, Newark and Jersey City.

RECREATION

Borough Park has baseball fields, a jungle gym, White's Pond, and an exercise course. The borough also has several tennis courts and a few other small parks. A new indoor recreational facility is being erected at the high school, which will be used for school activities during the day and by community groups at night.

ARTS AND CULTURE

The public library sponsors concerts and monthly art exhibits showing works of Bergen County artists.

CHILD CARE SERVICES

The borough has two private child care facilities.

SENIOR SERVICES

The Golden Age Club sponsors social activities.

RECENT DEVELOPMENTS

A condominium project that included the borough's first seven units of low-income housing was completed in early 1996.

DRAWBACKS

Twenty-nine residents in neighboring Allendale have sued the firing range on Pine Street, the town, police chief, and the Waldwick Pistol and Rifle Club, claiming their quality of life is affected and their safety is at risk. They are seeking to close down the range.

PROMINENT RESIDENTS

Dave Fiore of the San Francisco 49ers grew up in Waldwick and attended school here.

PHONE NUMBERS

Township clerk (201) 652-5070
School district (201) 445-3340
Public library (201) 652-510

— Hali Helfgott

Demographics

County: Bergen
Size: 2.1 square miles
Population: 9,757
Density: 4,678/square mile
Median age: 36
White: 94.5 percent
Asian: 4.6 percent
Black: 0.5 percent
Median house value: $204,900
Upper 25 percent: $239,700
Lower 25 percent: $180,700
Median year built: 1955
Median rent: $908
Single-family homes: 2,968
Condominiums: None
Median property taxes per household (1994): $4,987
Median household income: $60,000
Industrial property: 23 parcels
Sewers: Public and septic
Library: 45,242 books and periodicals, 486 videos, 112 music cassettes, 619 audiobooks on cassette, 332 compact discs
Media: The Record covers the town, as do the Ridgewood News, the Villadom Times, and the Suburban News, all weekies. Cable service is provided by TCI.
Fire and ambulance: Volunteer
Police: Paid
Crime rate per 1,000 (1994): 13.9
Violent crime rate per 1,000 (1994): 0.8

WASHINGTON TOWNSHIP

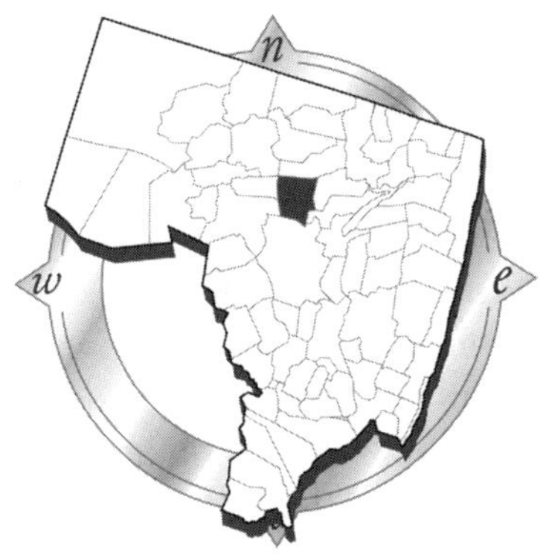

Solid and stable, the Township of Washington is a fully developed community that clearly enjoys the benefits of its mature status.

This former farming community is strictly residential, composed almost exclusively of single-family homes. A small shopping center offers convenience stores, a movie theater, a restaurant, and food shopping, while nearby highways, such as the Garden State Parkway and Route 17, furnish access to malls and New York City.

It's an ideal haven from metropolitan life, said Township Administrator Agnes Smith.

There is no industry — although the township was once a major source of flowers. Chances are if you received a carnation during the 1950s, it came from the Beuerleines farm in Washington. The four brothers who operated the farm made a practice of giving local children jobs each summer tending the blossoms that were shipped all over the world. Among them was Cheryl Todd, now the township historian.

The township's solid reputation ensures reliable home resale values. Additionally, an AA rating from Moody's helps keep property taxes stable.

Much of this economic security stems from the original contributions of senior members of the community, who long ago saw Washington through its growing pains. "They remain a very active part of the community," said Smith. A senior center was built recently to serve these longtime residents' needs, so together with the younger population, they continue to have an impact on the township's character.

Noteworthy Historical Events

Seven Chimneys, a Washington Township home built in 1748 by the Zabriski family, has been the site of several significant historical events. The township took its name from the fact that George Washington slept in the eight-room Colonial structure during the American Revolution. Almost a century later, the house served as a stop along the Underground Railroad for slaves fleeing to the North in search of freedom. Theodore Roosevelt was a frequent Seven Chimneys guest between 1915 and 1917, while visiting its owner, his friend Thomas L. Rowland. The house remains a private residence today.

Schools

The township is part of the Westwood regional school district, which has an enrollment of approximately 2,100 students at four primary schools and Westwood Regional Junior-Senior High School. It is the only regional school district for kindergarten through grade 12 in Bergen County, and schools Superintendent Joseph Fisler described the educational collaboration between the towns as "the model for how it should be done." The elementary schools and the combined junior-senior high school are governed by a single school board. This promotes more efficient management and helps to keep administrative costs down. Similarly, leaders from each of the six schools' parent organizations meet monthly to discuss districtwide initiatives in addition to school-specific plans.

The high school offers 196 courses, including nine advanced placement programs. Honors classes are offered in every subject in grades 6 through 12, except foreign languages, in which honors courses begin in the fourth year of study. There is also a preschool program for handicapped youngsters.

The high school is one of 22 Bergen County schools in the Interactive Television Network (ITN), which provides more than 30 televised classes ranging from advanced foreign-language courses to college-level physics and business classes.

A $6.9 million renovation is under way to spruce up the school buildings and provide new technology, especially Internet-access computers.

Eighty-seven percent of the high school graduates attend two- or four-year colleges; eight percent enroll in Ivy League schools.

With average SAT scores of 527 verbal, 546 math, the district easily beats the state averages.

In recent years, the district has emphasized greater student and community involvement in the educational process. The student government is very active in proposing and implementing policy changes. The Peer Mediators program actively involves students in adjudicating disputes, and the Pupil Assisted Leadership (PAL) program provides one-on-one guidance and counseling between students. Parents staff the buildings and grounds committees at each school, and there is strong participation in the Key Communicator, a school/community liaison organization.

Immaculate Heart Academy, a Catholic girls' high school, is located in Washington Township.

Houses of Worship

Abundant Life Assembly of God; Our Lady of Good Counsel Roman Catholic Church; Temple Beth-Or (Reform), and Valley Bible Chapel.

Houses

Houses come in a variety of styles, including Cape Cods, ranches, split-levels, bi-levels, and colonials. Most were built in the last 35 years. Prices typically remain close to the quarter-million-dollar mark but can range from $175,000 for a three-bedroom Cape to a half-million dollars for a new 3,000-square-foot center-hall colonial.

Transportation

The Red and Tan bus line provides transportation to and from Port Authority in New York City. New Jersey Transit provides rail service to Hoboken and the PATH system from nearby Westwood. There are no local bus lines or other public transportation.

Recreation

"Extensive and second to none," Smith declared of Washington Township's co-ed recreational program. For children, basketball, bowling, football, softball, and wrestling are offered, in addition to privately sponsored baseball and soccer leagues. Men's and women's adult softball also is available.

During the summer, the township conducts an eight-week children's recreational program that includes trips, games, and crafts.

The township has several small parks, including one with a baseball diamond that is lit for nighttime play. Washington Lake is available to members of the lake association for swimming, skating, fishing, and other activities. Each year an Easter egg hunt, a Christmas tree lighting, a Memorial Day parade, and a Ragamuffin parade are held. There is one local movie theater.

Arts and Culture

A YM-YWHA facility serving all Bergen County is located in Washington Township and sponsors recreational and cultural activities for adults and children. The Pascack Historical Society in Park Ridge maintains a collection of local artifacts, including many from the township. Community theater organizations are located in nearby municipalities.

The library hosts book discussions, lectures, and seminars, and features exhibits from the Pascack Art Association.

Child Care Services

The Westwood school district (serving Washington Township) hosts an after-school child-care program, run by the local YM-YWHA, in one of the elementary school buildings five days a week from noon to 7 p.m. Bus transportation is provided from each of the district's schools. Starting a day-care program at the high school for the children of school staff members is being explored.

Senior Services

The Golden Seniors sponsors social activities. The organization, which meets once a month at a Knights of Columbus Hall, will move into a new center on the first floor of the newly renovated Town Hall. The new center offers large meeting and activities spaces, a kitchen, and a recreational room.

No housing for seniors is available in town.

Recent Developments

The township is completing renovation and additional construction on its Town Hall. The original 1902 schoolhouse, which now contains the municipality's administrative offices, will be incorporated into the new structure. The township also is completing the refurbishment and resurfacing of its roads, and the local shopping center is being renovated with private funds.

Drawbacks

The high rate of development across Bergen County has had spillover effects on the township, resulting in increased traffic and a more citified feeling.

Phone Numbers

Township clerk (201) 664-4425
School district (201) 664-0880
Public library (201) 664-4586

— *Maria C. Zingaro*

Demographics

County: Bergen
Size: 2.91 square miles
Population: 9,245
Density: 3,179/square mile
Median age: 39.1 years
White: 93 percent
Asian: 5.7 percent
Black: 0.8 percent
Median house value: $254,200
Upper 25 percent: $304,600
Lower 25 percent: $209,500
Median year built: 1960
Median rent: $1,001
Single-family homes: 2,842
Condominiums: 338 units
Median property taxes per household (1994): $5,176
Median household income: $68,043
Industrial property: None
Sewers: Public
Library: 41,096 volumes
Media: The Record covers the town, as does the weekly Community Life. WCTV is a local television station. TCI provides cable service.
Fire and ambulance: Volunteer
Police: Paid
Crime rate per 1,000 (1994): 11.2
Violent crime rate per 1,000 (1994): 0.3

WAYNE

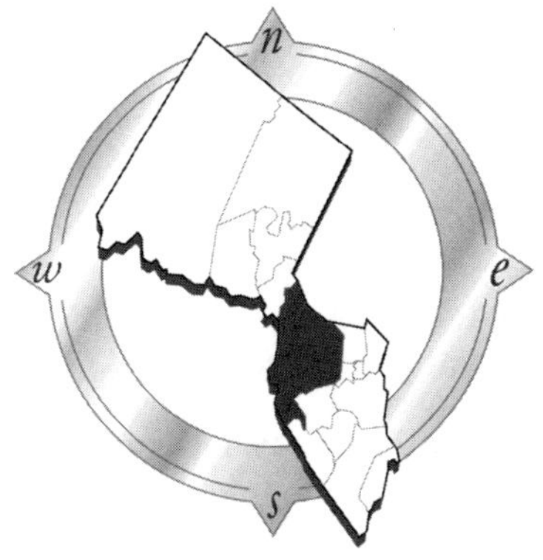

Wayne residents sometimes refer to their hometown as the crossroads of North Jersey — a place where anything and everything is just a five-minute car ride away.

Comprising 26 square miles of suburbia in northeast Passaic County, the mostly upper-middle-class community is divided between residential and commercial land situated at the heart of the spider web of highways and byways that snake throughout North Jersey. It is also home to a number of corporate headquarters of major firms.

"I think that's one of the main reasons things are so good here," said Mike Tomasulo, senior vice president for the township-based Gelesi Realty Corp. "All the major highways are right here or right up the street, making it attractive to people looking to reside here or commercial businesses looking to set up here."

Having blossomed from a sparsely developed farm town to a monster shopping mecca that is home to New Jersey's second-largest mall, Willowbrook, Wayne has become one of the state's largest retail hubs.

But residents say Wayne offers more than easy access to malls and markets, a top-notch school system, and a comfortable suburban locale close to New York City. It is a town rich in history and class diversity, with roots reaching past the American Revolution, said library director Barbara Pickell.

The town got its name from General "Mad Anthony" Wayne, a Revolutionary War hero who earned his nickname for his astounding courage in the face of battle, his daring (some would say suicidal) deeds, and his fearlessness.

Wayne came to Passaic in 1780 to meet with George Washington at the home of Theunis Dey, a Revolutionary patriot whose mansion was used by Washington as a secret meeting place.

"The whole town is almost directly in the middle of the military route from West Point to Valley Forge. That gives us a lot of history," said township clerk and longtime resident Jack O'Brien.

Noteworthy historical events

During the late 1980s, the township was a notorious hive of municipal corruption — a rap that stemmed from the jailing of ousted Mayor Louis V. Messercola on charges of extortion. Five former officials and three developers also pleaded guilty to taking part in bribery schemes. A federal investigation of corruption in the area continues to this day. Township officials responded to the scandal by filing a huge civil racketeering suit against the culprits, resulting in almost $300,000 in damage settlements.

Schools

The school system is considered well above average by residents and officials. There are eight elementary schools for kindergarten through grade 5, two middle schools (6 through 8), and two high schools, Wayne Hills and Wayne Valley. In New Jersey Monthly's 1996 ranking of the state's top high schools, Wayne Valley was 56th and Wayne Hills was 70th.

About 94 percent of high school juniors take the Scholastic Assessment Test. Average SAT scores for both schools are 437 verbal, 536 math. At Wayne Valley, about 76 percent of students go on to four-year schools, while 16 percent continue on to two-year colleges. At Wayne Hills, about 70 percent of graduates continue their education at four-year schools; 17 percent go to two-year colleges. Wayne Hills is also the magnet school for English as a Second Language students in the district.

Both high schools offer five language programs and advanced placement courses in foreign language, mathematics, science, computer science, and English. An accelerated math program begins in middle school for advanced students and eventually will run through AP calculus II by senior year.

"There's no question the school system is one of the biggest reasons why people come to Wayne," said Wayne Hills guidance chairman Mario Gillio.

Parochial schools include DePaul High School (Catholic) and Calvary Christian Academy.

Wayne is also home to the 250-acre campus of William Paterson State College, located in the township's northeast corner.

Houses of worship

Annunciation of the Blessed Virgin Mary Roman Catholic (R.C.) Church; Assembly of God Calvary Temple; Bethany United Methodist Church; Calvary Gospel Church; Chabad Center (Lubivitch); Church of the Annunciation of The Blessed Virgin Mary; Circassian Benevolent Association; Grace Fellowship Church; Grace United Presbyterian Church of Wayne; Holy Cross R.C. Church; Immaculate Heart of Mary R.C. Church; India Cultural Hindu Temple; Lakeland Unitarian University Fellowship; Mountain View Gospel Church; New Apostle Church; Orthodox Church of the Holy Resurrection; Our Lady of Consolation R.C. Church; Our Lady of the Valley R.C. Church; Packanack Community Church; Pequannock Reformed Church; Preakness Baptist Church; Preakness Bible Church; Preakness Christian Reformed Church; Preakness Reformed Church; St. Michael's Episcopal Church; St. Timothy Evangelical Lutheran Church; Seventh Day Adventist Church of Wayne; Shomrei Torah (Conservative);Temple Beth Tikvah; United Methodist Church in Wayne; Vivekananda Vidyapith Inc.; Wayne Christian Assembly; and Wayne Presbyterian Church.

Houses

Houses vary in style from Victorians to cottages. Prices range from $150,000 to more than $1 million. Neighborhoods range from modest to million-dollar: Mountain View and Hoffman Grove are low- to moderate-income, while such communities as Pines Lake occupy pristine, nearly parklike areas featuring towering trees within walking distance of several hiking and fishing spots.

Wayne also has a handful of condominium complexes and some commercial property, thanks to its proximity to highways and interstates. Most industry is relegated to the town's perimeter.

Transportation

New Jersey Transit offers direct bus service to New York City and train service to Hoboken. Wayne is accessible from Routes 23, 46, and 80. Route 287, an interstate highway under construction, likely will encourage additional growth in coming years.

Recreation

Recreation programs include soccer, baseball, softball, wrestling, basketball, and tennis for kids. There's also an adult softball league and an over-40 softball league. The James W. Roe Memorial pool, in Kilroy Park, is open to residents.

Other outdoor attractions are the municipality's many parks and baseball diamonds, as well as 12 lighted tennis courts (Wayne residents pay annually for a tennis badge).

The annual Wayne Day celebration, held in June, features craft fairs, athletic events, rides, and fireworks. Also in June, the Van Riper-Hopper Museum hosts a strawberry festival and crafts show.

Arts and Culture

The Van Riper Hopper Museum is dedicated to preserving the history of farming and farm life in Wayne, and features several old paintings. Nearby is the Van Duyne House, a prototypical Dutch farmhouse. Both are maintained by the town and the Wayne Historical Commission. The Dey Mansion is also open to the public, and The Schuyler-Colfax Home recently opened as a museum.

Art exhibits and musical and theater performances are held at the Sarah Byrd Askew Library and at the Ben Shahn Center for The Performing Arts at William Paterson College.

Child Care Services

There are 11 private child care facilities in Wayne.

Recent Developments

The community is under court order to provide some 1,000 low-cost units and is grappling with a Fair Share Housing Plan to map out how it will meet that mandate.

Other issues the township faces are updating the master plan and improving antiquated roadways and infrastructure. A major artery, Hamburg Turnpike, is in line for a multimillion-dollar face lift.

School administrators are investigating the merits of consolidation. The controversial topic must be addressed in the next few years, as the student population is expected to grow substantially.

Drawbacks

The southern section of town near the Pequannock River habitually floods, causing havoc during bad weather. But some say the local media blow the flooding way out of proportion.

"The flooding is a problem, but it pertains to a very small area of town," said Robert Brubaker, chairman of the Wayne Historical Society. "It's not the entire township of Wayne that floods every time we have heavy rains. The only major floods the whole town has had were in 1936, 1968, and 1984."

The town's population has increased steadily and often experiences traffic problems on Hamburg Turnpike and Route 23 during rush hours. Also, the cloverleaf of Routes 80, 46, and 23 becomes congested at peak times of the day.

In the northwest section of town, a dangerous thorium waste site is being cleaned up. The site was infected with the radioactive material when a company allegedly dumped it there around 1971.

Signs of hard times are evident in the going-out-of-business notices and vacant storefronts cropping up all over town.

Prominent residents

Cecil B. DeMille ("The Ten Commandments") spent some time in Wayne before becoming a famous movie producer.

Phone numbers

Township clerk (201) 694-1800
School district (201) 633-3031
Public library (201) 694-4272

— *Steven C. Johnson*

Demographics

County: Passaic
Size: 23.8 square miles
Population: 47,025
Density: 1,974/square mile
Median age: 37.7 years
White: 95 percent
Asian: 3.1 percent
Black: 1.1 percent
Median house value: $242,000
Upper 25 percent: $301,200
Lower 25 percent: $191,200
Median year built: 1962
Median rent: $693
Single-family homes: 12,895
Condominiums: 16,306 units
Median property taxes per household (1994): $5,383
Median household income: $59,290
Industrial property: 86 parcels
Sewers: Public and private
Library: 146,682 volumes
Media: The Record and the North Jersey Herald & News cover the town, as do several weeklies including the Independent News and Wayne Today. UA Columbia Cablevision provides cable service.
Fire and ambulance: Volunteer
Police: Paid
Crime rate per 1,000 (1994): 59.2
Violent crime rate per 1,000 (1994): 1.1

West Milford

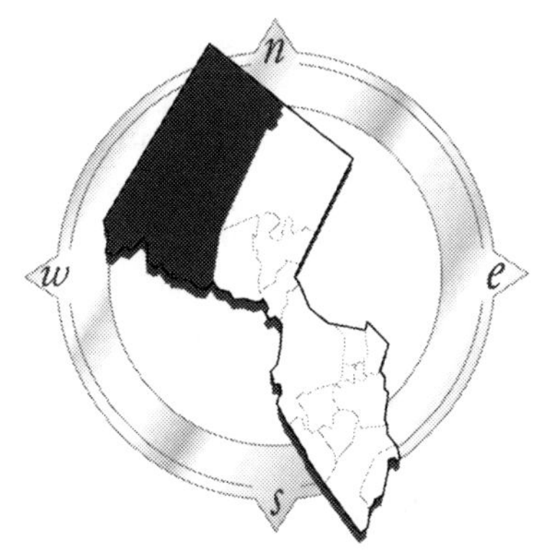

A landscape of more than 40 lakes and reservoirs, rivers, rocky ridges, and abundant wildlife draw many to semi-rural West Milford. The township's 80 square miles — much of it protected watershed, open space, and state forest — make it the largest municipality in Passaic County. For those among the town's 28,000 residents who work in New York City, the drive back home can feel like traveling to a different planet.

"It's an escape from reality," said Maria Harkey, a longtime resident and local councilwoman. "The fall is absolutely gorgeous, spring is lovely, summer is cooler here, even the winter is beautiful."

The up-county township is bordered by New York's Orange County to the east; Morris County to the west; Ringwood, Wanaque, and Bloomingdale to the south; and Sussex County to the north.

The township is composed of seven sections: Upper Greenwood Lake, Hewitt, Macopin, Newfoundland, Oak Ridge, Apshawa, and the town center, West Milford. Each area has its cluster of commercial development, with residential areas consisting mostly of single-family houses located on lots of an acre or more. The township is steering new development toward the existing clusters, focusing first on the town center, where most shops, restaurants, offices, and banks are located.

Large-scale development is limited by the township's elevation — ranging from nearly 450 to 1,500 — and its vast water resources and protected forests. The city of Newark owns 17,000 acres of watershed in West Milford, and no fewer than three state parks ring the township, providing residents with recreational opportunities such as mountain biking, cross-country skiing, hiking, boating, fishing, swimming, fishing, and horseback riding.

"You get more for your money here," said Susan Stinneford, a sales agent at Century 21 in West Milford. "We have a lot of summer, lakeside bungalows people are buying and converting to year-round. There are middle-range homes and newer, upscale areas around the lakes. We're accessible to major highways. ... It's a great country life, and you can still go to work in the city."

Noteworthy Historical Events

On February 23, 1936, a research engineer named Willy Ley conducted the first test of air mail delivery by rocket. The rocket was launched from Sterling Forest in New York, across the state line and over Greenwood Lake into the Hewitt section of West Milford. It carried 6,000 pieces of mail. The event gained worldwide fame among philatelists when the event was commemorated with a stamp.

Schools

West Milford's school district launched a major technology and computer literacy initiative two years ago.

The district, which serves 4,401 students, has six elementary schools, one middle school, and a high school. The Board of Education has submitted a plan to expand the middle school to include sixth-graders and integrate computer systems throughout the district. The district has not yet released cost estimates for the expansion.

The district touts its Learning Unlimited program for gifted and talented students in kindergarten through grade 12.

West Milford students in all grades also participate in the Odyssey of the Mind program, a competitive, team-oriented approach to problem solving and creative thinking. West Milford teams have gone to the world finals in the prestigious competition.

High school students choose from a variety of curricula, including college preparatory, vocational, or commercial programs, which include work-study experience. Electives include photography, interior decorating, computer mathematics, astronomy, oceanography, and data processing.

Special education programs are provided, including classes for neurologically impaired, perceptually impaired, and emotionally disturbed students.

In 1995, 72 percent of West Milford High School graduates went on to two or four-year colleges. About 75 percent took the SAT; the average scores in 1995 were 416 verbal, 476 math.

Houses of worship

Abbey of the Holy Name; Calvary Bible Church; Christian Life Center; Church of the Incarnation; Church on the Mountain; Echo Lake Baptist Church; Gilgal Bible Chapel; Green Pond Bible Chapel; Greenwood Baptist Church; Holy Faith Lutheran Church; Jehovah's Witnesses of West Milford; Jewish Center of Upper Greenwood Lake; Oak Ridge Presbyterian Church; Our Lady Queen of Peace Roman Catholic Roman Catholic (R.C.) Church; St. Joseph's R.C. Church; St. Simon the Apostle; United Methodist Church at Newfoundland; and West Milford Presbyterian Church.

Houses

The diverse housing choices range from log cabins and lakeside bungalows to luxury town houses and new 4,000-square-foot homes. The township is developing 24 affordable senior citizen condominiums. There are relatively few apartment units in town.

Transportation

West Milford operates three free community buses. Schedules can be obtained at the town hall. New Jersey Transit provides bus service from West Milford to Willowbrook Mall in Wayne and Port Authority in Manhattan. There are two park-and-ride facilities.

Recreation

The township has a full-time director of parks and recreation and recently hired a consulting firm to study recreation resources and enhance facilities, with a view toward marketing the town as a tourist destination.

Greenwood Lake — the second-largest in the state — offers water sports including sailing, fishing, water skiing, jet skiing, windsurfing, and swimming. A chain of smaller reservoirs and lakes provides drinking water to millions of North Jersey residents and affords beautiful vistas from the many hiking and biking trails that wind through the forest.

Three state parks ring West Milford — Hewitt State Park, Wawayanda State Park, and Norvin Green State Park.

At Bubbling Springs Recreation Area, residents can fish in the lower lake in spring and summer and ice skate in the winter. At Brown's Point Park, off Greenwood Lake Turnpike, facilities include a picnic area, playground, and Frisbee golf course.

Mt. Laurel Park, in the Upper Greenwood Lake section, includes softball fields, tennis courts, basketball courts, a tot lot, and picnic tables. The Hillcrest Community Center is the headquarters for the parks and recreation department.

Township-sponsored summer recreation programs include three two-week day camp sessions, tennis, swimming lessons, and swim team competition.

ARTS AND CULTURE

The West Milford Players present dramas, musicals, and comedies; the library sponsors afternoon jazz and blues concerts in nice weather; and the husband-and-wife team of Rich and Janet Dixon — better known as Dancin' Boots — teach country-western line dancing at the West Milford Elks Lodge.

The West Milford Heritage Committee is restoring a nearly 140-year-old church that once served as the town hall. The committee is collecting artifacts and donations and plans to rehabilitate the old building and reopen it as a museum.

The Friends of Long Pond Ironworks are restoring a Colonial-era iron furnace built in 1768 and abandoned in 1880. The ironworks produced cannonballs, stoves, and other equipment for the American army during the Revolution and was an important source of iron for the Union Army in the Civil War.

West Milford's annual Autumn Lights Festival began in 1995 as a tongue-in-cheek event celebrating the installation of the town's first traffic light. By the following year, it had grown into a major regional autumn festival, drawing hundreds to enjoy the flaming fall foliage and to participate in lots of recreational activities as well as historic and environmental exhibits and retail sales.

Child care services

There are 15 private child care facilities in West Milford.

Senior services

The township offers transportation and an escort service that takes homebound seniors to stores, banks, and doctors' appointments. Senior organizations include the Highland Seniors, Golden Jet Set, Golden Agers, and the West Milford Senior Citizen Advisory Committee. The township's office of Older Adult Services also sponsors recreational activities.

Recent developments

A $1.4 million, 25,000-square-foot youth recreation center is being built by the local Police Athletic League in cooperation with the township and is scheduled to open in 1998. The township also is developing 24 units of affordable senior citizen housing. An addition to the Macopin Middle School is in the planning stages.

Drawbacks

With 76 square miles of hilly territory pocketed with lakes and reservoirs, getting around can be difficult, especially during heavy winter snows. A spate of underground gasoline tank leaks has contaminated portions of aquifers in several sections of the township.

Prominent residents

Olympic Gold Medalist (Albertville, 1992) and 1996 World Champion moguls skier Donna Weinbrecht.

Phone numbers

Township manager (201) 728-2715
School district (201) 697-1700
Public library (201) 728-2820

— *Tim May*

Demographics

County: Passaic
Size: 75.4 square miles
Population: 25,430
Density: 337/square mile
Median age: 32.8 years
White: 97.2 percent
Black: 1 percent
Asian: 0.9 percent
Median house value: $167,700
Upper 25 percent: $350,000
Lower 25 percent: $80,000
Median year built: 1960
Median rent: $667
Single-family homes: 8,510
Condominiums: 923 units
Median property taxes per household (1994): $4,790
Median household income: $52,734
Industrial property: 29 parcels
Sewers: Mostly septic
Library: 27,681 volumes
Media: The Record and the North Jersey Herald & News cover the town, as do the bi-weekly Suburban Trends; the Greenwood Lake and West Milford News; and AIM Action Ads/News. Cable service is provided by TCI.
Fire and ambulance: Volunteer
Police: Paid
Crime rate per 1,000 (1994): 18.1
Violent crime rate per 1,000 (1994): 0.8

WEST PATERSON

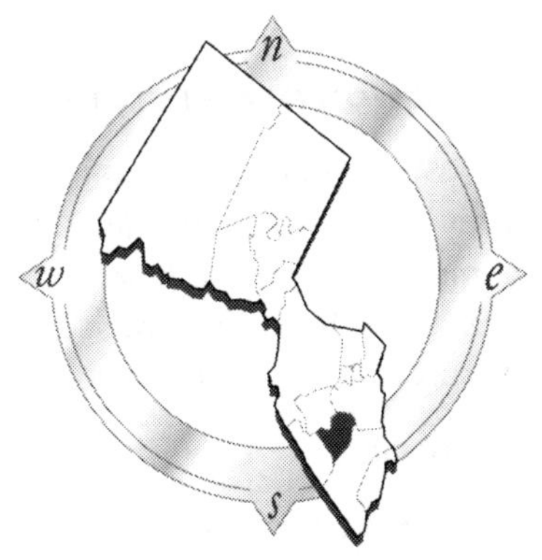

Residents of this working-class community say they have the best of two worlds — a town edged by parklands situated less than a half-hour from New York City.

"It's a close-knit, family-oriented suburban community that's conveniently located," said Mayor Matthew Capano. "We have wooded areas and parks, yet within a few minutes you can be at some of the largest shopping malls in New Jersey or in New York City."

"I think the best thing about West Paterson is that it is a small, friendly community," said Councilwoman Ruth Theodora, a longtime resident. "When you go down the street or into a store there is always someone you know to say hi to."

Many of its approximately 11,000 residents are blue-collar workers, predominantly Roman Catholic and of Italian, Irish, and German descent. Quite a few came here from the inner-city areas of neighboring Paterson, and they are quick to point out West Paterson's differing character.

Separated from its urban neighbor by Garrett Mountain Reserve, a county park, and bordered by the Passaic River and Route 46, West Paterson is primarily a residential community of modest but well-kept homes, large shade trees, and neighborhood parks with jungle gyms and ball fields.

There are a few town house developments and a 960-unit apartment complex. But both were bitterly opposed, for fear they would change the town's character.

"Throughout the years, West Paterson has served as an attraction for recreational resources," said Alfred H. Baumann, mayor for 26 years. "Today we still draw thousands of people to the mountain."

NOTEWORTHY HISTORICAL EVENTS

West Paterson occupies an area where George Washington's army stood guard during the American Revolution, giving Rifle Camp Road its name; where anti-aircraft guns were mounted during World War II; and where scenes from the first major silent motion picture, "The Great Train Robbery," were shot.

SCHOOLS

The West Paterson school system serves 839 students with two elementary schools and one middle school. Students in kindergarten through grade 4 attend Beatrice Gilmore School or Charles Olbon School. Grades 5 through 8 attend Memorial School. The district recently upgraded the computers in the middle school's computer lab and library and moved a dozen computers into the elementary schools. In addition to Internet access, the Memorial library also has an extensive collection of CD-ROM reference guides.

After-school enrichment programs in introductory Spanish, math enhancement, and art are offered. Three new sections of advanced reading were added in the 1996-97 school year to supplement an advanced mathematics program. And through a partnership with the Nestle corporation, after-school recreation programs, daytime tutoring, and field trips are offered.

Older children attend Passaic Valley Regional High School in Little Falls. (See the Totowa profile for further details on the high school.)

HOUSES OF WORSHIP

Appenzeller Methodist Church Korean Speaking Congregation; Calvary Assembly; Community Church; Community United Methodist Church; Holy Cross Church; Our Lady of Mercy Chapel; St. Ann's Melkite Catholic Church; and St. Michael's Cathedral Chapel.

HOUSES

These range from starter homes to upscale single-family houses in ranch, contemporary, and colonial styles; two- and three-bedroom town houses; and one large apartment complex.

Transportation

Manhattan is a 25-minute drive away on routes 46 or 80. The Garden State Parkway is also close, and Newark Airport and the Meadowlands Sports Complex are ten minutes away. New Jersey Transit provides regular bus service to surrounding towns, with connections to New York City in Paterson and at Willowbrook Mall. A bus to Port Authority in Manhattan departs from neighboring Totowa, a ten minute drive.

Recreation

One-third, or about one square mile, of West Paterson is taken up by two large county parks to the east. Both are popular locations for nature trail hiking and bird-watching. The Garrett Mountain Reservation offers views of the New York skyline on a clear day, and Rifle Camp Park contains a popular fishing pond.

A variety of team sports, from football to roller hockey, for grades K-8 are organized through the borough board of recreation and the Boys' and Girls' Club. Adult sports such as basketball, aerobics, and dance classes are available. Borough facilities include six playgrounds, one with chess tables; lighted football and soccer fields; and handball, tennis, and paddleball courts.

The borough cooperates with Totowa and Little Falls to provide activities for disabled children.

Arts and Culture

Situated in a historic house in downtown West Paterson, Nathan's Art Gallery displays works by area artists. The Barnes & Noble bookstore on Route 46 west frequently sponsors poetry readings and book signings.

Child Care Services

There are six private child care facilities in West Paterson.

Senior Services

The municipality operates free door-to-door bus service within the borough and to the ShopRite center on Route 46. During the holiday season, the bus also travels to Willowbrook Mall. The West

Paterson Seniors club meets every Wednesday morning in the West Paterson Boys' and Girls' Club for bingo, buns, and coffee. The club occasionally goes on outings or meets elsewhere for lunch. The Triborough Seniors, whose members are from West Paterson, Totowa, and Little Falls, provides free lunches for seniors on weekdays at the Boys' and Girls' Club. They also run the Meals on Wheels program.

Recent developments

The $1.8 million West Falls Plaza, a shopping center anchored by an A&P supermarket, recently opened on Route 46 west between Browdertown Road and McBride Avenue. But with an area of less than three square miles, a third of which is parkland, the borough has little space left to develop.

Nevertheless, one developer, invoking a state Supreme Court ruling requiring municipalities to provide low- and moderate-income housing, has announced his intention to construct 120 town houses on a wooded 20-acre site along Rifle Camp Road. Borough officials have said they will fight the plan.

Drawbacks

There is no senior or low-income housing.

Prominent residents

Many National Football League players live in West Paterson. Among them: Cedric Jones, Chris Calloway, Willie Beamon, Ray Agnew. Also Derick Coleman, former Nets player.

Phone numbers

Borough clerk (201) 345-8100
School district (201) 684-0331
Public library (201) 345-8120

— *Kelly David*

Demographics

County: Passaic
Size: 2.96 square miles
Population: 10,982
Density: 3,708/square mile
Median age: 35.8 years
White: 95 percent
Asian: 2.3 percent
Black: 1.4 percent
Median house value: $193,600
Upper 25 percent: $600,00
Lower 25 percent: $150,000
Median year built: 1950s
Median rent: $638
Single-family homes: 1,910
Condominiums: 296 units
Median property taxes per household (1994): $4,338
Median household income: $44,933
Industrial property: 30 parcels
Sewers: Public
Library: 36,600 volumes, 120 periodicals, 556 videos, 290 music cassettes and books on tape, 226 compact discs
Media: The Record and the North Jersey Herald & News cover the town, as does Today, a bi-weekly. TCI provides cable service.
Fire and ambulance: Volunteer
Police: Paid. The Borough Council has approved a cost-cutting plan to replace the department's top three brass with a civilian director, effective 1998.
Crime rate per 1,000 (1994): 46.7
Violent crime rate per 1,000: (1994): 2.9

Westwood

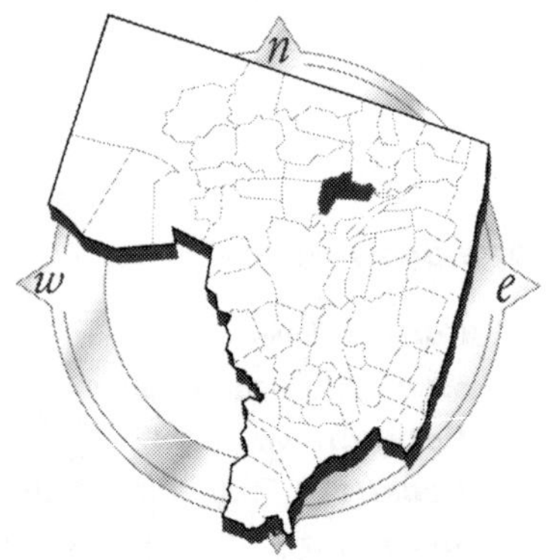

Known as the Hub of the Pascack Valley, Westwood offers affordable homes, a family atmosphere, and a thriving and charming downtown.

The borough comprises 2.3 square miles in north-central Bergen County and is bordered by Hillsdale, Washington Township, Emerson, and River Vale.

"I think we have a great quality of life in Westwood," said Mayor Bernard "Skip" Kelley, a 24-year resident. "From the bottom of my heart, I love this town."

From its new red-brick Borough Hall to the old-fashioned lampposts and well-swept sidewalks of its downtown business district, Westwood is an inviting place. "People come from all the towns around just so they don't have to shop at the malls," Kelley said.

There are affordable homes hugging the center of town and stately colonial houses (and a few mansions) in the Goodwin Park section, some of them overlooking historic Bogert's Mill Pond. No house or neighborhood is more than a mile's drive from the commuter train station and bus stop.

For parents and outdoor enthusiasts, there are seven borough-owned parks and the lush, 78-acre Pascack Brook County Park, which together offer fishing ponds, walking trails, tennis and basketball courts, and playgrounds.

"It's a very solid, upper-middle-class community and there's a lot of stability," said George Bedrosian, a real estate agent in town.

Noteworthy historical events

On Oct. 7, 1780, George Washington and his troops are believed to have stopped to refresh themselves at Bogert's Mill Pond in Westwood while marching from Tappan, N.Y., to Totowa.

Schools

The township is part of the Westwood regional school district, which has an enrollment of approximately 2,100 students at four primary schools and Westwood Regional Junior-Senior High School, located in Washington Township. (For more details on Westwood Junior-Senior High School, see the Washington Township profile.)

Houses of worship

Calvary Baptist Church; Grace Episcopal Church; Grace Korean United Methodist Church; Korean Hanil Presbyterian Church; Lebanon Baptist Church of Westwood; Mount Zion Baptist Church; New St. Mark AME Zion Church; Reformed Church of Westwood; St. Andrew's Roman Catholic Church; St. John AME Church; and Westwood United Methodist Church.

Houses

Most of the homes are pre-World War II, wood-frame colonials. There is a sprinkling of stately red-brick colonials, as well as some one-story condominiums, ranches, and bi-levels. A 43-unit, upscale town-house development is planned at the site of a former middle school.

Transportation

Red & Tan Lines runs bus service from Westwood to Port Authority in Manhattan — about a 45-minute trip. New Jersey Transit offers train service from Westwood to Hoboken, where PATH connections can be made to New York, Newark, or Jersey City.

Recreation

There are seven recreational borough parks, plus Veterans Memorial Park, a grassy expanse with a gazebo in the center of town.

The parks offer basketball and tennis courts, Little League and softball fields, playgrounds and picnic areas, a wooded walking trail and a pond for fishing.

An ice-skating rink is open year-round and offers figure- and ice-skating lessons and hockey clinics.

The borough's summer recreation programs include arts and crafts, basketball, Ping-Pong, field trips, and swimming once a week at the private Westwood Swim Club.

Arts and Culture

Summer concerts are presented in Veterans Memorial Park, sponsored by the borough and a local bank. Musical styles have included bluegrass, bell chimes, Caribbean, and big band sounds.

The Pascack Valley Art Association shows local artists' work in the park every June.

Child Care Services

There are five private child care centers in Westwood.

Senior Services

Westwood House on Madison Avenue offers 183 subsidized rental units. A senior citizens club meets twice a month.

Recent Developments

A $2.1 million red-brick colonial municipal building opened in October 1994. A new firehouse is planned.

Drawbacks

Houses in the Glenbrook section of town have experienced flooding over the years by the Pascack Brook, a problem borough and county officials are trying to solve. Some downtown shoppers and merchants say drivers don't yield to pedestrians enough at crosswalks downtown.

Phone Numbers

Township clerk (201) 664-7100
School district (201) 664-0880
Public library (201) 664-0583

— *Paul Rogers*

Demographics

County: Bergen
Size: 2.3 square miles
Population: 10,446
Density: 4,505/square mile
Median age: 37.6 years
White: 89.3 percent
Black: 6.6 percent
Asian: 3.5 percent
Median house value: $217,600
Upper 25 percent: $255,700
Lower 25 percent: $184,700
Median year built: 1955
Median rent: $721
Single-family homes: 2,602
Condominiums: 160 units
Median property taxes per household (1994): $4,682
Median household income: $46,866
Industrial property: 34 parcels
Sewers: Public
Library: 43,150 volumes, 5,543 periodicals, 332 videos, 3,118 cassettes, compact discs, and audiobooks
Media: The Record covers the town, as do the weeklies Suburban News and Community Life. TCI provides cable service.
Fire and ambulance: Volunteer
Police: Paid
Crime rate per 1,000 (1994): 24.4
Violent crime rate per 1,000 (1994): 2.3

WOODCLIFF LAKE

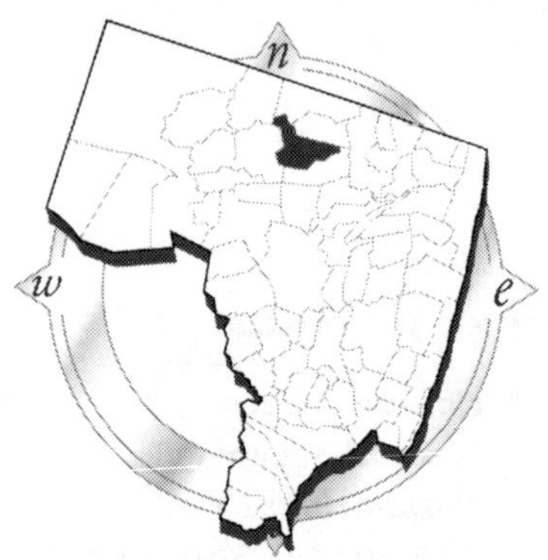

The cynical might remark that any town with a median family income of more than $88,000 per year *should* be idyllic, that any town with a homogeneous populace doesn't have to face the problems that beset communities with a more diverse makeup. The cynical would be wrong, however, if they believed that these two qualities are adequate to maintain a stable, vibrant community.

Nestled in the rolling hills of northern Bergen County, minutes from the New York State border, Woodcliff Lake offers the best that any suburban community can give its residents because its residents give the community the very best that they can offer.

"It's the ideal community to raise your children in," said Mayor Josephine Higgins. "Our citizens are committed to the community. We've got parents volunteering to be sports coaches, to help religious groups. Our fire department and ambulance corps are both volunteer. When federal funding allowed us to add handicapped access to one of our parks, parents volunteered to build a refreshment stand so the town wouldn't have to spend the money.

"One doctor even donates her time at our flu clinic every year."

Woodcliff Lake's elementary and middle schools are among the finest in the region, offering an array of specialized programs.

And, believe it or not, taxes in Woodcliff Lake are lower than in the surrounding communities of Saddle River, Hillsdale, and Montvale.

There has been a recent boom in growth, but the town monitors it carefully.

"We want to keep the community the same," said Mayor

Higgins. "We want to keep the area green."

Woodcliff Lake's rural atmosphere has not changed, although several corporations have located their headquarters here. Instead of a central downtown, three small commercial areas have slowly built up in the former farming community. Two of the borough's oldest families, the Tices and the Van Ripers, still operate retail farming businesses.

Noteworthy Historical Events

Until the late 19th century, fewer than 1,000 people lived in the area that is now Woodcliff Lake. Former President Richard Nixon maintained an office in the borough until his death.

Schools

The Woodcliff Lake school system comprises two schools, Dorchester Elementary School (kindergarten through grade 5) and Woodcliff Middle School (6 through 8). Both are on the same campus, along with several athletic fields and playgrounds. Woodcliff Lake teenagers attend Pascack Hills High School in Montvale. (See Montvale for details.) Membership in the Pascack Valley Special Education Council allows the school system to provide services to students with special needs. The Dorchester lab has a greenhouse and is staffed by a full-time science teacher. Beginning in the fourth grade, the foreign language program introduces students to French or Spanish. Project Impact's artist-in-residence program allows students to study with a working artist.

Houses of Worship

Apostolic Christian Church; Christ Lutheran Church; Jehovah's Witness Congregation of Woodcliff Lake; Our Lady Mother of the Church (Roman Catholic); and Temple Emanuel of Pascack Valley.

Houses

Some of the loveliest homes in Bergen County can be found in Woodcliff Lake. Stone mansions; large, airy Cape Cods; somber Tudors; and many fine examples of contemporary architecture sit on large lots.

Transportation

New Jersey Transit has direct bus service into Manhattan (about an hour's ride) and train service to New York City, Newark, and Jersey City via the PATH trains in Hoboken (45 minutes). Local NJ Transit buses run regularly through the municipality.

Recreation

Woodcliff Lake has three public playgrounds, four athletic fields, six lighted tennis courts, and one public swimming pool — Old Mill Pond. Use of the pool is limited to sponsored families and individuals. Residents and nonresidents must pay to use the municipal tennis courts. Other programs include a theater arts workshop, tennis lessons, bowling, baseball, roller skating, and a swim team. The borough also sponsors the annual Woodcliff Lake Day at Old Mill Pond, a picnic with contests and live entertainment.

Arts and culture

No programs specific to Woodcliff Lake. There is no library, although residents may use the library in any of the surrounding towns for a fee that is reimbursed by the town.

Child care services

Woodcliff Lake, in partnership with the Ridgewood YWCA, provides an after-school child care program at Dorchester School. Summer and preschool day camps are run by the department of recreation. There are also two private child care facilities in town.

Senior services

The Woodcliff Lake Senior Association meets monthly to discuss topics such as insurance for seniors, real estate, and patients' rights. The association also sponsors trips to such destinations as the Culinary Institute of America. The association has more than 100 members, who pay $3 annually in membership fees.

Recent developments

Woodcliff Lake is experiencing a burst of development that the town is watching very closely. Eighty-one houses are going up or have been built in the last few years, and Chestnut Hill Road has seen some commercial development. Under the Mount Laurel decision, some low- and moderate-income housing is in development, but none of this activity has significantly changed the community's quiet atmosphere.

DRAWBACKS

The opposition to a 15-bed Alzheimer's group home proposed for Woodcliff Lake was exacerbated because residents weren't notified until two days before work began on the site — even though borough officials had voted on a zoning variance months before. Residents have formed the Woodcliff Lake Concerned Citizens Group to challenge the developer's plan.

PHONE NUMBERS

Township clerk (201) 391-4977
School district (201) 391-6570

— *Marc Warren Watrel*

DEMOGRAPHICS

County: Bergen
Size: 3.3 square miles
Population: 5,303
Density: 1,592/square mile
Median age: 38.2 years
White: 94 percent
Asian: 4.9 percent
Black: 0.9 percent
Median house value: $401,100
Upper 25 percent: $500,001
Lower 25 percent: $298,700
Median year built: 1962
Median rent: $1,001
Single-family homes: 1,665
Condominiums: None
Median property taxes per household (1994): $7,403
Median household income: $88,670
Industrial property: None
Sewers: Public
Library: None
Media: The Record covers the town, as does the weekly Community Life. Cablevision provides cable service.
Fire and ambulance: Volunteer
Police: Paid
Crime rate per 1,000 (1994): 17.2
Violent crime rate per 1,000 (1994): 0.6

Wood-Ridge

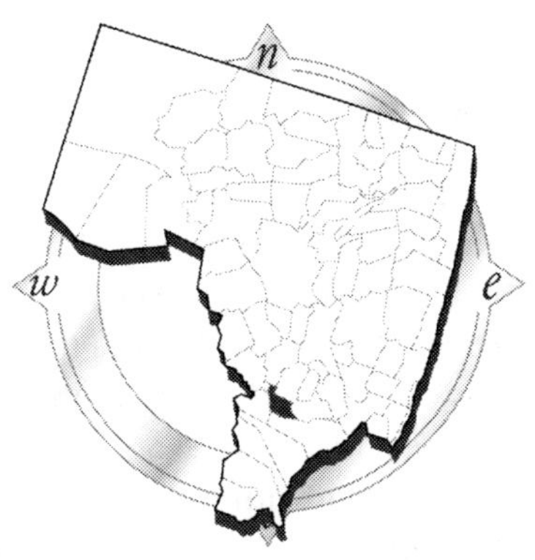

Budgetary concerns have forced many North Jersey towns to scale back programs. But despite shrinking resources, the small, southern Bergen County borough of Wood-Ridge has refused to let such difficulties diminish the quality of life.

"We stay within our budget and try to maintain the tax rate. We rely on our citizens' volunteerism to fill in the gaps," said Wood-Ridge Mayor Paul Calocino.

"We created a sidewalk program that allows citizens to get new sidewalks by paying for it through a personal tax assessment. The rest of the town doesn't pay for it. When we created Memorial Walk, we sold bricks for $25 and put people's names on them. And the Lion's Club donated a gazebo for the park on the boulevard."

The town has a large senior population, but there has also been an influx of young people with families. Homes are reasonably priced, and taxes are low.

"It's a quiet town with tree-lined streets," Calocino said. "I moved here from Weehawken and couldn't sleep the first two nights because it was too quiet."

Busy Route 17 cuts through the eastern end of Wood-Ridge. Wood-Ridge's small business district is along Valley Boulevard.

Noteworthy Historical Events

Wood-Ridge was once the hunting grounds for several tribes of Native Americans. The first European settlers arrived in 1669, and the land was used primarily for farming until the burgeoning of the railroad system after the Civil War. By the turn of the century, the borough had changed from rural to suburban.

SCHOOLS

The Wood-Ridge school district serves some 700 students in three schools: Catherine E. Doyle School for kindergarten through grade 4; Gretta R. Ostrovksy School, grades 5 and 6; and Wood-Ridge High School, grades 7 through 12. The two elementary schools offer a traditional curriculum; both recently added state-of-the-art computer facilities. There are gifted and talented programs at both schools, along with support programs for reading, language arts, and math. After-school tutorial programs are available.

Wood-Ridge High School recently restructured its course offerings to accommodate an interdisciplinary approach to teaching. Courses include many honors and advanced placement classes. Eighty-one percent of Wood-Ridge graduates pursue post-secondary education. Average SAT scores for 1995 were 379 verbal, 443 math.

Assumption Roman Catholic School is located in Wood-Ridge.

HOUSES OF WORSHIP

Assumption Roman Catholic Church; First Presbyterian Church; Jehovah's Witness Congregation of Garfield; and St. Paul's Episcopal Church.

HOUSES

Many Victorians remain from Wood-Ridge's earliest years of suburban development. The lots average 50 feet by 100 feet, and the homes are traditional stone and wood-frame structures.

TRANSPORTATION

New Jersey Transit provides bus service to Manhattan and rail transportation to Hoboken, where connections can be made for Manhattan and elsewhere. Nearby Rutherford has direct train service to Manhattan. NJ Transit also provides bus service to Newark and other North Jersey destinations.

RECREATION

The Wood-Ridge recreation commission is an all-volunteer organization that offers soccer, junior football, girls' softball, baseball (all ages), coed basketball (all ages), and cheerleading. Field trips and arts and crafts programs are added in the summer. Some programs are run jointly with neighboring Moonachie. Recreational facilities include Veterans Park, the 13th Street Park, and the Little League field, along with the school district's athletic fields.

Arts and culture

The borough has no museums or professional performing arts groups. Overview Ltd., located in Wood-Ridge, is a poetry publisher seeking new poets for publication.

Child care services

Wood-Ridge has no municipal child-care programs. There are several privately run facilities in town.

Senior services

There are three social organizations for Wood-Ridge seniors: Wood-Ridge Contemporary Club, Wood-Ridge Seniors, and the 60 Plus Club.

Recent developments

Wood-Ridge has been discussing regionalizing its school system with neighboring Hasbrouck Heights. Hasbrouck Heights voted 3-1 against the proposal a few years ago, but another vote is scheduled for spring 1997.

Drawbacks

Running a school system for a small number of students is expensive. The cost per pupil — $10,353 — is among the highest in Bergen County.

Phone numbers

Township clerk (201) 939-0202
School district (201) 933-6777
Public library (201) 438-2455

— *Marc Warren Watrel*

DEMOGRAPHICS

County: Bergen
Size: 1.1 square miles
Population: 7,506
Density: 6,824/square mile
Median age: 39 years
White: 95.9 percent
Asian: 2.6 percent
Black: 0.7 percent
Median house value: $190,200
Upper 25 percent: $224,500
Lower 25 percent: $166,800
Median year built: 1943
Median rent: $694
Single-family homes: 2,062
Condominiums: Approximately 160 units
Median property taxes per household (1994): $4,698
Median household income: $51,531
Industrial property: 11 parcels
Sewers: Public and private
Library: 33,339 volumes
Media: The Record covers the town, as do the weeklies the Shopper and the Wood-Ridge Independent. Cable service is provided by TCI.
Fire and ambulance: Volunteer
Police: Paid
Crime rate per 1,000 (1994): 18.5
Violent crime rate per 1,000 (1994): 0.4

WYCKOFF

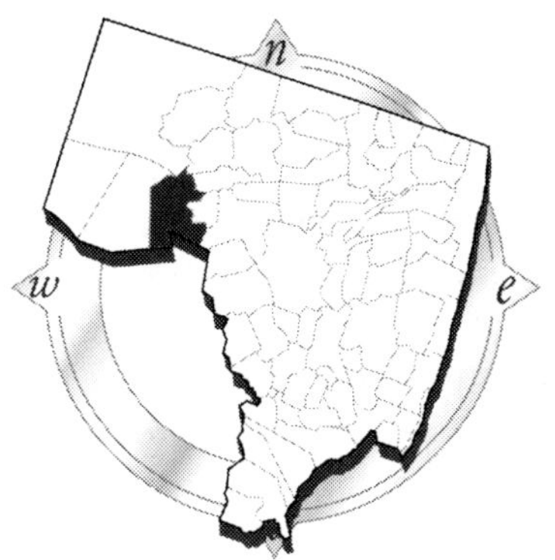

Snuggled in the foothills of the Ramapo Mountains in northwest Bergen County, Wyckoff is the epitome of upper-middle-income suburbia.

Located 25 miles from New York City, the semirural community has a strong business district, an excellent school system, good municipal services, and outstanding recreational facilities.

"Tree-lined streets, good schools, newer playgrounds, a wildlife center, and a broad range of homes characterize this countrified community," said Dale Migliore of Abbott & Caserta Realtors.

Councilman Walter M. Smith Jr. concurred. "This is the best town in Bergen County, with a great corps of volunteers and an administration that runs the town very efficiently," Smith said. "We are always looking to save tax dollars without negatively impacting our residents."

Wyckoff's quaint, 10-block business district, called the Triangle, has boutiques, chain stores, fast-food restaurants, and antique and specialty shops — many of them located in converted old Victorian houses. Its appeal is wide enough to draw people from nearby towns, sometimes causing minor traffic tie-ups.

The 6.5-square-mile community also offers leisure-time programs at a newly constructed recreational facility, the YMCA, and a wildlife center.

"Our stable tax rate and the services we offer make Wyckoff a great place to live," said Mayor Harold Galenkamp Jr. "But because of all the things Wyckoff offers — such as the business district, large post office, etc. — we're a victim of our own growth. The need for infrastructure updates is a direct result of this growth."

NOTEWORTHY HISTORICAL EVENTS

Settlers migrated to Wyckoff, a community built around a dozen ponds connected by brooks and streams, because of its fertile farmland. Farming and dairying were the chief occupations, although hunting and trapping were also common pursuits. Two farms still operate: Russell Orchards and Abma's Farm Market. Each maintains a country store, and Abma's also has a petting zoo.

SCHOOLS

More than 2,000 students attend Wyckoff's four elementary schools and one middle school, all recognized throughout North Jersey for their excellence. The schools are spread out geographically so that all elementary schoolchildren can walk to class.

The Wyckoff Education Foundation, an extremely active organization, recently awarded a $100,000 grant to the district to upgrade the schools' computers. Now, all four elementary schools will have a computer teacher, a fully equipped computer lab, and additional units in the media centers.

Eisenhower Middle School has three computer labs with three Internet hookups. Eisenhower also offers three modern foreign languages — French, German, and Spanish — plus Latin. Wyckoff's high school students attend Ramapo High, located in Franklin Lakes. The school was named ninth-best in the state in 1996 by New Jersey Monthly magazine. (For more details on the high school, see the Franklin Lakes profile.)

Private schools in Wyckoff include St. Elizabeth Interparochial School and the Eastern Christian School.

HOUSES OF WORSHIP

Advent Lutheran Church; Bergen Christian Testimony Church; Beth Rishon Synagogue; Bethany Church; Cedar Hill Christian Reformed Church; Christian Fellowship Center; Church of Christ; Convent Protestant Reformed Church; Faith Community Christian Reformed Church; Grace United Methodist Church; New Covenant Church; St. Elizabeth Roman Catholic Church; St. Nicholas Greek Orthodox Church; Second Reformed Church; Wyckoff Assembly of God; Wyckoff Baptist Church, and Wyckoff Reformed Church.

Houses

Houses in Wyckoff start in the low $200,000 range for ranches and small split-levels. "Then you can buy up as high as $900,000," said Migliore. Construction was scheduled to start in January 1997 at Barrister Farms, a 35-acre housing development that would include single-family homes and condominiums.

Transportation

Several bus companies offer service from Wyckoff to Port Authority in Manhattan and other destinations in New York State. New Jersey Transit train stations are located in nearby communities.

Recreation

Ball fields, lighted tennis and basketball courts, soccer fields, and other facilities are plentiful — and almost always packed. More than 1,300 children participate in the soccer program, and approximately 2,500 people take part in some activity offered by the recreation department.

Arts and culture

The Van Voorhees-Quackenbush-Zabriskie House, which dates to 1824, was bequeathed to the township in 1973. The house now serves as a museum of Wyckoff history and culture and is open Fridays during the school year.

The James A. McFaul Environmental Center, an 81-acre park established in 1962, offers an exhibit hall, meeting rooms, wildlife exhibits, hiking trails, botanical gardens, and a picnic area. Many of the center's programs are designed for young children.

In 1993, Wyckoff received a gift of 13 acres of ponds, woods, and meadows to be used as a horticultural center.

Child care services

Wyckoff has no municipally run child care programs. There are numerous private preschools.

Senior services

The Wyckoff Senior Citizen Club, with about 90 members,

meets weekly at the public library. It offers a variety of recreational activities, including trips, line dancing, arts and crafts, and speakers' programs. Christian Health Care Centers is working on a plan to add an assisted-living facility for seniors to its nursing home on Sicomac Avenue.

RECENT DEVELOPMENTS

Wyckoff's Township Council is working with the county to improve intersections in the community; the one at Franklin and Godwin avenues was scheduled for improvement in spring 1997.

The council has saved thousands of dollars by cutting back garbage pickup to once a week from November through April, then resuming twice-a-week pickup from May to October.

DRAWBACKS

Because the community has an interesting and strong retail district, including two large supermarkets, residents of other towns are drawn to the Triangle, adding to traffic congestion. The town is not accessible by any major highways except Route 208.

PHONE NUMBERS

Township clerk (201) 891-7000
School district (201) 848-5700
Public library (201) 891-4866

— *Barbara Williams*

Demographics

County: Bergen
Size: 6.55 square miles
Population: 15,372
Density: 2,347/square mile
Median age: 39.3
White: 96.4 percent
Asian: 2.9 percent
Black: 0.5 percent
Median house value: $333,800
Upper 25 percent: $432,700
Lower 25 percent: $251,600
Median year built: 1958
Median rent: $927
Single-family homes: 4,811
Condominiums: Approximately 150 units
Median property taxes per household (1994): $6,026
Median household income: $75,905
Industrial property: 18 parcels
Sewers: Public and private
Library: 70,094 volumes
Media: The Record covers the town, as do the Gazette, the Ridgewood News, the Suburban News, and the Villadom Times, all weeklies. TCI provides cable service.
Fire and ambulance: Volunteer
Police: Paid
Crime rate per 1,000 (1994): 10.2
Violent crime rate per 1,000 (1994): 0.3

GUIDE TO ADVERTISERS